"This is a book that inspires hope. Its contributo[illegible] motivated by restlessness with a dysfunctional s[illegible] state of the caring and therapeutic professions in [illegible] often on the margin, they offer profound an[illegible] theory, practice and research. Their combined efforts will encourage readers not to yield to the dispiriting trends which permeate our fractured society or to the straitjackets which increasingly threaten therapeutic creativity. It is refreshing to meet a group of writers who celebrate the whole person and have retained the vision of a more compassionate society."

Emeritus Professor Brian Thorne, University of East Anglia, UK; Lay Canon, Norwich Cathedral

"In an age where the psychological therapies seem increasingly boundary-focused, it is a delight to read a book that allows you to breathe once again. Bringing together formidably articulate writers, Nolan and West facilitate the reader beyond the limitations of therapy and explore aspects of our work in a refreshing and engaging way. They demonstrate that while good helping is about being grounded in strong ethical practice, work that empowers and truly facilitates is informed by much wider horizons. An excellent and welcome read."

Dr Andrew Reeves, Chair of BACP. Associate Professor in the Counselling Professions and Mental Health, University of Chester, UK

"This book takes readers on a refreshing journey of reflection, 'beyond' the customary 'packaged' mainstream ways of understanding counselling and psychotherapy (which are well-rehearsed and culturally constrained), to alternative ways of thinking that are born out of the wisdom that comes from experienced practitioner-reflexivity and wider-informed practitioner development. Any therapist, who has grown beyond the bounds of defensive practice to become more grounded and authentic in their way of being and thinking with clients, will find resonances with, and permission-giving in, the text."

Professor Peter M. Gubi, Professor of Counselling, University of Chester, UK

EXTENDING HORIZONS IN HELPING AND CARING THERAPIES

This vital new book examines how healing encounters might further the horizons of practice and extend innovation in professional interpersonal relationships. Highly qualified contributors explore ways in which insights into individual, cultural and community meanings open further perspectives on human being and help clarify what can feel a confusing present and an increasingly unpredictable future.

Divided into parts on Personal and Professional Identity, Culture and Personal Context, Practice Research, and Clinical Practice, each chapter opens up thinking on crucial contemporary issues, informed by personal and clinical practice case-study examples and by findings from leading-edge research investigations, adding to the current literature on both theory and practice.

This book brings together voices from the margins, offering alternative practice perspectives that look beyond protocol and statistics-based therapy, emphasising the relational richness that informs professional interpersonal encounters in the support of mental health and wellbeing. It will be of immense value to counsellors and psychotherapists in training and practice, as well as for related mental health professionals and those with an interest in the caring professions.

Greg Nolan is Visiting Lecturer in Counselling and Psychotherapy at the University of Leeds, MBACP Senior Registered Practitioner and Fellow of the Higher Education Academy. He has a teaching career spanning over 45 years and has research interests in the phenomena of micro-moments in practice and clinical supervision. He has published on therapeutic practice, clinical supervision and counsellor training.

William West is a Visiting Professor to the University of Chester and Honorary Senior Research Fellow in Counselling Studies at the University of Manchester, where he was most noted for his interest in counselling and spirituality and for his work with doctorate and PhD students. He has published extensively and remains passionately interested in the overlap between counselling and religious pastoral care.

EXTENDING HORIZONS IN HELPING AND CARING THERAPIES

Beyond the Liminal in the Healing Encounter

Edited by Greg Nolan and William West

LONDON AND NEW YORK

First published 2020
by Routledge
2 Park Square, Milton Park, Abingdon, Oxon OX14 4RN

and by Routledge
52 Vanderbilt Avenue, New York, NY 10017

Routledge is an imprint of the Taylor & Francis Group, an informa business

British Library Cataloguing-in-Publication Data
A catalogue record for this book is available from the British Library

Library of Congress Cataloging-in-Publication Data
A catalog record has been requested for this book

ISBN: 978-1-138-38745-4 (hbk)
ISBN: 978-1-138-38746-1 (pbk)
ISBN: 978-0-429-42625-4 (ebk)

Typeset in Bembo
by Newgen Publishing UK

Printed and bound by CPI Group (UK) Ltd, Croydon, CR0 4YY

Greg – This book is dedicated to my wife Angel, and Jessica and Jacob, who make life complete

William – This book is dedicated to my wife Gay Morton for all of her support over many years

CONTENTS

ILLUSTRATIONS

Figures

Box

ACKNOWLEDGEMENTS

There are many people over the years who have profoundly contributed to our understandings of the issues explored in this book. In the first instance, we are grateful to our authors, as inspirational and professional exemplars who, having accepted our invitation, have dedicated their time, diligence and inspirational wisdom in offering their experiences and observations on practice and research in the support of others' mental health.

In addition we wish to mention some who have inspired and informed our drive toward the idea of this collection: Colin Agnew, Pete Armstrong, Liz Ballinger, Fenia Christodoulidi, Gala Connell, Cody Coyne, Cemil Egeli, Keith Gibbard, Val Haigh, Sue Hill, the late Grace Jantzen, the late Chris Jenkins, Nikki Kiyimba, Nick Ladany, Diane Lawson, Jeff Leonardi, John McLeod, Lynn McVey, Roy Moodley, Emily Morton-West, Moss Pinder, Andrew Reeves, Joy Schaverien, Adam Scott, Bobby Silverman, Richard Summers, Penny Tharratt, Brian Thorne, Jean White and Janice Wilson.

And not forgetting past student trainees and postgraduate researchers who have inspired us with their commitment and enthusiasm, as representing the best in people, and who selflessly offer their professional humanity in the care and service of others' wellbeing.

Also we would wish to say a particular thank you to the editorial staff at our publishers, Routledge Mental Health: in the first instance to Joanne Forshaw, Charlotte Taylor and Alec Selwyn; and also to our copy-editors at Newgen, Kelly Winter and Rachel Carter – together, their help and advice, diligence, careful attention to detail and gentle 'nudges', have helped guide us through to completion of this process. And a final thank you to our anonymous reviewers for their generosity and commitment in offering helpful feedback and supportive comments.

CONTRIBUTORS

Liz Ballinger is Honorary Lecturer at the University of Manchester. Before her retirement, she acted as Programme Director for the MA in Counselling, alongside supervising doctorate and masters students' research and providing input on the counselling and educational psychology doctorate programmes. Her belief in the importance of the social context in the shaping of human experience has led her to an ongoing critique of therapy. She identifies herself as coming from a working-class background, and has a long-standing interest in the relationship between social class and therapeutic processes and outcomes.

Allison Brown is a British Association for Counselling and Psychotherapy Senior Accredited therapist. She is in private practice in Yorkshire working with adults, children and young people and has a particular interest in attachment, bereavement and loss within therapy and supervision.

Friday Faraday is a writer and adjunct professor in the City College system of Chicago who, with David Paul Smith, is the co-author of chapter 2. Efforts have been made to protect Friday's anonymity.

Phil Goss is Director of Counselling and Psychotherapy at the University of Warwick, and a Jungian Analyst (AJA London and IAAP member) and UKCP-registered psychotherapist. He is the author of two books, *Jung: A Complete Introduction* (2015), *Men, Women and Relationships: A Post-Jungian Approach* (2010), and of a number of book chapters in collections such as: *The Routledge International Handbook of Jungian Film Studies* (edited by L. Hockley, 2018); *What Counsellors and Spiritual Directors can Learn from Each Other* (edited by P. Gubi, 2017); and *Alchemy and Psychotherapy* (edited by D. Mathers, 2014).

Lynn Learman has worked as a psychological therapist and service manager in the third sector for 35 years. She is a BACP Senior Registered Practitioner who also works as a supervisor and trainer. She has a particular interest in trauma and complex trauma, an expertise in accessing hard to engage client groups and a commitment to equal access and cultural competency. Her professional doctorate focused on the impact of the interpreter in the therapeutic triad. She is currently the Service Manager of the Student Counselling Service at Liverpool University where one in four undergraduates are international students. Until last year she managed Seedlings, a specialist CAMHS service for traumatised children in primary schools, and Spinning World, which provides therapy for asylum seekers and refugees with complex trauma at PSS in Liverpool.

John Lees is Senior Lecturer in Mental Health at the University of Leeds School of Healthcare. He is a UKCP-registered psychotherapist and BACP-accredited senior practitioner, was the founder editor of the Routledge journal *Psychodynamic Practice*, has edited a book series, edited or co-edited five books and published numerous book chapters and peer-reviewed articles. His research interests include the links between therapy and complementary and alternative medicine and approaches to practitioner research based on investigating the microphenomena of practice. He works in private practice.

George MacDonald The late Dr George MacDonald was a counsellor, psychotherapist and group therapist in private practice. He carried out doctoral research on 'Culture as a positive resource in therapy' at the University of Manchester. In previous lives he worked as an engineer and manager in the chemical industry and a management consultant working with global companies. He maintained a lively interest in technology and its influence on the individual and the nature of society.

Lynn McVey works as a BACP-registered therapist in private practice and is a Researcher at the University of Leeds, School of Healthcare. She is interested in reverie, empathy and the micro-phenomenal nature of client–therapist/participant–researcher interactions and has first-authored several journal articles in the field. Lynn undertook the qualitative research outlined in this chapter as part of a Masters in Psychotherapy and Counselling at the University of Leeds, before going on to complete a PhD in Psychotherapy and Counselling at Leeds in 2018. ORCiD: https://orcid.org/0000-0003-2009-7682

Rachel Mallen is Lecturer in Counselling and Psychotherapy at the University of Salford, Fellow of the Higher Education Academy and BACP-registered counsellor. She teaches on undergraduate and postgraduate professional counselling training programmes, and supervises MSc and BSc students. Her research and teaching interests include bereavement and loss, heuristic research and transpersonal psychotherapy, in particular the link between traumatic loss and spiritual phenomena.

Greg Nolan is Visiting Lecturer in Counselling and Psychotherapy at the University of Leeds, MBACP Senior Registered Practitioner and Fellow of the Higher Education Academy. He has a teaching career spanning over 45 years, including 30+ years as a therapist, manager of counselling services and counselling training programmes, freelance counsellor, clinical supervisor and trainer. He has research interests in phenomena in micro-moments of practice and clinical supervision and has published and co-edited books, chapters and peer-reviewed articles on therapeutic practice, clinical supervision and training counsellors. ORCiD: https://orcid.org/0000-0002-2308-2702

Barry O'Sullivan is the Coordinator of Education and Outreach and a counsellor and psychotherapist at St Luke's Centre in Manchester, UK, a centre devoted to the psychological wellbeing of members of, and candidates for, the Roman Catholic clergy and religious orders in England, Scotland, Ireland and Wales. Ordained as a Roman Catholic priest in 1987, he is a qualified counsellor and an expert in safeguarding. He is a Visiting Lecturer at Pontifical Gregorian University in Rome, and a member of the British Association for Counselling and Psychotherapy.

John Prysor-Jones is a counsellor, psychotherapist and Anglican priest. He lectures in Counselling Psychology in the School of Psychology, University of Bangor, North Wales. He has been researching hope in counselling in the United Kingdom and in different cultures for many years and has presented widely at international conferences. An accredited and registered member of the British Association of Counselling and Psychotherapy he has worked for over 40 years in a variety of mental health settings. He is Secretary of the Executive Council of the International Association for Counselling. He lives on the edge of Snowdonia.

David Paul Smith is a clinical psychologist in private practice in the Chicago Land area. He also works with staff in hospitals in his capacity as health psychologist and clinical supervisor. He is a member of the Society of Psychotherapy Research and the Society of Clinical and Experimental Hypnosis. In addition, he works as the chief editor of the *International Journal for Traditional Healing and Critical Mental Health*.

Bridget Tardivel is a systemic practitioner and BACP-registered psychotherapist with a particular interest in death anxiety, currently working in palliative care in the UK. In the 1980s she trained as a registered mental nurse and practised for some years within an NHS forensic setting. Since then, alongside her role as a mum, she has worked in various voluntary sector contexts including education, mental health and criminal justice, as well as with those challenged by the asylum process. She has a BSc in psychology, an MA in counselling and psychotherapy and a PG Cert. in systemic practice.

James N. Tebbutt is a Methodist minister who has served in a number of ministerial and chaplaincy appointments, including from September 2019 as the Chair of the Cumbria District of the Methodist Church. Initially a London solicitor, but also with degrees in theology and some preliminary psychotherapeutic training, he brings a number of perspectives to his interest in the interface between psychotherapy and counselling, and pastoral care and theology. This led to a PhD (undertaken with Professor William West) on an aspect of the experience and practice of deep listening, as referred to in his contributed chapter.

William West is a Visiting Professor to the University of Chester and Honorary Senior Research Fellow in Counselling Studies at the University of Manchester, where he was most noted for his interest in counselling and spirituality and for his work with doctorate and PhD students. William has written 34 academic papers, 22 book chapters and 35 professional articles. He has (co-) written/edited six books, the most recent one being *Therapy, Culture and Spirituality: Developing Therapeutic Practice* (co-edited with Greg Nolan, 2015). William remains passionately interested in the overlap between counselling and religious pastoral care.

FOREWORD

In an age in which we constantly question and reinvent what it is to be human, we have become accustomed to the transmission of knowledge, thoughts and ideas at an extraordinary speed, and with a reach that encircles the globe. This helps solve problems, but it also helps create them.

So-called wisdom and knowledge can be collected and consulted, no experience necessary. Those collections of knowledge have saved an enormous amount of time. We do not have to discover for ourselves, all over again, what our ancestors have already learnt. Literacy liberates: it allows people to learn anything from anywhere, and to imagine lives and futures differently. In an era of growing liberty, we find ourselves in the face of cultural intolerance.

With that liberty come challenges, and responsibilities. And what is lost as we skate across the surface of received knowledge, not born out of constructed wisdom? Large doses of empathy and empathic resonance one might contend, with a subsequent impact on the ability to stimulate, facilitate and rehabilitate healing in self and other.

In this most recent edited text, Nolan and West, with their contributors, diligently remind us of the importance of being earnest and conscientious learners, no matter how experienced or wise we believe we are. We must continue to seek wisdom, check our sources, revise our opinions and gain new understandings of ourselves and others. This is much more than toleration. Therapeutic relationships, beyond the liminal, mean that we learn that we are all one, and just as we care for ourselves and our loved ones, in turn that human agape infects those around us; those we are invisible to, as well as those with whom we have a shared intentionality. Mutual repair.

Dawn Freshwater
Vice-Chancellor and Professor of Mental Health
University of Western Australia

INTRODUCTION

Greg Nolan and William West

As editors we have gathered together a series of chapters, authored by practitioners and researchers-in-practice that present ways in which those in the helping professions might push forward the current horizons of therapeutic practice, offering insights from practice, findings from their research and reflections on case study examples.

Mental health practitioners continually face challenges of limited resources and funding, working with clinical issues that stretch the coping capacity of organisations and individual practitioners when they are with the stories, narrative complexities and enormity of social realities that clients bring to their door – always assuming that, if outside of statutory services, clients have the personal resilience, access to third sector provision, or the financial wherewithal to access practitioners in private practice.

Arguably a crucial task for therapists is for the client to be supported in making sufficient sense of themselves and their world. However, in these times of huge changes in our societies, the typical questions of 'Who am I?' and 'What is my world?' are open to more confusions than ever. For example, in our current social media age, understandings of what it is to be a human and what we mean by I or Self has changed, probably irrevocably. So much personal contact for so many people now depends on an electronic link or connection and how we present ourselves to the world that often now has a strong electronic and imaged element. For the younger generation especially, careful handling of social media has become a crucial part of their mental health and wellbeing.

Life pathways are continually potholed by events beyond our control, some incidental, some impactful, others overwhelmingly awful, which together feed a collective fragility into the social zeitgeist. Today's tomorrows can feel threatened by uncertainties of instant (dis)information, the puzzle of weighing media hype against what may (or may not) be imagined realities. Cumulatively, these factors can drive despair in the aloneness of our own temporality. The continuing social drift toward polarised extremes of power, wealth and poverty demands that mental health practitioners maintain and promote a balanced perspective in the face of others' knee-jerk reactions. Psychotherapist Susie Orbach (2019) offers succinct reflections on these social dynamics and the consequent psychological anxieties so provoked, noting that

> [h]istory tells us what happens when economies in decline, with mounting social and economic anxiety, are captured by oversimple populist slogans which cast out those who don't agree or are deemed not to look or sound right.
>
> *Orbach, 2019, p. 10*

Extending Horizons in Helping and Caring Therapies is concerned with how healing encounters can stretch the edges of understanding. The impact of rapid social and community change, fed by exponential growth in global media interconnectedness, has appeared to polarise international politics and people's belief systems, challenging their cultural values. Together, these factors distort how power and control are exercised over individual and collective autonomy. Our contributors explore ways in which insights into individual, cultural and community meanings open further perspectives on human being, helping clarify what can feel a confusing present and an increasingly unpredictable future.

In this book we explore some of the challenges of modern life as reflected in the therapeutic practice, research and thoughts of the contributing authors. We are concerned with how interpersonal healing encounters might flex the edges of our understanding, extend our experiencing and challenge our meanings. Each chapter draws on ideas from practitioners and their experiences, exploring ways in which, by extending our horizons of understanding, the liminal boundaries of 'being' might further journeys of discovery through clients' life challenges. This book brings together some voices from the margins, offering alternative practice perspectives that look beyond protocol- and statistics-based therapy.

When collective and individual identities are being questioned, perhaps more now than ever previously, the role of psychotherapists, counsellors and other helping professionals and volunteers remains crucial. Continuing to offer the very best help and support to clients' needs demands that we redevelop, re-think, re-imagine, and see to re-structuring our therapeutic practice in order to remain relevant for a changing world.

Extending beyond our earlier interests around spirituality, race and culture (Moodley & West, 2005; Nolan & West, 2015; West, 2000, 2004 & 2011), in this book we include chapters from therapists and practitioner-researchers in the helping and caring professions who open up our thinking around crucial contemporary issues and add to the current literature on both theory and practice, informed with clinical experience examples and in shared findings from their leading-edge research.

The book is divided into the following parts:

I Personal and Professional Identity
II Culture and Personal Context
III Practice Research
IV Clinical Practice

Each section progressively reflects a trend of thinking: from the emerging challenges of change in personal and professional meanings; seeking ways to locate client and practitioner in contemporary context; how frontier research projects can inform therapeutic interventions; and how each of these areas might be contributing in current practice.

Beginning Part I on *Personal and Professional Identity* is Bridget Tardivel, a psychotherapist in palliative care, who reflects on her personal journey of experiencing, both in the UK and when immersed in a contrasting Middle-Eastern culture. She explores how a 'dominant Western collective mindset towards death' might be challenged by a different perspective on what it means to 'be', how one might find ease with the prospect of 'not-being', and thereby live life more fully. Developing along the theme of identity and the person, David Paul Smith and his pseudonymous African American client, Friday Faraday, offer a refreshing perspective on agendered identity in Friday's exploration of his remembered life and struggles with depression, attempted suicide and subsequent hospitalisation. Through the practice of hypnotherapy, drawing on Jungian archetypical imagery and an open-mindedness toward an ancient god, together they discover 'a more coherent sense of self and purpose' and a deeper understanding of creative potential.

Clients' storying of traumatic bereavement and loss can make vast demands on a practitioner's emotional energy. Rachel Mallen explores her experiencing of traumatic loss in her candid reflections on a transformational personal journey, inspired through Jung's active imagination and notion of archetype, enabling a bridge between the imaginal and material realms of trauma, and finding reconnection with 'the temporal experience of being human'. She offers a case example from therapeutic practice in showing how her journey released potential for deeper immersion within her client's grieving process.

As with David Paul Smith's thoughts on gendered and agendered identity, Phil Goss reflects on the possibilities for a plurality of identities, in both individual and collective senses of 'I' and 'self'. Taking an integrative discussion across psychotherapeutic theories, he reflects on examples from practice that directly impact on our persona(s), including the notion of 'trans-relational' communications on the internet and social media that can 'facilitate connections between us, individually and across groups and communities', when seeking transformational shifts in self-meaning.

Given the necessity that practitioners remain mindful of the wider contexts in which their clients and patients are attempting to cope, Liz Ballinger begins Part II on *Culture and Personal Context* by focusing attention toward the seldom-addressed issue of class, placing in historical context its effects on systems within which mental health support is provided. She questions 'the relevance of psychological therapies in their current form', highlighting how intergenerationally perpetuated social inequalities and a socio-economic 'class gradient' both impact on a person's autonomy when attempting to gain access to mental health services, offering suggestions for potential ways forward.

The endemic pervasiveness of child sexual abuse within communities throughout the globe, in all its forms, continues to swell the statistics of helping professionals in attempting to help clients ameliorate the worst aspects of its effect on so many peoples' lives. Barry O'Sullivan, as priest and counsellor, considers findings from his doctoral research on holding difficult conversations in the context of 'the effects of clergy child sexual abuse on non-offending priests' and coping with the psychological effects of such scandals as clergy continue their vocation. His chapter 'explores what we should do when we do not know what to do', in particular as priests struggle to 'deal with brother priests who had betrayed them and with the Church which was both a victim and a perpetrator of betrayal'.

The late George MacDonald's doctoral research into culture as a 'positive resource in therapy' is considered in two chapters: in Part One he conducts a psychoanalytic look at culture and metaculture, challenging notions of fixed definitions – in social constructionist terms, 'each individual has access to a multiplicity of competing discourses', having some choices where 'they can accept or resist being interpolated or called into place as subjects'; he explores metaculture as a universality of features 'that are common to some or all of mankind'. In Part Two, he considers findings from his doctoral research on 'Culture as a resource in the creation of meaning', in which participants were encouraged to map their cultural life. A three-stage process encouraged co-created narratives at each stage that aimed to: establish facts; identify the cultural resources available to the participant; and identify and describe the superordinate metacultural themes active in the lives of the participants. He cross-correlates his findings of metacultural commonality in the need for 'belongingness' and 'growth', citing these as evident in case example narratives of three individuals: from Mid-Western USA; mixed Afro-Caribbean and white British; and Islamic Middle-Eastern ahead of integration into the UK.

Part III on *Practice Research* opens with John Prysor-Jones' doctoral investigation into counsellors' liminal experiences of 'hope' and 'hopelessness', specifically of 'hope present, hope as relational and hope lost'; the client's perspective is suggested as already incorporating a degree of hope by their arrival in the counselling process. Practitioner-participant voices are explored, reflecting on instances of the sometimes immense struggle in maintaining a sufficient vector of intentionality toward change, hope 'tussling' with hopelessness. On other occasions hope is experienced as 'an embodied, visceral and transitory experience' for both client and therapist, where 'the spirit in somebody comes through'; seen as embodied and relationally dynamic, it allows deep connectedness. This depth of connection can also be accompanied by 'dread and blackness', of professional dissatisfaction and failure. He concludes with a discussion on how practitioners might manage and live with these liminal extremes of 'safe uncertainty'.

Therapist and university researcher, Lynn McVey, investigates the nature and relevance of the psychoanalytic notion of reverie to both therapeutic encounters and to qualitative research. She focuses specifically on the experiencing within a liminal moment that arose from within a video-recorded interview between one of her practitioner-participants and herself as researcher-participant. She describes the extended moment as 'opening up a bright space for exploration and discovery', and further examines the implications for reflexive qualitative methodology that might 'extend the horizon of reverie from clinical practice to research'. The analysis of this example and further similar findings from this investigation in 'imaging/imagining the "real"', later served to inform and refine the research methods applied in subsequent doctoral research.

James Tebbutt's investigation into moments of deep encounter emerged from curiosity into experiences as a therapist and Methodist minister, occurrences being 'spread across a number of therapeutic and pastoral approaches' within psychotherapy and counselling and Christian ministerial contexts. This doctoral research focused questions on what might facilitate these moments and, in their unfolding, 'how they might be understood or interpreted'. Elaborating on methodology and the analysis, his detailed findings emphasise how an open-minded approach in the dialogue can facilitate meanings beyond what might be termed 'transpersonal', 'spiritual' or 'psychodynamic' practice, such open-mindedness being 'therapeutically more beneficial than applying a rigid interpretive or theoretical framework'.

One of our editors, Greg Nolan, opens Part IV on *Clinical Practice* in an exploration of the potential for agape love alongside its counter equivalent, destructive hate, when within the dynamic intimacy of clinical supervision. He links these emotional phenomena with ideas that emerged from Carl Jung's personal transformational journey toward individuation, elaborated in the text and images in *Liber Novus: The Red Book* (Jung, 2009). Jung's ideas of the 'third' and the 'fourth' are discussed, seen as relational phenomena that give evidence to our 'interconnectedness in the struggle toward individual meaning-making'. These notions are explored alongside a case example from supervision that generated edge of awareness phenomena, originating from within a recalled client's narrative, then reified from the clinical session within an extended moment of parallel processes. Reflections on these 'developmentally insightful' phenomena are seen to have helped personal discovery and sense-making 'for each in the relational supervisory triad'.

Practitioner Lynn Learman presents her findings from doctoral research that arose from experiences as a psychological therapist within the voluntary/3rd sector when working with refugee asylum seekers and a translator. She cites from the three voices – the therapist, the interpreter and the traumatised asylum seeker – finding that all participants identified significant moments of encounter that had little to do with linguistic issues; emotional connection was created non-verbally and tended to occur in silences and within moments of emotional distress. Her discussion raises issues on the role of the interpreter, identifying that, when being at ease with emotional distress and having an awareness of the potential for vicarious trauma, interpreters as additional skilled professionals can act as 'brokers between at least two cultures', enhancing the therapeutic process between counsellor and client in helping understand the distress and trauma that may be impacting on asylum seekers and their mental health.

Counsellor therapist and supervisor Allison Brown considers the supervisory relationship from the perspective of the supervisee, storying in the third person her developmental journey through clinical casework and the inevitable interweaving of the personal with the professional self. She reflects on the dynamics of attachment and the unconscious elements impacted upon by life events, of grief and loss unfolded in the transferences and countertransferences generated from proximal immersion in client narratives, that re-emerge in relational supervision. Also illustrated is how openness and trust within the supervisory frame may overcome occasional fallibility and allow a deepened trust, and that 'being sufficiently secure and yet vulnerable' is a prerequisite for insight and change. She concludes by juxtaposing these personal and professional experiences alongside consideration of theoretical perspectives on therapy and supervision, offering observations toward evolving good practice when at the far reaches of relational trust.

John Lees, psychotherapist and assistant professor, reflects on a single-case research study with his client, perceived through the multiple lens of anthroposophic psychotherapy (originating in the work of Goethe and Rudolph Steiner) and incorporating many of the findings of recent developments in the helping therapies, 'particularly the psycho-social aspects of the integration between therapy, sociology and politics and the biological aspects of the integration between therapy and medical science' – but also incorporates a spiritual world view, suggested as 'a bio-psycho-social-spiritual approach to practice' linking together contemporary innovations in psycho-social humanistically inclined relational psychoanalysis and recent psychosomatic research and practice. The chapter explores how anthroposophic psychotherapy purposefully circulates between the therapeutic relationship and the existential phenomenological situation of the client, enabling each as co-researchers into sufficient meaning.

Our other editor, William West, concludes the collection with reflections on the therapist as an 'edge dweller' – practitioners who share this aspect with many client perspectives in dwelling on the edge of the social and personal frameworks that help enable meaning to existence. He observes that this need not necessarily be 'a wholly negative experience', but perhaps 'a choosing to not belong or be in one situation', giving examples from personal and clinical experiences and those of therapists and others. Reflections on edge-dwelling are offered as also encompassing thoughts on the later stages of life and of our own inevitable death, that mystical bliss and suffering co-exist, and that there is hope, suggested in an analogy with flowers, that 'they all die but their seeds do have a chance to germinate'.

We hope that these thoughts and reflections, gathered from a range of therapists and researcher-practitioners in the helping and caring professions, give a collective flavour of some developments in the field. Their personal and professional openness to experiences and insights have arisen from courage, wisdom and vision in risking their views from the 'liminal edge', extending perception, awareness and sufficient meanings to differing ways of managing and living life as fully as is possible, offering ways of extending horizons of practice in the helping and caring professions.

References

Moodley, R. & West, W. (Eds) (2005) *Integrating Traditional Healing into Counselling and Psychotherapy*. Thousand Oaks, CA: Sage.

Nolan, G. & West, W. (Eds) (2015) *Therapy, Culture and Spirituality: Developing Therapeutic Practice*. London: Palgrave Macmillan.

Orbach, S. (2019) No direction home. *The Guardian Review*, 26 January 2019, 54, pp. 6–10.

West, W. (2000) *Psychotherapy and Spirituality: Crossing the Line between Therapy and Religion*. London: Sage.

West, W. (2004) *Spiritual Issues in Therapy: Relating Experience to Practice*. Basingstoke: Palgrave Macmillan.

West, W. (2011) *Exploring Therapy, Sprituality and Healing*. Basingstoke: Palgrave Macmillan.

PART I

Personal and professional identity

1

REFLECTIONS BEYOND THERAPY

To be or to not-be, is *that* the question?

Bridget Tardivel

It is late and I should be sleeping. But your words are grumbling around in my head, – "She told me I had two months to live. Well, that was over six months ago now … and I'm *still here*. Since then I feel like I've just been waiting … I'm *still* waiting …" – I can see him clearly in my mind; furrowed brow, heavy-lidded eyes searching some distant middle ground ahead, his words falling into the space between us, "So tell me … what is this … *waiting*?"

It's such an interesting question. Working as a therapist within a palliative context I have heard these, or similar words many times, and they inevitably linger with me. It's clear that the 'waiting' ends at death. But when and where does it begin? Surely, on some level, we are all waiting? I know that I am. Hopefully, if we are leading a reasonably sustainable lifestyle, we are doing lots of other things besides. But I have to own, that, just like the gentleman above, there is a quintessential part of me that sits, and waits. Although unlike him, I haven't experienced the grim reality of being presented with a terminal diagnosis. So to date, my prognosis remains blurry and indistinct.

For me, there is no clear distinction between living and dying. It does not exist in my mind. I find it easier, and more helpful, to see myself living *and* dying simultaneously; they sit side-by-side on a continuum, not following on one after the other. However, I have come to realise that this mindset is not the norm.

I am interested in the notion of a *tipping point* beyond which someone is considered to be dying rather than living, in who decides where this tipping point lies, and in how it impacts upon the living/dying experience of those within its clutches. In the Western context in which I live, we tend to regard ourselves as either living *or* dying, but generally not both together. Around me I witness frenetic energy spent attempting to separate and sift death out of life so that dying becomes a carefully segregated process that happens later, immediately prior to death. It is sometimes post-traumatic and short-lived, but more commonly follows the identification of an irreversible and progressive deterioration in health, often topped off with a terminal medical diagnosis. In general, only those in receipt of palliative care can truly call themselves dying, and even then they will probably find themselves surrounded by those who will try to persuade them otherwise. So, immersed in this wider culture, for me to regard myself as dying from the moment I was born, living *and* dying as I breathe, while mindful that at some future time I will 'not-be', feels curiously discordant and off-kilter. Populist terminology currently refers to palliative illnesses as 'life-limiting'. But the reality is that *all* life is limited and death is a part *of* life, not apart *from* life, no matter how much we might wish otherwise.

But I am not only a counsellor. Among other roles, I am also a mother, a sister and a daughter. As I stumble through my 57th year, my life is becoming littered with bereavements and loss. At times it feels positively cluttered. It is rare these days to have a conversation with friends or family that will not reference some imminent death or sad 'passing'. Recently I watched my Dad dying in hospital. He *was* very old, and as I keep trotting out, like a broken record, "he *did* lead a full and interesting life". Like that makes it somehow okay. They say hindsight is a wonderful thing, but looking back, I remember it dawning upon me, way before it became apparent to medical and nursing staff, that he really *was* going to die very soon.

It stole over me as I sat next to his hospital bed in the days before his death; a cold creeping realisation that I was witnessing his life-force trickling away. I had, I realised with crystal clarity, been observing this process for many years. More than I dared to remember. But these were the final dregs of life; those last few drops of blood red wine being drained from the bottom of the bottle. The light was clearly fading from his eyes.

And I think he knew it too. Sitting there I became increasingly baffled that nobody around us in the busy hospital ward seemed to see what I was seeing. The daily routine of propping him up in the chair next to his bed and offering him countless plastic beakers of tea and plates of mushy food continued way past the point at which he was able to politely decline. I'm sure I recall his last coherent words to me: "I'm *so* tired. *Please* just let me lie down." I felt I was dragging the medical team behind me toward the pearly gates of palliative care. "Keep up!" I wanted to shout at them over my shoulder. "He's not going to wait for you!" A few short hours before he drew his last breath, almost as though conceding defeat, they reluctantly wrote the phrase 'palliative care' in his notes so he could be wheeled into a side room to be left in peace to relinquish life, and die with some semblance of dignity. For me and my family, the whole process felt unnecessarily complicated, exhausting, and, for everyone involved, including fellow patients and clinical staff, potentially traumatising.

After he died, I sat holding his still-warm hand, and watched him for a long, long time. I couldn't tear my eyes, or myself, away. I have never before felt as calm and centred as in those moments of peace and tranquillity, like sitting at the eye of a storm.

Dad had a no-nonsense attitude toward life and death, and he had often talked about dying. It had interested him. I am positive that this was helpful for both of us in so many ways. Proud of his humble French 'peasant' (his word) rootstock, he would occasionally spatter his exchanges with the odd phrase of Breton Patois. One such; '*chacun à son tour par monter en carrosse*', loosely translates as 'each has his turn to climb into the hearse'. He was definitely waiting. In fact I used to joke that he'd had his coat on and bag packed for years before his final departure date.

Back in 1927, German philosopher Martin Heidegger wrote: 'just as one who flees death is pursued by it even as one evades it, and just as in turning away from it one has to see it nonetheless' (Heidegger, 1927, p. 404), and I find myself wondering about his words; while intuitively we might busy our lives with much fleeing and evading of death, there will also, for some of us, be those times when we find ourselves stopped in our tracks, waiting for it to catch us up.

Death *is* interesting though. Or perhaps it is our relationship with it that makes it so? In contemporary Western civilisations we play with it in our imagination, indulging ourselves through fiction and drama. Here, it is always carefully controlled and staged, the impact barely brushing our skin. It feels permissible to watch death unfolding from a distance, on a screen, stage, or in a book, presumably because it is happening to the other, and not to me.

Then there are the 'non-fiction' times too, the death of someone we know, and occasionally, someone very close to us; painful, gut-wrenching, heart-breaking. These are the times we feel ripped apart and hung out to dry, times we have to remind ourselves to keep breathing.

Reflecting here on the page, I feel my mind drifting down deeper into reverie; ghosts begin to creep between the lines (see Ibsen, 1881, *Ghosts*, Act II), snapshots from a different time of loss, in a different faraway place, a time of yesteryear which yet still feels like yesterday …

> … And now the dawn calling to prayers is filtering through the open window and into my consciousness. I am in the wake of a dream; scooping up the remnants before they skitter and disperse out into the morning light. In my dream I am ill and dying. It is a lonely vigil. I hang about on the periphery of living. Being with others, I find they are either sickeningly simpering or icy cold. It is easier to be on my own. At some point in time I take my leave and slink away to curl up in a ditch and wait for death like an old cat. I can sense relief waiting in the wings; relief that this exhausting process will all soon be over. But as I lie there I realise that I do not know what it is I am waiting for; I don't know what it looks like. After a while I become restless; I am cold and hungry, and there are indefinable things I need to be doing. So I get up and brush myself down before heading back towards the others. The dream drips with aching isolation which clings to my skin long after I have dragged myself wearily out of bed towards the day ahead …
>
> Cairo 2015: a vast and sprawling city, the colour of dirty honey, grown up out of fertile river mud and spilling out into the surrounding desert sand.

It is teeming with life and death, a kaleidoscope of soul and vitality. The air tastes earthy and brackish. Here I am, visiting my oldest daughter who lives in Egyptian Cairo. I have been drawn to pull myself towards her in the immediate aftermath of a family bereavement. Death looms large in my mind. Here I am, a very small fish out of water, gasping and flapping about, fazed and dissonant, senses drenched through. I am drowning in a sea of raw guttural noise as the sound of passionate and colourful Arabic expression drums into my ears and reaches right down inside my body. Those around me lean into their exchanges, animating them with life and fluid arm movement. In contrast, my limbs hang redundant and stiff by my side. I move cautiously through the narrow streets of the Islamic Market, pushing myself further into the busy space beyond. I have donned an air of unconvincing confidence as I duck and weave in amongst the mass of people, animals and vehicles. Together, we circumnavigate stalls piled high with bottles and jars, hessian sacks of brightly coloured powders, dead insects and dried entrails. A large sweet-smelling cauldron of spicy soup simmers and bubbles. Piles of sleepy tortoises and sliding snakes move about sultrily inside glass tanks. Wide-eyed kittens mew sadly and small birds chitter frantically from behind the bars of flimsy cages. Mounds of rubbish bake in the sun and puddles of dirty water steam gently underfoot whilst skanky cats scratch about amongst scraps. Is that a rattling lock I hear inside my head, an urgent whisper through a keyhole in my mind? Or is it just dancing shadows and my own shallow breath playing tricks on me as I stumble about in this strange space? Death sits sneering, lolling head and rolling eyes, smirking and sniggering in the corner of my eye …

Blistering heat engulfs me as I move from here to there, tentatively placing my feet on uneven ground that is opening up in front of me as I go. Quickening now, I am tripping along plunging further forwards into the throng that envelopes me in its midst. I am concentrating hard and averting my eyes from the stares and demanding questions that come crashing through my British stiffness: "Lady! Lady! Where are you from?" "Hello Lady! What is your name?" Gripping on tightly to my urge to dip and hide beneath my headscarf, I am desperate to blend in with those about me, to become invisible and disappear. I cower inside a stammering standoffishness which belies what is happening within. Timidly I creep and peep out from under my covers, anxious and alert for signs of hostility. Yet here there is nothing but insistent curiosity and slowly, slowly, as my frostiness thaws, I am tempted out, and drawn up into the warmth that smiles all about me in welcome …

Venturing from here to there, my confidence begins to grow. A staple diet of polite etiquette begins to unfurl inside and I am surprised to awaken within myself a natural aptitude for sharpness which enables me to fend off the most persistent enquiries, and maintain my personal space with firm and steady clarity. I am learning to trust in the rules of the game. "La!" I pronounce assertively, whilst eyeballing my over-enthusiastic inquisitor. There is no need for reprisal and upset, we understand each other perfectly and the message is heard. Walking out into the boiling traffic to cross the road with arm outstretched, I am forging my own space between cars as, with horns blaring, they manoeuvre around me. The process appears to work well and I begin to feel visible and valid. I am here and my presence is affirmed ...

Of course I realise that here, I am a foreign woman, and as such, I am awarded special privileges that native Cairene women are not. The voices I hear are masculine in the main, and I have to strain to hear softer female tones. Eyes downcast, women tread lightly here, and remain carefully covered up underneath swathes of cloth. I do not underestimate, nor claim to understand, the challenges for women living in this cultural melting pot, brimming with a rich and complex tincture of multi ethnic and mixed religious ingredients. I am well aware that there is much I am not privy to on the streets of Cairo; that there are areas of the city where my presence would not be welcome, and places where it is safer for young girls to hide their femaleness and disguise themselves as boys. Whether illusion or reality, to a certain extent, I feel protected by my foreign differentness. Yet I am also mindful of a paradoxical deep pull to blend in and belong; to cover myself up and become less visible as a woman ...

There is something too about my age being afforded an unspoken regard; I realise I have gravitas here and I begin to revel in it. It highlights a growing recognition that back in my home-culture I have been relinquishing a steady drip-drip of credibility; a sense that sometime around my half century I have been shunted from ascent into descent. Back home, I have been feeling under pressure to disguise and reinvent my Self; to repaint and gloss over my fading colours with a veneer of brassy cosmetic false hope. In contrast, here in Cairo, I find myself wearing my age with comfortable authenticity, and in return I receive something akin to respect ...

Egyptian silt begins to settle more comfortably into the folds of my skin as I become immersed in this strange and vibrant city. Flitting from now to now, '...the harmless endless succession of nows that just runs on...' (Heidegger, 1927/2010, p. 404), I am hungrily chasing fragments of new and vibrant experience before it is my time to leave, like a bird gathering crumbs with a wary eye out for the garden cat. Here, I have a vivid sense of reaching out towards something just beyond my grasp; something that remains unseen and undressed, though not completely naked, because in my thoughts and dreams, I am already clothing it in colourful expectation ...

And now I am alone, interring myself deep inside the great Pyramid of Giza. Here lay King Khufu, who spent much of his life making preparations for his onward journey beyond death. He left behind a tyrannical reputation as he shored up his existence; pouring his power into the creation of this huge iconic monolith. Built over four thousand years ago, it pays homage to eternity ...

Panting, I slowly clamber up through the steep passageway towards the King's Chamber, Khufu's final resting place (although ironically not his last);

a small dark recess beckoning from up above through the dim electric light. Nothing disturbs the quiet stillness other than my heavy footfall and the laboured breath which falls out of my mouth and hangs all about me in the warm oppressive air. As I stumble through the low entrance into the chamber, my eyes already adjusting to the pale shadows before me, I realise I am not alone. A tall sinewy woman stands squarely in the middle of the room, facing the broken stone sarcophagus. She remains stock still, arms hanging loosely by her sides, head and gaze tilted up towards the huge slabs of limestone resting above our heads. Quieting my breath, I take my place in a shadowy corner to watch and wait. I am an intruder whichever way I look at it, an uninvited voyeur vicariously stealing intimate moments from this woman's commune with the dead king. Time elapses as we share the crushing stillness all about. I have no sense of Khufu's soul here; no feelings that enable me to capture his missing presence. His remains and accompanying precious trappings have long since been stolen away. All is empty and gone …

Now, I am here in Tahrir Square; symbol of erupting passion and rage, of spilt blood and splintered bones, both historically and more recently in 2011 during the so-called Arab Spring. Since then, traffic is being carefully diverted away from the Square and the nearest metro station remains closed. So I have walked through sweltering heat to get here and as I linger to look about me I do not feel welcome. All feels eerily sterile and cleansed of emotion, and yet, like a pregnant pause, there remains a simmering tension in the air, and some clear reminders of recent unrest. A group of uniformed soldiers hang about desultorily, close by a line of sleeping tanks. They eye me as I eye them. To one side of the square, the imposing grand façade of the Egyptian Museum looks out from behind a scrolled up wall of razor wire. To the other, like a dirty smudge against the crisp blue sky, a burnt-out blackened block of flats discolours the picture. Uncomfortable and intrusive ghosts creep about restlessly at the edge of my mind as I move out from under this scorched memorial to pick my way towards the Museum ticket office …

Inside the Museum, I am quickly overwhelmed by the quantity and richness of historical artefacts that have been collated inside this vast quiet space. I come ill-equipped with insufficient capacity to digest and take it all in. After careful consideration, I move purposefully towards the gallery housing the exhibition of Egyptian Mummies. Approaching, I feel an uneasy mix of excitement, embarrassment and irreverence at the prospect of seeing these dead bodies; the ancient remains of cadavers, removed from their burial chambers and displayed in glass chill-cabinets under stark electric light for all the world to see. There is no earth-to-earth, or ashes-to-ashes going on here. And as I move slowly and blandly around the room from mummy to mummy, I feel I have become automated and slightly disconnected. I realise I am holding my breath as I struggle to locate my Self in this strange place …

I find myself tutting sharply at a young man who is trying to take a 'selfie', all bright smiles, with the remains of an Egyptian queen. He catches my stern look and drops his gaze and his Smartphone sheepishly. "So sorry …", I murmur to the dead queen as he slopes away towards the next exhibit. I am uncomfortable here in my voyeurism, and yet cannot help but be drawn to this dead person, laid out, exposed and vulnerable in her glass tomb. As my indignation begins to dissipate, I push the remnants of my discomfort aside and, just like the young man before me, lean in close to gaze into the casket. Intently, I begin to search your dead face and those empty eye sockets that lie so close to mine. For what, I wonder, am I searching? Signs of a life lived, or clues to a death died?

I have read that after your demise, it took seventy days to tend to your body; an attempt to preserve you and keep you intact; to hold on to some semblance of your presence. It took seventy days to drain and desiccate your viscera, to pack your cavities and to soak and wrap your skin in strips of swaddling cloth, jewels and precious stones carefully pressed into the folds, just in case perhaps? But they remain unspent and your body appears desolate. Is it the reluctance of the living to let go of life that is churning about in my gut; that yearning to challenge mortality and cling on for, and to, dear life? I hope you were handled with a gentle tenderness, and that tears fell and mingled amongst those gems. As I watch you, I welcome the familiar sensations of grief that well up from the depths of my being, and I am transfixed as the enormity of the space between us begins to shrink and shrivel. We are as one, you and I, as I reach in tentatively with my feelings and touch you softly, following the contours of your sunken cheeks and carefully stroking your ancient leathery brow …

And now it is dusk as my black cab speeds along the Sharia Salah Salem. We race and weave amongst the noisy throng of vehicles flying towards the Citadel way up above the city, and ahead I look out over the Northern Cemetery, where thousands of Cairenes have made their homes in and amongst a swathe of darkening mausoleums and tombs that stretch away and fade into the distance. I am hunkered down safe in my seat, remote and riding high, until suddenly we are pulling off the fast road and dropping down towards this City of the Dead. The weight of traffic forces us to slow, and as we crawl past this macabre housing estate, I peer out through my open window to snatch at illicit and enticing glimpses of the narrow streets and ginnels that disappear deep inside the labyrinth of stone edifices all about me. I wonder how it would be to live, and breathe, and sleep so closely in and amongst the bones of my ancestors; to dwell with the dead. In my mind's eye I am leaving the safety of my cab, and as I skulk towards the dark alleyway that draws me towards its depths, my head bowed and hidden beneath my head-scarf, I still my shallow breathing and quickening heartbeat to steal in amongst the shadows and begin to stalk that presence that watches my approach …

Now I am standing at the Citadel walls looking out into the deepening orange skyscape above the city spread out before me. The sun has lost its bluster and is dipping fast towards the sprinkling of darkening domes and

> minarets below. The intricate detail and minutiae of daily grime and grind is fading with the light. Far away across the disappearing purple city, the pyramidal peaks of Giza blink at me enquiringly through the haze. I wonder what my exit will be like. How will we part? Will we be graceful and dignified? Or will we scrabble about messily, clutching at straws and dousing ourselves in white lies? My time is approaching. It circles me slowly, watching and waiting. I can feel it in my bones.
>
> The prospect of leaving feeds a growing knot of fumbling emotion buried deep within my chest walls. I hold my breath and grip on to it tightly but it has already begun to unravel and creep up to clot and lodge inside my throat. Salty tears pool and prickle behind my eyes as, from a mosque below, a single mournful wail slowly ascends before me to cut through the night sky. Gradually, other voices call out as though in response and together they thicken into a glorious cacophony of soulful sound that settles like a blanket over the sprawling cityscape. Tonight I must wrench myself away and take my leave from this spellbinding place where life and death sit side by side, to chase my shadows back home from whence they came …

My time in Cairo was, for me, a pivotal period of reflection and of reckoning; an experience that enabled me to take back into myself responsibility for the way I wish to be. Once upon a time in my life, death appeared far more peripheral than it is now. It would take me by surprise, creeping up behind me, tapping me on my shoulder. These days I sense it following me around doggedly. Occasionally I think I catch a glimpse out of the corner of my eye. I know that some day it will finally trip me up and I will fall into its arms. Death has a shadowy form in my mind, and if I concentrate really hard and focus in on it, I can almost begin to contemplate the oblivion that lies beyond; the not-being.

At times, I have found myself using the concepts of *death* and *not-being* interchangeably and, while they are inextricably linked, I acknowledge the distinction between them which, I think, merits further attention here. If we consider the term *death* more closely, strictly speaking it alludes to a moment at which life ceases to be, addressing a specific date; a point in time when the final breath escapes the body. There is a clear distinction between a before, and an after. The body remains, but the person has gone. Or in Lucretian terms, the soul-atoms have abandoned the vessel. We may find ourselves rushing to a bedside to bear witness to this momentous event; the moment that crystallises the sharp distinction between life and death. Death has physicality and finitude. It has a form which has tangible attributes; legacies, remains and residue, imprinted upon those custodians who remember. Once the moment of death is past, it lodges in the minds of those left behind.

In contrast, *not-being* is much more slippery. Elusive and ethereal, it is a void. I can play with death as a concept, but when I try to describe not-being, my imagination becomes scrambled, and my words sparse. While I can perceive of death as an event that happens to others and will happen to me, the concept of not-being remains tantalisingly personal and intimate, yet virtually inaccessible. As concepts go, death is the sharp edges and stench, to not-being's odourless gas in a blacked-out room with no walls.

These days my being is interlaced with awareness that at some unspecified time in the future, I will not-be. From this time on my being will exist only in the memories and minds of others. I will no longer be embodied within my Self. Nor will I exist in my own mind. I find this concept terribly difficult to grasp. It is relatively easy to write the words here on the page, but processing them into meaning is tricky. As such, I find my Self here, being, somewhere within the space between birth and death, contemplating not-being as I go. My death awareness has taken on many different guises over the years, but has become increasingly salient of late. Recently, someone asked me how many times I think about death in a day. For me, that is the wrong question. Death, (or is it not-being?), is in my mind all the time. Perhaps it's an 'age thing'. I'm really not sure, except to say that these days, I reflect upon my entire life, past, present and future, through a prism of death awareness.

It dithers about on the edge of consciousness, partly obscured by the more shadowy areas of my mind. It is a shape-shifter moving through dappled undergrowth at the bottom of the garden. Rustling through leaves, snapping twigs, it watches me from the depths. I can peer at it cautiously through the lace curtains of my awareness, but I cannot quite pinpoint or define it. It is elusive and vague. Nonetheless, it remains a major player in the substance of my story, embedded within the essence of my spirit; that which permeates the boundaries of my skin and mind, and fetters my sense of self into the landscape within which I move about.

This relationship with death began at the moment of my conception. It is a built-in contract, a part of the package. I might collude in tidying the fragility of life away among the tiny type-script of a footnote at the bottom of a page, but it remains a small caveat, a tiny fingernail scratching at the inside of my skull. I know it is there; its angst is a part of my Self.

The level of my angst, or anxiety, ranges up and down accordingly. I am never without it, it feels fundamental to my being; an integral and primal part of what it is to be human, reminding me I am alive. How each of us experiences and expresses this anxiety may well vary, but it exists, nonetheless, in all of us. Of course I can't prove this in any gold-standard randomised-controlled trial, but as a hypothesis it works well for me; it's one that I find useful to my own being, and it helps me process what I evidence all around me.

I have grown to perceive this sense of temporality as a valuable asset; burying it underground wastes energy and compromises my capacity to experience emotion in relationships at a deeper, more meaningful level. If I ignore it, over time my existence can begin to feel superficial and monotone. And if I avert my eyes for too long, it sneaks in under my skin, wreaking havoc in the most innovative of ways; those creaking joints, that weighty malaise upon waking, or that ill-timed decision to step off the kerb in front of that car. Resilient and persistent, my temporality will always find creative ways to remind me it is still there. Never static, this awareness requires constant monitoring and nurturing to keep it from sliding into sickness. In return,

I am rewarded with a sense of vitality, not always comfortable, but nevertheless rich in feeling.

In Western culture, reported anxiety-related sickness is on the rise. Anxiety itself has bad press these days, and is generally regarded as a state to be excised. Perhaps we have always experimented with alcohol and non-prescription drugs as a means of self-managing our anxiety. No doubt we will continue to do so. But increasingly, these days we appear to hand over the reins of responsibility to the expert 'other'. Our angst has become pathologised and is treated with pills, potions and psychological therapies. Personally, I fear that this is a dangerous trend for a society to endorse. Arguably, the pharmaceutical approach toward anxiety operates skin-deep, providing a cultural sticking plaster that is frankly losing its 'stick'. In my view it is so entangled with monetary profit and the finance industry that it begins to corrode the ethical principles that scaffold both individual and collective responsibility toward health and wellbeing. The pull to collude in this powerful dynamic is strong, and while anxiety remains such big business, and money the chosen currency of value, individual needs can become muffled and blurred.

Don't get me wrong, I acknowledge that medical advances continue to enhance and enable longevity of life, and on occasions, quite literally offer a lifeline to many whose living experience is blighted by pain and suffering. However, I worry that a cultural passivity is eroding our capacity to listen to our bodies and trust in our own voices. Relinquishing responsibility for personal wellbeing to the 'expert' other is, I feel, becoming endemic, whether medical, political or spiritual. Indwelling and self-reflection has become passé; an extra-curricular activity as opposed to a fundamental component of healthy living. I am drawn toward Paul Tillich who, in post-war 1952, described anxiety as 'existential', and as such, that which 'cannot be removed', and incapacitating anxiety, a 'neurosis … an avoidance of nonbeing by avoiding being' (Tillich, 1952, p. 12). I feel his words are ever more poignant in light of current trends.

So, to clarify, I am not proposing a culture without medical advances, far from it. Instead, I am advocating one where a sense of temporality, with all its associated anxiety, can thrive and be respected as an *essential* component for health and wellbeing; where being 'well' involves assimilating the prospect of not-being into the self. Neither am I recommending specific ways of working in therapy. As practitioners, we all work differently and have our own individual approaches depending upon who we are, and who we encounter within the therapy setting. However, if you accept the premise that death anxiety permeates our culture underlying everything we do (and you may not), then inevitably, it will play a significant role deep within any therapeutic encounter. If we, as therapists, fail to address our own relationships with mortality, then I would argue that we also risk failing in our responsibility toward those who seek out our services.

In an ideal world my professional role would become totally redundant. There would be no need to *manufacture* therapeutic spaces in which fundamental existential questions of life, and death, can be addressed. Instead these would be integrated into everyday living. Perhaps only then, the 'waiting', whenever that begins, rather than an arid state of passivity, might be more easily relished as an opportunity to take stock, and focus attention on what it is we want from life, for *all* of the time in which we have it. It is only through acknowledging the inevitability of not-being that we will find the 'courage to be' (Tillich, 1952, p. 17).

References

Heidegger, M. (1927/2010) *Being and Time*, trans. J. Stambaugh. Albany, NY: University of New York Press.

Ibsen, H. (1881) *Ghosts*, Act II.

Tillich, P. (1952) Anxiety, Religion and Medicine. *Pastoral Psychology*, 3, pp. 11–17.

2

'MAGICAL' CONSCIOUSNESS

An ancient god, synchrony and anomaly in service of the ego

David Paul Smith and Friday Faraday

Psychotherapy often focuses on techniques applied to eradicating symptoms. Symptoms are often conceptualized in mechanistic fashions, e.g., cognitive and behavioral categories. Trained in applied behavioral analysis many years ago, I make use of these approaches which I find very effective. However, I often utilize hypnotic techniques in my practice and have frequently engaged vistas of psychological processes that are only done justice to by viewing them in a depth psychology framework and in particular a Jungian framework.

This chapter will review a case that touches on religious imagery, Western magic and archetypical conditions. In approaching this case from a Jungian perspective, I feel it allowed me and my client to make progress, where other approaches would have run the risk of pathologizing the process. Furthermore, on suggestions from a colleague, I offered my client to participate in collaborating in writing this chapter. As a writer, I asked Friday to author descriptions of *their*[1] experience and to take full license to creatively portray *their* side of the process. I hoped that this would both further the therapeutic process and convey our experience in a more effective fashion.

My client is a tall, muscular African-American individual who came to see me around the time *they* were beginning graduate school for a degree in creative writing and English. Friday was living with a woman but had recently moved back to *their* parents' home as *their* partner's mother moved into the apartment both were living in. Also, Friday needed to save money while finishing *their* degree. Friday worked in the city at a stable job. However, the most salient feature of *their* presentation was that *they* asserted *they* could remember very little of *their* life prior to living with *their* partner. Friday only remembered parts of high school and nothing from *their* childhood. This amnesia and *their* struggle with depression is why Friday decided to come see me.

My first assumption, considering *their* history, was that Friday would be dealing with some suppressed trauma. Also, in spite of being big in stature, Friday was soft-spoken and had a gentle demeanor. My intuition suggested *they* may be struggling with gender identity issues. I began our work, as I do with anyone, to gather what history I could. We talked about recent history, *their* relationship, *their* job in the city, and *their* plans for the future. Friday wanted to be a writer. *Their* present job was in a field related to what *their* father had done for a living. On *their* free time, Friday had finished a bachelor's degree and was now working through an online university for *their* masters in writing.

During the early period of therapy, Friday had a tendency to succumb to anxiety. Friday obsessed on applying for jobs online. *They* wanted to get a better job and move out of *their* parents' house. Friday's parents tended to fight and bicker and the father is an alcoholic. Exposure to the stressful stimuli, which I was sure *they* had dealt with through *their* life, continued to fuel *their* depression.

In therapy, I encouraged Friday to meditate which *they* said *they* were already practicing. We discussed ways to gain some relief from the stress and began to look at *their* depression, anxiety and relationship with *their* parents. Friday also decided that living at home while in school had advantages that would be lost by prematurely moving. Friday needed to save money and finish *their* degree.

I introduced Friday to hypnotic techniques. I would periodically make a recording that *they* could listen to at home. These efforts provided imagery and suggestions to cope with stress and solve problems in order to make confident progress toward graduating and moving into a type of work that was in line with Friday's ultimate goals.

We entered a second phase of therapy that involved a stable presentation. Friday was dating and felt "okay". *Their* work in school was going very well and things at home were stable. *They* wanted to start coming on a biweekly basis. It was around this time that Friday had missed a session and then I was notified that *they* were in the hospital. Friday had tried to take an overdose of medication but luckily notified a friend and went to an inpatient unit at a local hospital. Friday's parents were concerned and sympathetic but they would tend to argue with each other and blame each other for their child's condition. The parents were lost in a coping strategy that externalized their own frustrations and problems.

Friday returned to weekly sessions. *They* told me that *they* had plateaued and felt stuck. Then *they* were grabbed by despair. Friday wanted to succeed and get out on *their* own. Often, *they* felt as though things were not moving quickly enough. *They* would start to doubt *their* own ability to be successful.

In the course of working with hypnotic techniques and encouraging *them* to meditate, a fascinating course of intersubjective phenomena unfolded that I feel helped move the therapy along and engaged us in a more intimate and shared psychological process.

On one occasion, I was reading a book by Scott Jones (2014) titled, *When the Stars Are Right: Towards an Authentic R'lyehian Spirituality*. It is the author's personal presentation of a spirituality which he bases on ideas and imagery from the works of H.P. Lovecraft. Lovecraft originally published in pulp magazines such as *Weird Tales* and *Astounding Stories*, and is one of the most influential writers of horror in America, having been included in the Library of America (*H.P. Lovecraft: Tales* volume 155, 2005). His work has influenced modern authors such as Stephen King, Alan Moore, Neil Gaiman and many others. Lovecraft introduced a new theme to horror, breaking from Gothic narratives, and developed stories that talked about ancient gods, apocalyptic threats from under the ocean and the deep realms of space. Lovecraft suffered medical and psychological trauma and both of his parents were committed to mental institutions from which they were never released. Nightmares that he suffered from the age of five influenced his writing and his work is clearly amenable to depth psychological analysis. His ideas have fueled a virtual industry in the modern age, inspiring movies, Animae, video games and modern occultism (Steadman, 2015)

I would describe Jones' (2014) book as a spirituality of work with the Shadow, borrowing from a concept of Carl Jung (Zweig and Abrams, 1991); Jones shares aspects of his own psychological process which led to his interest in the works of Lovecraft.

Jordan Stratford, in the 'Foreweird' in Jones (2014), describes a dream from when he was around 14 years old and encountered repetitively, described as follows:

> I awakened into the dream and found myself standing at the edge of a barren cliff. A glance behind revealed a hammered sheet of sand and bare, dusty stone that stretched to the limit of my sight. The view ahead was similarly flat and massive: the sea, the western sea (for somehow I knew I faced that direction), insistently wore away at the base of the cliff. This was a place of boundaries, of drawn, stepped horizons: the lifeless land of sand and stone, the cliff edge where I stood; below, the cliff base, the shoreline, and below that, further along the curve of the earth, the edge where sea met sky, leagues away. I breathed deeply, tested the air with my tongue. Salt and ancient decay; strange fragrance as of scorched metal resting on stiff shelves of breeze.
>
> *Stratford, cited in Jones, 2014*

Later that same week I met with Friday. Friday had shared some impressions *they* had from meditation or dreaming earlier in their week. I suggested we try a hypnotic session to engage unconscious processes that might lead to some insight to what *they* were hiding from, what may be holding *them* back emotionally. Hypnosis can unlock memories or engage images that can be useful in analyzing fears, make us face what we don't want to face. This is shadow work. In 1945, Jung defined the Shadow as "the thing a person has no wish to be" (Samuels, Shorter and Plaut, 1986, p. 138). It is the sum of all unpleasant qualities one wants to hide.

I conducted a basic hypnotic regression and Friday would share in a whispered and trance state, what *they* were imagining. This is a standard technique in hypnotherapy. *They* described finding themselves on a dark beach with vast expanses of sand and water. The water was black and viscous, *they* felt stuck and had difficulty wading through it. The sky was a night sky and everything went on forever.

As Friday described it, the passages I had read earlier in the week came to mind. The similarities in delving into the dark recesses of dream imagery were striking, i.e., the ocean, sand and blackness. The similarities in characteristics related to the Shadow were also striking – deep and expansive darkness, powers outside of perception. Jones goes on to describe hidden powers submerged beneath the murky depth; for my patient, difficulty moving forward in the restrictive murkiness of depression.

Friday described *their* own repetitive dream which involved a dark figure that caused them fear and continued to haunt them. This proved to be a foreshadowing of the following incident which became a very significant development in the therapeutic process.

Anubis/Hermanubis

It was after their hospitalization that we had an even more curious session. Friday came to the office somewhat tremulous. Friday had been meditating and told me *they* sensed a presence in the room. In *their* mind's eye *they* had seen a canine-headed person. However, *they* said it was visceral, very real. It was as though this entity was in the room with *them*. When Friday closed *their* eyes, *they* saw this person, a canine-headed entity wearing an armored outfit of bygone years. Behind this entity flowed the universe, stars and galaxies swirling in the background. The entity told Friday to be true to *themselves*, to find *their* own power. This became a theme in interactions with this god.

My first reaction was to de-pathologize the experience. To normalize it I explained that when meditating or during hypnotic techniques we can have powerful experiences but that was okay, to be expected. Furthermore, we could examine this together and figure out what to make of it. I let Friday know we were in this process together.

After seeing patients that day, I went to a local pub at the University of Chicago where I ritualistically get a late dinner and relax. I opened a book by Gordon White (2016) that I had been reading, *The Chaos Protocols*. I opened it and continued reading from where I left off. I was completely unaware of what the next part of the chapter had to offer. The following section of the book was titled "Hermanubis" and reads as follows:

> Ah, Hermanubis, the most magically useful god you have never heard of. Emerging from the sometimes-literally psychedelic period of Greco-Egyptian syncretism, Hermanubis is a hybrid form of the Egyptian Funerary god, Anubis, and the Greek messenger-trickster, Hermes. The combination of the two provides a psychopomp par excellence. He is depicted as having the body of Hermes and the head of Anubis. His most famous surviving statue is viewable in the Vatican Museum.
>
> Cynocephalic (dog-headed) gods are supremely ancient and wide-spread. As for Hermanubis specifically, his origin is something of a moving feast.

> Plutarch, for instance, identifies Anubis with Hermes and with the star Sirius (the dog star). But the dog/messenger/Sirius connection is found at least as far back as the early New Kingdom where we see cynocephalic figures greeting the rising sun at the four doors of the eastern horizon on one of Ramses II's obelisk. The rising of Sirius marked the beginning of at least two of Egypt's simultaneous calendar systems.... This calendric notion survives into the Egyptian concept of the decans—mighty spirits that hold sway over sections of the night sky. The sequence of decans begins with Hermanubis, and here we can see his role as psychopomp and opener of the ways. He appears from the underworld and travels across the sky at the head of the entire parade of star gods.
>
> *White,* 2016, *pp. 87–88*

My patient had a profound and personally disturbing event. Jung warns that encounters with the collective unconscious and the archetypes can be powerful and challenging to the cohesiveness of the self. The usual compensatory mechanism of the psyche is challenged by forceful impingement of unconscious imagery (Samuels, Shorter and Plaut, 1986, p. 123). My patient experienced what Harry Stack Sullivan called an autochthonous experience, the intrusion of imagery and impressions that come from outside ones sense of self (Sullivan, 1996, p. 150). This can lead to chaotic and psychotic processes that render the individual unable to integrate the material into a coherent sense of self. However, the process, arguably normal from a Jungian perspective can be facilitated in therapy and lead to psychological and spiritual growth.

Jung also referred to events such as this particular example as "synchronistic". Jung defined this in several ways, initially as an "acausal connecting principle" (Jung, 1952/70). He suggested it referred to events that were meaningful but not causally related, not coinciding in time and space. He also defined the synchronistic as referring to events that coincide in time and space but can also be seen to have meaningful psychological connections. It involves the linking of psychic and the material worlds (Samuel, Shorter and Plaut, 1986, p. 146). Anubis or Hermanubis entered both our lives in different ways, and he became a substantial ally in the therapeutic work.

Friday started to have more anomalous, trancelike and hypnotic imagery when meditating, dreaming and, at times, during the work day. Friday had a few spontaneous experiences of trance involving derealization and disassociation. We worked together to interpret and make sense of this process.

On one occasion, during a bus ride downtown to work, Friday dozed off and felt like *they* were rising up in the air, levitating. The experience was visceral and disorienting. Friday explained that it took some time to ground *themselves* when *they* got off the bus and *they* even had some difficulty gaining *their* balance.

Around this time Friday had a persistent image of Superman encased in ice. *They* identified with the image and said they felt they were in a block of ice but eventually the ice broke or melted and they broke free, flying away.

There is a tendency in the literature to pathologize these types of experience. In Farias and Wikholm (2015) *The Buddha Pill*, there is a whole chapter dedicated to "the dark side of mindfulness". They argue that meditation is not all that it is cracked up to be. For example, they describe a young yoga teacher whose experience of her "sense of self" changed. This led to depression and psychiatric treatment. The authors explained she spent 15 years being treated for psychotic depression. They also give examples of two teenagers who became emotionally disturbed because their meditation practice unleashed emotional material that they could not deal with. They refer to one study by David Shapiro that examined 27 people and found that 63% had at least one negative effect and 7% suffered profoundly adverse effects. Negative effects included anxiety, panic, depression, increased negativity, pain, feeling "spaced out", confusion and disorientation (Farias and Wikholm, 2015, p. 145). The authors give other examples that include psychotic symptoms such as ego dissolution, dissociation and hallucinations.

One may ask, if mindfulness techniques are psychotherapeutic, why are there so many side effects? If a pill made symptoms worse in 7–63% of the population, would it ever get approval from the FDA (US Food & Drug Administration)? However, is the point of practice to relieve symptoms? Let's examine the definition of mindfulness. Baer (2006, p. 5) defines mindfulness as "the nonjudgmental observation of the ongoing stream of internal and external stimuli as they arise". The author goes on to articulate that acceptance refers to "a willingness to let things just be as they are the moment we become aware of them". As any good teacher will tell you, it does not matter if what you observe is positive or negative, just notice it. It is an examination, an examination of consciousness itself. To borrow from Plato's analogy of the cave, it is a shift from looking at the shadows on the wall to noticing the light that is creating them.[2] It is an examination of the processes of our own minds to see how reality is constructed and an examination of how our reality of "self", is constructed. One could and should argue that this examination is a cure to our own ignorance, our own stuckness in the world.

As any good psychotherapist will tell you, the struggle to understand yourself is not always fun. Our habits are challenged; and our accustomed sense of self is threatened. People appear disturbed by threats to one's sense of self, one's equilibrium and the status quo. Defending threats to our view of reality is part of how our heads are wired. Research shows that growth of the mammalian brain is bound to sensory stimulation from the environment which then shapes the structure and functional organization of the brain. Once the organism reaches sexual maturity, the "existing structures tend to be enduring and resistant to change" (Wexler, 2008, pp. 58–59.) Techniques that help continue change and growth can be scary, in the least. They may be disturbing but they are manageable in the therapeutic process.

Also, these anomalous experiences can be construed as psychotic but if occurring in a functional human being and during the therapeutic process, they are better defined as mystical. As Jung and the Jungian influenced mythologist Joseph Campbell suggested, schizophrenics drown in the same pool of water that the mystic jumps into, swims around in and benefits from.[3]

After this stage of therapy, Friday started to remember bits and pieces of repressed material. *They* remembered being fearful when *their* father was very drunk and mistook their closet for the bathroom. Images that were painful came to the surface and we discussed them.

A particular painful memory that was visceral and volatile was of an extended family member who had touched Friday inappropriately. This was material we talked about but *they* felt they could not share with *their* parents or family. *They* felt family would doubt *their* story or react in a manner that would make Friday's present life worse rather than better.

Friday shared memories, playing with girls and feeling more at home in their world than the world often pushed on *them*. Friday was inclined to artistic efforts but *they* were always pushed toward sports, mechanics or computers. None of those worked for *them*. Friday even went to a school for game design but eventually enrolled *themselves* in college and then eventually, an MA program in creative writing.

Here is a description of the process in Friday's own words:

> It all began with a dream. Which was odd for me because I often don't dream. A man of shadows in the living room. He was broad and unmovable like a mountain, and made no attempt to leave his station, looking out the window into the clear night. I stood behind him as if that was always my place. In that moment, I wondered if it was fear or undeniable awe that controlled me as I stared at his rigid back, unable to move. That hesitation must have been known to him. The frozen stance that made him nothing more than a statue began to thaw. A hand on my shoulder came at unnatural speed, jarred me awake, and I went about my life, chalking it up to a bad dream.
>
> It wasn't until after my suicide attempt and 72-hour hold in the hospital that led me to meditate more and have another encounter with the man in black, or better yet, the Egyptian god Anubis. The night was calm and still, almost to the point that you assumed nothing would happen, but with my legs tensely crossed and my eyes sealed shut, he came; dark leathery skin that gave off a warmth and pulled me in close, it was hypnotic and lit a flame across my own skin. More of his animalistic face came into view; sun-color eyes had no restraint and cut to the soul. The lines of his mouth were barely noticeable, yet he spoke, "listen to your heart" and stared a fury into me. Tears painted my skin, but my eyes remained closed. His face soon faded back into the black and his body, muscular just as the shadow man that I saw years ago. Although, I didn't make the connection that seemed obvious.
>
> I let the experience fade into the rest of the night and wondered if I made it up, or was I just seeing things? For days, I didn't meditate. It was a fear that coursed through me like a poison, and the moment I decided to dive back in, I had no antidote. It took minutes before he came again, staring with those blazing eyes that could burn you if he wanted. The same message came from those fused lips "listen to your heart." My mind searched, it practically begged

for another explanation than the sight before me. What did it take for a mind to lose itself in the bout of depression, sadness, and anxiety? It was a question among many that I asked myself in a blur of uncertainty. I knew the answer, but it seemed more unbelievable than what I saw within my minds-eye. With that sense of fiction, I believed to be just that, fiction. I kept it to myself.

A change came forth. A change that I didn't want but knew that I needed. That drive became a pull of gravity that gave me no choice but to move forward. The world became something I never expected to be. It twisted into possibilities—roads that broke apart and divided into unknown paths. As beautiful as it sounded, it whipped me with a fright that came with having faith in something unknowable. Yet just as unknowable, I unwittingly gave into small compulsions to do the things that I wanted. The things that I was afraid to do. The iciness of fear started to thaw. I didn't see how much until I found myself being more social. Not just going out when I received an invitation but setting things up and taking charge. The moment that I learned to be still, breathe and feel the moment, something was unlocked. A path that was once shrouded in fog began to part, and I could hear the urge to keep moving from that same booming voice belonging to an old god that I didn't worship. However, a roadblock of my own creation formed, and I willingly slammed into it. That's when I learned that only one person can halt your own personal progress. Yourself. I stopped meditating and I kept the progress to myself, not even telling my therapist. Bad habits coursed like a virus that had free rein. It's when you let cruelty win that you see how much it changes you.

Restarting my weekly sessions instead of the bi-weekly schedule I started became the first step to setting things right, but it also led to something that my mind couldn't grasp. On the advice of my doctor, I meditated. The first time in days that I did so. My body groaned under the lotus position, it practically begged me to stop and do something else. Like a cruel taskmaster, I made myself sit and focus. That act didn't solve anything, and it kept the self-destructive wheel turning. A self-conscious brake was applied. I floated in a starry void that looked like the universe itself—peace and calm melded into me. A drum sounded that awakened a part of me that was long lost. Light took over the dark and I was in a room. I went down a small staircase and into a circular space that held a large cylinder in its center; blanketed in ice there was something inside that looked familiar. A figure. An image. A person, I came to realize. It was me, frozen in thick aged ice. I had no idea what it meant, and like most events, I was quick to dismiss it as another symbol of imagination.

However, that image repeated in other meditation sessions, and with each look at that block of ice and the figure within it, new feelings flooded around me and unlocked a confidence. It wasn't a superman level confidence that made me feel as if I could leap a building in a single bound, but it paved a road through struggles that I had long tried to run from. I would like to say that going down that road was easy and quick. I would like to say that there weren't times that I wanted to give up. Therapy and the admission of all I had seen encouraged me to keep going, but to have the balance of not putting too much pressure on myself as I continued down that road. That it was important to be kind to myself as I walked.

Which I did, most of the time. I wasn't immune to the cracks in the road that threw me off course. They took the form of relationships that I used to take my mind off the progress I made, or at least that was the lie. Every flirt, date, hook-up was an excuse to take a break on the road. That break became longer with each time that I gave my full focus to someone else and not myself. That block of ice became thicker and that version of myself that no doubt held secrets that I needed to get to became harder to see, but like most storms, they didn't last for long even when a small part of yourself wants them to, and often fights against the clearing of the day. Break-ups and the feelings of emptiness even when you are in bed with another person are true enough signs that a change is happening, and you cannot fight against it. So, when they ended, I was left with the same images in my head waiting for me like they knew what was going to happen before it did. It was a merry-go-around; no matter where I sat, I was going to go in the same repeating circle unless I decided to get off.

There is always a pattern with life if you look closely enough to see it without judgement. Part of me always sensed that but I lacked the courage to look because that meant that I would have to face many truths about my journey, and I thought that I wasn't ready to do so, even as therapy was going well, and I slowly grew stronger. On a bus ride to work, the wheels galloped at their normal speedy pace, and I watched the roving landscape out the window. It signaled a rather normal morning, but out of the ordinary, I got sleepy after I downed a large cup of coffee that I had after a miraculous nine hours of sleep. I tried to fight it, so I wouldn't miss my stop, but the urge ruled, and I submitted. My mind went to a place that it only goes when I meditate. Back in that room, where in the center of it stood that cylinder of ice with an unknown version of myself inside. I moved closer and saw the cracks travel like a wandering lightning bolt around the ice. There was no destination for it, around and around it went in a daze until it exploded in front of my mind, and it took off and soared into the sky like a lost god, and I woke up with a lightness and daze that couldn't be explain. However, it was the beginning of something more. The change came with an acceptance of who I was, and the things that my mind protected me from.

During our work, Friday obtained *their* MA, did very well and graduated with honors. Although in the Honors Society and post graduate credentials, Friday received very little praise or acknowledgement from family. We discussed how *their* efforts likely fell on deaf ears, not so much that Friday's family did not care about *them*, but that they really could not relate to Friday, and very likely never understood who *Friday* truly was. However, during Friday's education and during therapy *they* began to grow into *their* own identity, one that *they* felt comfortable in.

Friday is drawn to art and had a clearly artistic personality. *They* also identified with certain classically feminist perspectives. We discussed complexities of gender identification and the process of settling into an identity that felt true. *They* began to paint their nails and *they* put a poster on the wall in their room that said, "Feminist as Fuck". Friday's mother was bothered and made them take it down although she admitted she didn't know what a feminist was. She was unnerved by *their* nails. She asked Friday if *they* were gay. Friday was angry at the unaccepting quality of *their* parents' response, mom and dad's confusion related to self-expression. This resulted in more discussion of how Friday felt uncomfortable as a 30-something year old person, who was living with *their* parents, parents who continued to bicker and fuel Friday's depression. However, Friday continued to make progress, publishing several pieces and exploring options for varied employment.

Friday was drawn to T-shirts and lapel pins that jokingly depicted images of the dark arts. One had a group of children playing in a pentagram which poked fun at religious warnings of such things as Ouija boards being dangerous and not a toy. A popular expression on the south side of Chicago is "Not Today Satan!" Friday wore a pin that read, "Yes, today Satan!" Friday felt the religious community and *their* family were hypocritical. People made value statements about how to live one's life, although *they* did not attend church or practice what they preached. In an existential sense they proved inauthentic, while Friday was trying to find authenticity.

We discussed the similarities in Friday's interests and the process of therapy. In a way, we were raising demons, memories and fears that Friday had put out of mind or had not been able to integrate into *their* conscious. We were confronting their demons and in a preconscious manner, Friday was expressing in *their* clothing and accoutrements *their* work at facing the repressed, dark side of self. From a Jungian perspective, Friday was confronting the Shadow.

As *they* proceeded to express *their* artistic self, I encouraged Friday to explore opportunities in the city that would allow *them* an outlet for artistic expression and meeting people that were like minded. Friday became engaged with gender LGBTQ groups and social rights. Friday continued to send out work for publication and explore better vocational opportunities. *Their* father was diagnosed with congestive heart failure and actually cut down on his drinking.

Friday realized that *they* did not want to become *their* dad and feared they would if *they* did not accomplish *their* goals. That is, Friday feared working at the same job and never leaving home. However, Friday eventually came to accept that *their* parents may never understand who *they* really are and *they* could still be the person *they* were meant to be. In actuality, although it took time, Friday was now emerging into the person *they* were comfortable with, a writer. Friday was a writer and could engage all the possibilities that would accompany this role.

Although Friday's family provided very little acknowledgement of *their* obtaining a Master's degree, *they* continued to publish and move forward. On the writing of this chapter, *they* attained a job teaching at the college level working as an adjunct professor for the Chicago college system. Friday told me *they* love teaching and feel at home in this work. Our schedule changed to part-time as moving forward as a professor and working multiple jobs made the schedule complicated. As Friday progresses in a new career, *they* are preparing to get *their* own place and leave home.

In conclusion, I tell my patients, "When you meditate or practice clinical hypnosis, sometimes weird things happen". The experience may and ought to challenge your view of reality (see also endnote 3), and open a person to the possibilities inherent in the psychotherapeutic process. The process can involve anomalous experience and can be disturbing yet profound. I believe that modern psychiatry tends to pathologize these processes that are better defined as spiritual, albeit sometimes spiritual emergencies (Grof, 1989). The depth psychological tradition refers to it as "regression in service to the ego" (Kris, 1936/52, p. 60). I think this is the better way to view them.

Notes

1 In this chapter *they/them* is used as a gender-neutral replacement for *he/she* and *him/her*, as has become common parlance in contemporary literature sensitive to agendered identity. Efforts have been made to protect the anonymity of Friday. However, all clinical details have been presented exactly as they emerged in therapy with the author's permission.

2 "The psychotic drowns in the same waters in which the mystic swims with delight" (Campbell, 2000, cited in Grof, 2000, p. 136).

3 Plato's analogy of the cave is a parable of education and ignorance. Prisoners are chained in a cave from birth. Their reality consists of shadows cast on a wall. They are unable to turn and see the source of light, a fire. A prisoner is freed to see the fire and objects casting the shadows and ultimately to go outside the cave and see the sun. The light is painful to the eyes, the fire and then the sun even more so. The truth takes time to adjust to and Plato suggests the other prisoners would be reticent to leave their chains. However, once the truth is confronted, the option of a chained existence would never again be acceptable.

References

Baer, R. A. (2006). *Mindfulness-Based Treatment Approaches: Clinician's Guide to Evidence Base and Applications*. Burlington, MA: Academic Press.

Farias, M. and Wikholm, F. A. (2015). *The Buddha Pill: Can Meditation Change You?* London, UK: Watkins Publishing.

Grof, S. (2000). *Psychology of the Future: Lessons from Modern Consciousness Research*. Albany, NY: State University of New York Press.

——. (1989). *Spiritual Emergency: Where Personal Transformation Becomes a Crisis*. New York: Putnam Penguin.

Jones, S. R. (2014). *When the Stars Are Right: Toward an Authentic R'lyehian Spirituality*. Location 196. Amazon Digital Services LLC: Martian Migraine Press.

Jung, C. G. (1952/70). Synchronicity: An Acausal Connecting Principle. In: *The Structure and Dynamics of the Psyche CW8* (2nd Edn), Trans. R. F. C. Hull. Princeton, NJ: Princeton University Press.

Kris, E. (1936/52). The Psychology of Caricature. In: *Psychoanalytic Explorations in Art*. New York: International Universities Press.

Samuels, A., Shorter, B. and Plaut, F. (1986). *A Critical Dictionary of Jungian Analysis*. New York: Routledge & Kegan Paul.

Steadman, J. L. (2015). *H.P. Lovecraft and the Black Magickal Tradition: The Master of Horror's Influence on Modern Occultism*. San Francisco, CA: Weiser Press.

Sullivan, H. S. (1996). *Harry Stack Sullivan: Interpersonal Theory and Psychotherapy*. London, UK: Routledge.

Wexler, B. E. (2008). *Brain and Culture: Neurobiology, Ideology, and Social Change*. Boston, MA: MIT Press.

White, G. (2016). *The Chaos Protocols: Magical Techniques for Navigating the New Economic Reality*. Woodbury, MN: Llewellyn Publishing.

Zweig, C. and Abrams, J. (1991). *Meeting the Shadow: The Hidden Power of the Dark Side of Human Nature*. New York: Penguin Putnam Inc.

3

THE IMMERSION OF THE MERMAID

A heuristic autoethnographic approach to working therapeutically with active imagination and traumatic loss

Rachel Mallen

Introduction

This chapter is concerned with the Jungian concept of active imagination as a medium of working therapeutically with traumatic loss. This chapter appears in two parts to emphasise the very real, fragmentary process of trauma. In Part 1, the author explores her personal journey as the mermaid and her interweaving experience from immersion into the imaginal realm of trauma, to resurfacing in the material realm in constructing a narrative of coming to terms with and processing trauma. The mermaid metaphor provides a bridge between the two worlds. Part 2 will consider the wider social context in relation to the author's experience, looking at client interactions in a collective sense of working toward integration and reconnection following trauma, and a sense of being 'torn from the communal fabric of being-in-time' (Stolorow, 2011, p. 146).

Phenomenological methodology, i.e. heuristic autoethnography enables a depth of reflection interlinking personal and collective experiences of trauma, alongside authentic depiction and acknowledgement of the temporal experience of being human. The six stages of heuristic research (Moustakas, 1990) will be addressed throughout this chapter. This methodology facilitates 'seeing with fresh eyes' (Finlay, 2012, p. 175) for the researcher practitioner through interactions with others and the external world. It is hoped that this chapter will assist other practitioners to enhance their competency to be present with clients experiencing such phenomena.

Part 1

Initial engagement

Three months into counselling training, my Mum died suddenly and traumatically at the age of 48. This is the most painful loss I have experienced to date in my life, the trauma having long-term effects on myself and my family, grief resurging in waves. Reminiscent of Stroebe and Schut's (1999) Dual Process Model, identifying as a mermaid, I oscillate somewhere between the loss-oriented (delving into the watery depths) and restoration-oriented (coming back to land and living on earth) phases. My personal experience of trauma has influenced me to work psychotherapeutically with the trauma of others; active imagination being a significant technique emergent in this process. Stolorow (1999) and Stolorow et al. (2002) explore the pain and estrangement associated with trauma, describing the experience of hearing that 'the world was divided into two groups: the normals and the traumatized ones' and the inability for a 'normal to ever grasp the experience of a traumatized one' (Stolorow, 1999, p. 465).

> Because trauma so profoundly alters the universal or shared structure of temporality, the traumatized person quite literally lives in another kind of reality. Torn from the communal fabric of being-in-time, trauma remains insulated from human dialogue.
>
> *Stolorow, 2011, p. 146*

My mermaid identity works at ease with this duality and understands the importance of honouring this process; she has journeyed between life and death, or metaphorically speaking, between land and the oceanic depths of grief. She reconnects emotionally to her own grief and vulnerability alongside clients; paradoxically this personal experience of grief can enhance empathic attunement with clients. Loss is a reminder of the value of life; and by enduring such loss, I have gained increased spiritual awareness and an ongoing connection to my Mum, her death activating a series of meaningful coincidences, or what Jung described as synchronicities.

A month after my Mum died in January 2011, my only focus appeared to be Jung's (1969) *Psychology of the Transference* in which he explores the therapeutic relationship as a potentially transformative encounter. Reading this one evening, I finished at the section *The Return of the Soul* comprising an image of a hermaphrodite corpse and two birds, one half immersed in the ground and the other on the ground. Soon after reading this section, I fell asleep. When I went downstairs the next morning, my Dad[1] recalled his dream from the night before in which he went downstairs from his bedroom to go to the toilet. He recalled walking in darkness upstairs toward the light in the living room downstairs where my Mum was sat in her usual seat. My Dad said, 'What are you doing you daft bugger – get yourself to bed' upon which he noticed that she had a sparrow on her right shoulder and a chaffinch in her right hand. She was smiling but didn't speak. My Dad then said, 'I'm going to bed anyway'. My Dad described this dream clearly and in detail stating that it felt very real to him, from the darkness on the stairs to the light in the room where my Mum was sat. He stated that Mum was very alive in his dream, every bit of her looking real and even the birds' wings were fluttering vividly. He couldn't quite make sense of his dream apart from the very real quality of it.

PHILOSOPHORVM
ANIMÆ IVBILATIO SEV
Ortus seu Sublimatio.
Hie schwingt sich die sele hernidder/
Vnd erquickt den gereinigten leychnam wider-
L iij

FIGURE 3.1 *The Return of the Soul*, Jung, 1969, Fig. 9, London: Routledge

Astounded, I ran upstairs, grabbed my book and showed my Dad the image that I had viewed the night before (see Figure 3.1). We were both lost for words, finding this mutually meaningful; experiencing this as a message from Mum that she was okay. This shared experience dissolved the need for rational explanations which, from years of academic study, became my default worldview. This three-way interconnection was a great source of comfort for both of us, being a highly emotionally charged or 'numinous' experience, the type that often accompany synchronicities (cf. Main, 1997; Joseph, 2009). My perception of the 'rational world of knowledge' (Colman, 2011, p. 472) was instantly transformed, and I saw the world afresh, in a childlike awe, reconnecting with the 'imaginal world of meaning' (ibid.). Boyd (2015), Jung (1960) and West (2011) all highlight the experiential aspects of spirituality; synchronicities such as the above example are 'not even thinkable in intellectual terms' (Jung, 1960, p. 103). Furthermore, 'it is the living experience and consequent transformation that enables spiritual development rather than dogma or belief' (Boyd, 2015, p. 25).

Von Franz (1980) describes a 'unitarian reality' where the 'physical and psychic realms coincide within the synchronistic event' (p. 98). Joseph (2009) highlights *Animal Ostenta* as powerful archetypal symbols, stating that 'birds signify spiritual transition, of which dying is only one kind … imply[ing] the soul taking leave of its physical home' (p. 59).

The archetypal mermaid is born.

The immersion of the mermaid – the watery depths

The immersion in the bath is another 'night sea journey' … a descent into Hades and a journey to the land of ghosts somewhere beyond this world, beyond consciousness, hence an immersion in the unconscious (Jung, 1995, pp. 83–84).

ROSARIVM

corrūpitur, neq; ex imperfecto penitus ſecundū
artem aliquid fieri poteſt. Ratio eſt quia ars pri
mas diſpoſitiones inducere non poteſt, ſed lapis
noſter eſt res media inter perfecta & imperfecta
corpora, & quod natura ipſa incepit hoc per ar
tem ad perfectionē deducitur. Si in ipſo Mercu
rio operari inceperis vbi natura reliquit imper
fectum, inuenies in eo perfectionē et gaudebis.
Perfectum non alteratur, ſed corrumpitur.
Sed imperfectum bene alteratur, ergo corrup
tio vnius eſt generatio alterius.

Speculum

FIGURE 3.2 *Immersion in the Bath*, Jung, 1969, Fig. 9, London: Routledge

The Painting of Death: *life imitating art*

In context

I completed *The Painting of Death* (Figure 3.3) after a relationship breakdown in 2008. The disconnection in this painting is demonstrated by roots floating away and not being anchored within a cluster of flowers, also by the fragmented female body to the bottom left of the painting.

There are no stems or connectors to life from the roots to the flower heads. Throughout the process of painting, I felt disconnected from the outside world and so felt the need to express myself by emptying my emotions on to the canvas. The pain that I experienced during this time is, I believe, reflected through the work and from receiving feedback from others that the painting was disturbing. It is also interesting that I painted poppies, poppies being collective cultural symbols of death and remembrance.

My Mum had what might be described as a countertransferential reaction to this painting in that she intuitively grasped my emotional state as symbolised in this

FIGURE 3.3 *The Painting of Death:* life imitating art

painting and consequently named it '*The Painting of Death*'. I believe that this was an accurate title in that it symbolises the death of a phase of life due to the breakdown of a relationship. My Mum didn't particularly like this painting; however, I placed it on the wall of our family bathroom having completed this. I believe that this was an assertion of my independence and identity, as well as an indication that I was alone but not alone (Winnicott, 1958), that our relationship was strong enough to endure the difference. I believe that this is reflected by the one flower to the right of the picture which is flourishing but still connected to the other flowers. Once I felt that my painting and my feelings had been accepted by my Mum, I removed *The Painting of Death* from the bathroom wall and put it away.

Two years later, after the sudden death of my Mum, I was to learn that my placing of *The Painting of Death* on the bathroom wall was a synchronicity although not existing in the same space and time. The painting was no longer on the wall at the time, but my Mum died suddenly one evening in December 2010 in the bathroom where the picture had previously hung. This is what Jung describes as a synchronicity existing 'where a psychic event occurs, and a corresponding physical event takes place in the future' (Main, 1997, p. 21).

> Close-bonded archetypal relationships such as those between mother and child or between lovers often produce synchronistic telepathic communication.
>
> *Jung, 1976, pp. 398–400*

Immersion in images

My initial engagement in Jung's (1969) pictorial exploration of the *Rosarium Philosophorum* was specifically activated by *The Return of the Soul* image (see Figure 3.1), sparking my interest to engage further in these images, with relevance to relational transference phenomena as explored by Jung. The images: *The Naked Truth*, *The Conjunction*, and *Death* depict aspects of my archetypal journey; *The Naked Truth* (Figure 3.4) representing relationships and love:

> Two elements have each paired off, presumably with their opposites … with no false veils or adornments of any kind. Man stands forth as he really is and shows what was hidden under the mask of conventional adaptation: the shadow.
>
> *Jung, 1969, pp. 76–77*

This particularly resonates with me via the image of the naked couple, their nakedness representing their vulnerability and openness to each other; for me this symbolises an openness to having a dialogue with the 'split' aspects of myself, becoming more in alignment with my authentic self. As per the above citation, I began to accept and integrate my shadow self – those previously rejected personality aspects I didn't like about myself, which I recognised in heightened awareness in others. This illusion of separation started to disintegrate, illuminated via the

PHILOSOPHORVM.
ſcipſis ſecundum ęqualitatē inſpiſſentur. Solus
enim calor tēperatus eſt humiditatis inſpiſſatiuus
et mixtionis perfectiuus, et non ſuper excedens.
Nā generatiōes et procreationes rerū naturaliū
habent ſolū fieri per tēperatiſsimū calorē et ęqua
lē, vti eſt ſolus fimus equinus humidus et calidus.

FIGURE 3.4 *The Naked Truth*, Jung, 1969, Fig. 3, London: Routledge

moonlight (as per the symbolism of this image), consequently initiating an integration and ownership of these traits in my conscious awareness.

Following on from this, Figure 3.5 *The Conjunction* demonstrates more physical initimacy and depth of feeling; a merging and integration of, in this image, both masculine and feminine elements which might be perceived as a merging of the logical and felt/intuitive senses: 'the real meaning of the *coniunctio* is that it brings to birth something that is one and united' (Jung, 1969, p. 86). In my process of grief, this links to a deep connection with my felt and embodied grief, and an acceptance of this as part of my whole being; an integration of all aspects of the self.

Eventually separation must occur via *Death*: 'no new life can arise, say the alchemists, without the death of the old' (Jung, 1969, p. 95). This refers to a process of letting go, leaving behind outdated patterns, in my case initially via physical

CONIVNCTIO SIVE
Coitus.

O Luna durch meyn vmbgeben/vnd süsse mynne/
Wirstu schön/starck/vnd gewaltig als ich byn·
O Sol/du bist vber alle liecht zu erkennen/
So bedarffstu doch mein als der han der hennen.
ARISLEVS IN VISIONE.
Coniunge ergo filium tuum Gabricum dilectiorem tibi in omnibus filijs tuis cum sua sorore Beya

FIGURE 3.5 *The Conjunction*, Jung, 1969, Fig. 5, London: Routledge

death and relationship breakdowns, gradually the impact of this coming to light in terms of my relationship with myself, via expression of my values and an authentic way of being.

These images and accompanying words demonstrate an affinity with Goethe's *Archetypal Phenomenon* (*Urphänomen*), 'to be understood as … embracing both idea and sensory experience' (Naydler, 1996, p. 103), 'not a spiritual experience as distinct from a sensory experience, but rather in conjunction with a sensory experience' (ibid., p. 110).

Immersion in images and dreams, exploring the felt sense via active imagination and connecting to archetypal themes has been a significant means of working toward acceptance and processing grief, personally and professionally. These images have been poignant conduits in connecting to and working through the aforementioned archetypal themes. Heuristic research methodology has accelerated this process, with incubation periods being necessary so as not to become enmeshed in this, also enhancing meaning making emergent in this process.

PHILOSOPHORVM.
CONCEPTIO SEV PVTRE
factio

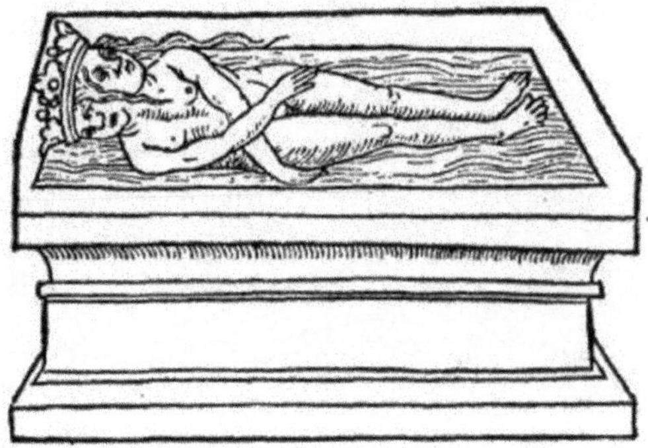

Hye ligen könig vnd königin dot/
Die ſele ſcheydt ſich mit groſſer not.

ARISTOTELES REX ET
Philoſophus.

NVnquam vidi aliquod animatum creſcere ſine putrefactione, niſi autem fiat putri* dum inuanum erit opus alchimicum.

FIGURE 3.6 *Death*, Jung, 1969, Fig. 6, London: Routledge

Incubation

Mermaid reading on a rock

Space away from images allowed further research into relevant literature, in order to make greater sense of these images and to connect with others' experiencing of similar phenomena, synchronicity being a prominent interconnected theme.

According to Jung (1960), synchronicity occurs when an individual's psychic state coincides with an objective event external to the individual's psychic state, manifesting in concrete, material reality and can appear 'in the form of a dream, idea or premonition' (p. 31). Hogenson (2005) highlights a consequence of synchronicities as the 'emergence of meaning and a transition in the individual's state or understanding of the world' (p. 280).

> It's as if the threshold of consciousness is lowered, which then allows the unconscious and its contents to show themselves in conscious life.
>
> *Jung, 1976, pp. 398–400*

In other words, synchronicities can be described as 'congruent correspondence in meaning-making … between the inner and outer events' (Colman, 2011, p. 472), showing up to assist in living life authentically, or 'mov[ing] into alignment with synchronicity' (Hunter, 2011, p. 13).

Gorsedene (2015) discusses Jung's findings on synchronicities – as 'occur[ing] more frequently around powerful archetypal factors such as birth, falling in love or loss' (p. 43). Grof (2000) notes that 'uncanny coincidences' are common to those experiencing 'spiritual crises' (p. 161) and Joseph (2009) reports death to be one of the most common activators of synchronistic experiences and observes a 'connect[ion with] this life with the beyond' (p. 130).

Reflective mermaid

As a predominantly reflective learner (Honey & Mumford, 1982), I need space alone to process my experiencing and learning, and to find the words to convey my experience, following immersion in the imaginal realm. Relevant to the heuristic research process, a period of incubation enables increased insights. I came out of the oceanic depths and back to land, reflecting on the safety and stability of a rock. By suspending my immersion, freezing images in time, revisiting and observing, new data emerges.

Immersion via both the written word and the imaginal realm has facilitated a deep connection with myself, images helping me to connect in an embodied way. A subsequent incubation process allowed me to make sense of and gain insights into this experience and find the words, ultimately finding a way to articulate and illuminate my experience and to consequently reconnect with others, developing my awareness of the interplay between the personal and collective.

> These spheres of heightened emotion occur within archetypal situations such as death … or relationship crises, which demonstrate innate 'patterns of behaviour that are universal in character, arousing the same feelings in everyone'.
>
> *Jung, 1976, pp. 398–400*

It might be said that all of the above archetypes are experienced universally by everybody at some point in their lives; falling in and out of love via relationship breakdowns or separation by physical death. This results in the deconstruction of life as we knew it which, hopefully, becomes reconstructed in the process of learning to accept and live with loss (see Worden, 2018). My mermaid continually interweaves deconstruction and reconstruction, embracing the duality inherent in this process.

Part 2

Illumination of the mermaid

Although *The Painting of Death* was completed in 2008, this painting provides continual increased awareness for me. Not only does this highlight a synchronistic connection with my Mum beyond the grave but also resonates very strongly with my feelings of grief. I felt like I had lost my anchor, floating around aimlessly, my mind and body fragmented. Death seemed more apparent than life. The mermaid was lost at sea. I had tapped into this previously due to a relationship breakdown but now I really knew what it was like to be a 'traumatized one' (Stolorow, 1999). Experiencing the physical death of my Mum led to an intense period of isolation; I felt very alone, often not understood, as observed in a parallel process when writing this chapter, at times overstating my experiences to be understood. This also resonates via the symbolism of the poppies being opiates; a man-made sleep representing a denial of real and raw feelings stemming historically from the wider family dynamics. I see that my poppies were a rebellious expression of transgenerational trauma in an environment that wasn't ready to acknowledge this; hence this medium being necessary for me to purge, heal and wake myself up to my individual self. Emptying my emotions onto a canvas captured the essence of my experiencing in a moment in time, allowing me to '"reframe" the perceived problem and to relate to it in a different way' (McNiff, 2004, p. 98).

The synchronicity of *The Painting of Death*, although initially unwanted, ultimately helped me to feel like I belonged to something bigger than me, the 'collective unconscious'. I experienced this as a spiritual awakening, synchronicities played an extremely significant part in raising my consciousness in an intense process of integration of what was previously split off, or what Jung would call the 'individuation process' in which 'a person becomes a psychological "in-dividual", that is, a separate, indivisible unity or whole' (Jung, 1968, p. 275). This process extended beyond the purely rational; I felt it viscerally in my body and in my art via the archetype of death. This can be symbolised by the metaphor of a mermaid; via my initial sense of duality and subsequent acceptance of and integration of inhabiting two worlds – delving into my emotions and grief while continuing to live my life and re-anchoring my roots and sense of groundedness on earth.

> As the archetypes are relatively autonomous, they cannot be integrated simply by rational means, but require a dialectical procedure, a real coming to terms with them.
>
> *Jung, 1968, pp. 39–40*

This 'dialectical procedure' involved image making and subsequent processing. In the words of McNiff (2004, p. 9) 'art heals by accepting the pain and doing something with it' and was my way of using Jung's 'active imagination' which 'is based on the image-producing *function* of the psyche, that is, the imagination' (Chodorow, 1997, p. 5). From a neuroscientific perspective, the right prefrontal cortex 'enables us to communicate and understand emotional meaning through metaphors and images' (Sunderland, 2008, p. 6). 'The left hemisphere removes things from context and analyzes them in "bits" ... it is primarily concerned with what it knows, whereas the right is concerned with what it experiences' (McGilchrist, 2009, p. 78, cited in Kalsched, 2013, p. 173). Furthermore, the right hemisphere is 'involved in the suffering and working through of real emotional pain – an essential part of the working through of trauma' (ibid., p. 176).

Jung (1968) and Winnicott (1971) recognised the emotionally healing potential of the imagination and the benefits of working creatively alongside this. I also use active imagination with my clients to enhance the consciousness raising, therapeutic process. I do this by revisiting dream accounts or using images to assist clients to go deeper into that space and the feelings aroused as a result (see 'Client K' discussion below). In the context of grief theory, this approach I see as working in alignment with Worden's (2018) first two tasks of mourning.[2]

> The great joy of play, fantasy and the imagination is that for a time we are utterly spontaneous, free to imagine anything. In such a state of pure being ... Nothing is 'unimaginable'. That is why play and the imagination tend to put us in touch with material that is ordinarily repressed.
>
> *Chodorow, 1997, p. 5*

Explication: the mermaid comes out of her shell

Increased engagement in the heuristic research process, alongside active imagination exploration enabled me to 'come out of my shell', expressing myself with increased understanding and consciousness; the explication phase becoming more defined.

The Two Birds and *The Painting of Death* show a transition from black and white thinking to broader nuances of colour and depth of experiences, as can be symbolised by the shift from black and white to colourful images. This process has enabled deeper insights and sense-making, via an emotional processing of my loss in relation to others. When creating *The Painting of Death*, I wasn't fully conscious of the significance of the symbolism of the poppies; unconsciously I was connecting to the archetypes of death and rebirth. The rebellious poppy floating away from the collective represents letting go of a persistent inner conflict as expressed in my wider family dynamic, the inner parts of the poppies resembling eyes observing, and the roots (i.e. my roots) pointing in a specific direction, indicating long held, and to me outdated, belief systems which I felt I needed to let go of.

The archetypes of love, death (loss) and rebirth have emerged for me repeatedly and synchronistically, extending to my professional work; my self-awareness of my own sense of this being an important facet of working effectively with others' experience of trauma collectively.

Synchronicity, archetypes and the collective unconscious

Jung (1960) suggests that synchronicity involves unconscious contents becoming conscious which is reflected by events occurring externally to the individual. Jung came across the notion of synchronicity while exploring the phenomena of the collective unconscious and discovered them to have a transpersonal, archetypal quality: '… a meaning which is *a priori* in relation to human consciousness and apparently exists outside man' (Jung, 1952, pp. 501–502, cited in Main, 1997, p. 14).

Jung observed synchronistic events occurring 'in situations in which an archetype is active or "constellated"' (Jung, 1952, para. 847, cited in Main, 2007, p. 361). Main (2007) elucidates the role archetypes play in the process of individuation through '*compensation*, whereby any one-sidedness in a person's conscious attitude is balanced by contents emerging from the unconscious, which, if successfully integrated, contribute to a greater psychic wholeness' (ibid.). This can be demonstrated by my personal reflections and insights gained from my experience of *The Two Birds* – a shift from a dominant rational epistemology to an increased trust in the felt sense.

Jung describes the 'collective unconscious' as a 'phylogenetic substratum' in 'the deeper layers of the unconscious'. 'It is the mind of our unknown ancestors, their way of thinking and feeling, their way of experiencing life' (Jung, 1968, p. 286). This idea conceptualises a continuation of our relationships with deceased loved ones and indeed our ancestors, their energies existing alongside us (see Steiner, 2006) and shared collectively, as will be demonstrated below.

Trauma in practice – the world is the mermaid's oyster

Client K – Using active imagination

Client K came for counselling because of various traumas she had experienced including physical and sexual abuse which were debilitating her, including not being able to have an outlet to express her feelings. From around session 4, Client K described to me dreams which she started to experience in between sessions. Active imagination has helped Client K to understand her deeper processes and to integrate these into her conscious awareness.

K described her dream of riding a blue tricycle with two friends. She is travelling very fast downhill and she feels scared as she looks behind her, but she doesn't know why. She pedals forwards and can see a target, but she can't seem to reach the destination. She jumps off her bike and runs through some water. She looks down at her feet and her white trainers are dirty and covered in mud and water. (She recalls these white trainers are a present from her daughter and we recognise aspects of day to day life intertwined with her dream life.]) She describes ending up in a house made completely of wood like the table that we are sat next to in the session.

The scene changes …

Client K dreams she is in her wedding dress. She can see her children when they were younger. She is no longer married to this man, but she stands there in her wedding dress but alone this time. She speaks as K out of the dream state and becomes emotional, telling me she is still in love with her ex-husband and is baffled by what this dream could mean.

Therapeutic reflections

Client K's dreams enabled her to work on her feelings, which were echoed in the counselling process. Exploring her dreams via active imagination helped her to understand and to begin to explore some emotional traumas from the past. Client K had been reviewing her past abusive relationships in sessions and exploring the trauma of this. Her dreams were a way for her to come to terms with the past and recounting her dreams in sessions helped to reconnect with parts of herself that have been kept unconscious. Graves (2009) emphasises the importance of 'find[ing] out how the presence, the dream, or the vision impacted on the client' (p. 173). 'An overall impression is of development towards more connectedness and integration ... both by synchronicity and between it and other human experiences ... it seems, they choose you' (Gorsedene, 2015, p. 48).

Client K's story touched me deeply. As I reflect upon this now, I'm in touch with my own emotions associated with a past abusive relationship, echoes of this also emerging recurrently in my dreams. Bogart (2009) describes 'retrospective' dreams as 'icebergs of the past, helping us understand early traumas and undigested memories' (p. 3). My clients' stories appear to be mirroring mutual experiences, their impact seeming to have a mutually therapeutic effect. In this context, Frank (1995) writes about the need to 'allow our own injuries to increase the potency of our care of patients, to allow our personal experiences to strengthen the empathic bond with others who suffer' (Charon, 1994, p. 158, quoted in Frank, 1995, p. xii). Working at this transpersonal level, 'we apprehend the numinous through the relationship with another person – a relationship in which both I and the other are transformed' (Rowan & Jacobs, 2002, p. 73).

Creative synthesis: duality and integration

The integration of the mermaid

In this chapter, I have explored personal experiences of synchronicity, interweaving with my clients' stories of traumatic loss. I have reflected on the archetypes of death, love and loss, via imagery, extending to a collective experience of them, and the impact of the harsh reality of the loneliness, disconnection and trauma experienced as a result, taking into account the potential duality of the 'traumatised' and the 'normals'. I note a connection between the 'traumatised ones'' experiences of psychological and emotional distress and consequent potential for spiritual development, reconnection and increased compassion for others experiencing grief, and the impact of this in therapeutic practice. I have explored the concept of 'active imagination' and put this into practice as a method of exploring and processing grief. I now wish to further reflect upon the concept of 'opposites' experienced throughout the grief process, this duality depicted via the archetype of the mermaid interweaving throughout this narrative. Jung refers to 'archetypes of transformation' which symbolise 'an enantiodromian structure ... and so present[s] a rhythm of negative and positive, loss and gain, dark and light' (Jung, 1968, p. 38).

Duality is significant in my choice of images, narratives and personal descriptions. Kalsched (2013) refers to the wider social context of trauma and 'the fragmenting reality of human conflict' (p. 1). He refers to splitting as a 'self-care system' stating that 'trauma results from the fact that we are often given more to experience in this life than we can bear to experience consciously' (Kalsched, 2013, p. 10). This links with Stroebe and Schut's (1999) Dual Process Model, a theory emphasising duality as a normal coping strategy in the processing of grief.

From an existential perspective, Van Deurzen (2010) refers to the inevitability of psychological disturbance, emphasising the potentiality of breakdown preceding breakthrough. In the words of Parkes and Prigerson (2010), 'the pain of grief is … perhaps, the price we pay for love, the cost of commitment' (p. 39), both being two sides of one coin. I propose that with loss, there is also gain, if we choose to accept this. 'Flatlining' is physical death, yet life has its waves, unpredictably and beautifully so, this temporal human experience highlighting the gift of life. How we choose to ride these waves is down to individual choice in their individual contexts. By embracing death, my mermaid chooses life:

> Balance is at once life and death. For the completion of life a balance with death is fitting. If I accept death, then my tree greens, since dying increases life. If I plunge into the death encompassing the world, then my buds break open. How much our life needs death! … Therefore I behold death, since it teaches me how to live.
>
> *Jung, 2009, pp. 266–267*

Waving, not drowning: heuristic mermaid

Heuristic methodology has been an additional therapeutic medium, enabling expression of challenging and opposing feelings in a creative and liberating way, resulting in increased insights and leading to reconnection with myself and others. Phenomenology is 'a way of seeing how things appear to us through experience' and 'demands an open way of being' (Finlay, 2012, p. 173). As Colman (2011) asserts, this involves being 'phenomenologically real in a way that includes the external world, not just the psyche' (p. 477). In heuristics, Moustakas (2001) emphasises that the inner and outer worlds aren't mutually exclusive, stating 'it is "I" who is the person living in a world with others, alone yet inseparable from the community of others' (p. 264).

Heuristic periods of *Incubation* have facilitated a deep level of reflection and reflexivity, extending to a parallel process with my client work, and resulting in increased insights, or *Illumination* into my research process and experience of and coming to terms with grief. Periods of *Incubation* have enabled clarity and *Explication*, subsequently facilitating articulation of the experience into words, culminating in a heightened transformational process via *Creative Synthesis*.

This is not without challenge, the immersion stage being a painful process in which I connect deeply to my grief and that of others; at times floating around when the mermaid is lost at sea. This dissolution of structure was an organic part of this process, the experience of which gradually clears the way for a necessary reconstruction. Having a loose structure (i.e. the heuristic stages and theoretical constructs) has enabled me to ground my reflections and gain perspectives of others to minimise the potential for solipsism, a potential critique of this methodology. Grounding in this way has led to an 'active participation in the process' (Moustakas, 1990, p. 42) and a sense of integration. My mermaid is waving, not drowning; she is now more streamlined, following a clearer structure. The initial fragmentation of this chapter (Parts 1 and 2) has expanded to multiple nuances of colour, leading to an understanding of the bigger picture. The distance from immersion has helped my mermaid to build a scaffolding which guides her. I exist in a societal context where external influences inform my practice, also helping to challenge my assumptions as well as minimising the potential boundlessness of the reflective process. Reflective learning, when there is no external experience, is very 'slippery' and subject to the influence of an even more slippery entity, emotion (Moon, 2004, p. 93).

I allow myself immersion into the feeling realm, but I know I can always come back to the safety and the structure of the land when I need to. I am the mermaid who revisits the rocks, still with access to the watery depths, but firmly grounded in myself and with my clients. This chapter has been a reflective learning tool giving me enough freedom and safety to immerse myself in the oceanic depths, and I have come out of this process with increased insights and self-awareness in relation to the wider context. This indeed has been a precious journey of personal and professional development.

> Our concern with the unconscious has become a vital question for us – a question of spiritual being or non-being … the treasure lies in the depths of the water … As they must never forget who they are, they must on no account imperil their consciousness. They will keep their standpoint firmly anchored to the earth and will thus – to preserve the metaphor – become fishers who catch with hook and net what swims in the water.
>
> *Jung, 1968, p. 24.*

Reflections for practice:

- As practitioners, are you open to using active imagination as a medium of working therapeutically with clients encountering traumatic loss?
- What is your perception of the potential links between traumatic loss and transpersonal phenomena?

Notes

1 My Dad consented to be identified as my Dad within this chapter.

2 Task 1: To accept the reality of the loss; Task 2: To work through the pain of grief (Worden 2018).

References

Bogart, G. (2009) *Dreamwork and Self-healing: Unfolding the Symbols of the Unconscious.* London: Karnac.

Boyd, J. (2015) Asking for help is a sign of weakness. In: G. Nolan & W. West (Eds) *Therapy, Culture & Spirituality: Developing Therapeutic Practice* (pp. 24–37). Basingstoke: Palgrave Macmillan.

Chodorow, J. (Ed.) (1997) *Jung on Active Imagination.* Princeton: Princeton University Press.

Colman, W. (2011) Synchronicity and the meaning-making psyche. *Journal of Analytical Psychology*, 56, pp. 471–491.

Finlay, L. (2012) Unfolding the phenomenological research process: iterative stages of "seeing afresh". *Journal of Humanistic Psychology*, 53(2), pp. 172–201.

Frank, A. (1995) *The Wounded Storyteller.* Chicago: The University of Chicago Press.

Gorsedene, C. (2015) Synchronicity. In: G. Nolan & W. West (Eds) *Therapy, Culture & Spirituality: Developing Therapeutic Practice* (pp. 38–55). Basingstoke: Palgrave Macmillan.

Graves, D. (2009) *Talking with Bereaved People: An Approach for Structured and Sensitive Communication.* London and Philadelphia: Jessica Kingsley Publishers.

Grof, S. (2000) *Psychology of the Future: Lessons from Modern Consciousness Research.* New York: State University of New York Press.

Hogenson, G. (2005) The Self, the symbolic and synchronicity: virtual realities and the emergence of the psyche. *Journal of Analytical Psychology*, 50, pp. 271–284.

Honey, P. & Mumford, A. (1982) *The Manual of Learning Styles.* London: Peter Honey Publications.

Hunter, A. (2011) *The Path of Synchronicity: Align Yourself with Your Life's Flow.* Forres, Scotland: Findhorn Press.

Joseph, F. (2009) *The Power of Coincidence: The Mysterious Role of Synchronicity in Shaping our Lives.* London: Arcturus Publishing Limited.

Jung, C. (1960) *Synchronicity: An Acausal Connecting Principle.* Princeton: Bollingen.

——. (1968) *The Archetypes and the Collective Unconscious, CW9, Pt1* (2nd edn), Trans. R. F. C. Hull. London: Routledge.

——. (1969) *The Psychology of the Transference.* London, New York: Routledge.

——. (1976) *Letters, Vol. 2 1951–1961.* Hove: Routledge.

——. (1995) *Memories, Dreams, Reflections.* London: Harper Collins.

——. (2009) *The Red Book Liber Novus – A Reader's Edition.* London: W.W. Norton & Company.

Kalsched, D. (2013) *Trauma and the Soul: A Psycho-spiritual Approach to Human Development and its Interruption.* London: Routledge.

Main, R. (1997) *Jung on Synchronicity and the Paranormal.* Princeton: Princeton University Press.

——. (2007) Synchronicity and analysis: Jung and after. *European Journal of Psychotherapy and Counselling*, 9(4), pp. 359–371.

McNiff, S. (2004) *Art Heals: How Creativity Cures the Soul.* Boston & London: Shambhala.

Moon, J. (2004). *A Handbook of Reflective and Experiential Learning: Theory and Practice.* Abingdon: Routledge Falmer.

Moustakas, C. (1990) *Heuristic Research: Design, Methodology and Applications.* London: Sage.

——. (2001) Heuristic research, design & methodology. In: K. Scheider, J. Bugental & J. Pierson (Eds) *The Handbook of Humanistic Psychology: Leading Edges in Theory, Research and Practice* (pp. 263–274). London: Sage.

Naydler, J. (Ed.) (1996) *Goethe on Science: An Anthology of Goethe's Scientific Writings.* Edinburgh: Floris Books.

Parkes, C. M. & Prigerson, H. 2010. *Bereavement: Studies of Grief in Adult Life* (4th edn). Hove: Routledge.

Rowan, J. & Jacobs, M. (2002) *The Therapist's Use of Self.* Maidenhead, Berkshire: Open University Press.

Steiner, R. (2006). *The Dead Are With Us*. Forest Row: Rudolf Steiner Press.

Stolorow, R. D. (1999). The Phenomenology of trauma and the absolutisms of everyday life. *Psychoanalytic Psychology*, 16(3), pp. 464–468.

Stolorow, R. D. (2011) *World, Affectivity, Trauma: Heidegger and Post-Cartesian Psychoanalysis.* New York: Routledge.

Stolorow, R. D., Atwood G. E. & Orange D. M. (2002) *Worlds of Experience: Interweaving Philosophical and Clinical Dimensions in Psychoanalysis*. New York: Basic Books.

Stroebe, M. S. & Schut, H. (1999) The Dual Process Model of coping with bereavement: rationale and description. *Death Studies*, 23, pp. 197–224.

Sunderland, M. (2008) *Draw on Your Relationships: Creative Ways To Explore, Understand and Work through Important Relationship Issues* (illustrator Nicky Armstrong). Milton Keynes: Speechmark Publishing.

Van Deurzen, E. (2010) *Everyday Mysteries: A Handbook of Existential Psychotherapy* (2nd edn). London: Routledge.

Von Franz, M. (1980) *On Divination and Synchronicity: The Psychology of Meaningful Chance.* Toronto: Inner City Books.

West, W. (Ed.) (2011) *Exploring Therapy, Spirituality and Healing*. London: Palgrave.

Winnicott, D. W. (1958) The capacity to be alone. In: D. W. Winnicott *The Maturational Processes and the Facilitating Environment* (pp. 29–36). London: Karnac.

——. (1971) *Playing and Reality*. New York: Basic Books.

Worden, W. J. (2018) *Grief Counselling and Grief Therapy: A Handbook for the Mental Health Practitioner* (5th edn). New York: Springer Publishing.

4

SELFIES, SELF-DEFINITION, THERAPY AND THE TRANS-RELATIONAL QUEST FOR MEANINGFUL CONNECTION

Phil Goss

Introduction

Is the freedom to define ourselves a gift or a curse, or a bit of both? In this chapter I will scrutinize the individual, as well as relational and trans-personal, psychology of the way in which the capacity to define ourselves, to 'I', as well as to 'you', 'we' and 'they', has become a dominant theme arising from a pervasive set of influences on westernized culture in recent times. I am referring to the paradoxical phenomena of the priority of individual self-definition on the one hand and the deepening nexus of connection between people, communities and cultures (usually described in the catch-all term 'globalization') on the other. In both cases, these trends have been hastened and deepened by the emergence of the World Wide Web in the 1990s, which is now such an established part of the personal and social landscape that for many the idea of not having access to social media, emails and other smart phone technology at a moment's notice might almost feel like having lost a part of themselves; a virtual 'limb' suddenly not there anymore.

In this regard, the scope to define who we are to others can be sculpted, and proliferate, through the use of social media identities, where it is possible to literally 'make up' who we are and 'be' someone we are not – something that in psychodynamic terms could be seen as a manifestation of usually unconscious aspects of ourselves (Jacobs, 2006), or in Jungian terms of a person's *shadow* (Jung, 1951/1968). It can also be seen in the phenomenon of expressing gender and/or sexual identity which may previously have been hidden from the awareness of others, such as transgendered, same sex, bisexual or queer, 'coming out' of a person's underlying experience of their gendered or sexual identity which is *really* who they are. This sometimes impacts not just on their self-identity but on their named identity – such as the trend for people who see themselves as 'non-binary' to term themselves as 'they' rather than 'she' or 'he'.

It also feels relevant to highlight what seems to be a marked inter-generational shift in perception around gendered and sexual identity and the agency of the individual to determine what this 'is' and how to express it. In my training role it is not uncommon to read a student's case study of a client where they might write that 'n' (client) 'identifies as a woman' (or 'man') rather than just writing that she or he is female or male. In this way, what had been the most fixed of gendered identities is loosened from its anchorage and can float as a psychological and emotional free agent which could swim to either shore of the river. In this gendered way, choice of identity penetrates deeply into old assumptions about fixed limitations to this.

I also want to posit a third way in which this is happening, and that is through counselling and psychotherapy (and other ways in which people 'explore self' – complementary therapies, mindfulness, religious and spiritual activities, and so on). In this respect, the freedom to be reflective and reflexive facilitates inward-looking 're-definitions' of self which can be multiple across a lifetime. I argue that in all three ways highlighted here these opportunities can also act as pressures to 'be' in ways that may become demanding, elusive and confusing. I also suggest that these phenomena reflect a deep-seated yearning for *transformation*, which, in turn, is an archetypal feature of being human and has very deep psychological and spiritual roots in the collective human story.

The taking of a Selfie, meanwhile, provides an everyday representation of the trend of expressing and recording the 'I' of self-identity, in the way it allows those many of us who carry phone devices to take a self-portrait, say in front of a building, landscape or cityscape, or to capture a moment of pleasure or excitement in our faces, or a snapshot of us alongside another person (could even be a famous person) we wish to keep a memento of. But it *also* acts as a symbol of the emphasis on self-realization, as it symbolizes the freedom to choose how 'I' want to represent myself to the world and record my own presence and significance in it.

So – with phone device in hand, ready to snap a Selfie when the mood strikes, we will explore how we might understand the nature of 'real' identity/identities and how far we may have a transformative capacity to inhabit and express our 'real selves', including in the therapeutic context.

I will explore this matter primarily through a Jungian lens (as well as drawing on other perspectives) and explore the tension between plurality and wholeness. I will address three questions arising from the wider social, as well as specifically therapeutic context: First, does the more permission and facility we have to redefine ourselves make genuine connection with self and others more or less *real*? Second, how could these challenges of our time facilitate or block connections between counsellors/psychotherapists and their clients and impact upon therapeutic growth and change (and how might we work with this)? Third, how could our experience and insight into the nature and impact of identity shifts and the search for personal transformation help us understand better what is happening in this area of contemporary life, individually, therapeutically and across families, groups and communities, in support of what I will sketch out as meaningful trans-relational connections?

Identity, identification and the search for the real 'I'

To want to experience who we really are is an aspiration with instinctual roots that seems to be ubiquitous in the way that Shakespeare's (1599/2005) bidding for us 'To thine own self be true' resonates strongly within contemporary western culture. That is not to say that it is necessarily archetypally prevalent across all cultures, especially where in some traditional Eastern cultures 'sacrifice of self', in terms of identity as well as responsibilities taken, is seen as crucial for the sustaining of family and community life. I want to assert the thought that an archetypal aspiration for transformation does operate across all cultures (e.g. via spiritual transformation in traditionally religious cultures). Also, the move toward greater, freer self-expression and renewal of identity (which may be argued to have its recent historical roots in the 1960s) operates in an archetypal *manner*, if we take Jung's formula that archetypal activity has an instinctual 'pole' and also an image-based one (Jung, 1948/1968).

The instinctual, bodily based need to express self – feelings, thoughts, sexual and aggressive drives – whatever social or psychological constraints may be in place, is hard to dispute, and in the phenomena being described in this chapter, these seem to turn into a focused aspiration – such as to change gender, create a new online identity, or express sexuality in a new way, or to explore one's feelings and experiences in therapy – as the underlying feeling or drive becomes focused on an idea of who one would like to be, or really is. This self-image of the *real* or *other* version of 'me' then seems to determine how the person sees themselves, and the wish arises that others would see them likewise and accept their new or different identity. This has implications for therapy and what people may come in to it for – such as to have their transformed/alternative identity accepted as who they are.

Of course, within the psychotherapeutic field there is the desirability of authentic living; from Rogers' (1961/2004) emphasis on self-actualization, to Jung's notion of individuation (1960/1969) and existentialism's emphasis on both free will and the accepting of responsibility for our lives (Van Deurzen, 2009). However, does the reaching for our true identity or *identities* (to recognize the plurality of possibilities within us) always operate in a way that brings us closer to 'being authentic?' In psychodynamic terms the notion of identification presents us with a challenge to assuming a person knows best who/what their authentic self 'is' (Rycroft, 1995). According to this perspective, unconscious or 'out of awareness' influences can lead us up a kind of garden path that appears to take us to fuller expression and authenticity of self but actually might be more of an acting out of an identification with what, in Winnicott's terminology, is another 'false self' (1965), like the inauthentic presentation of self a person may be trying to get away from, as I will illustrate in the discussion of therapeutic practice presented below.

However, I am less interested in pursuing this line of thought, as I am certainly not suggesting that the underlying drive to bring out into the open what is experienced in the depths of mind or body is not 'real', say, in respect to a change of gender identity or fresh declarative expression of sexuality, but rather am interested in what happens to us when we express a new identity, choose to create another version of self, or immerse oneself in a *voyage interior* to try to get hold of who we 'really are'. The ways we can identify with what we *think* a new identity represents and 'is' will be very influential in shaping how we perceive ourselves, express ourselves to others and generally navigate through life. An example in the case of the person who creates a new, different, identity online is that this could become an outlet for aspects of self that they struggle to express in their 'face to face' relationships and possibly reflect – further generate even – a sense of split in their view, and experiencing, of themselves. However, it could also work in a compensatory way, enabling for example a more flamboyant or maybe didactic voice to express itself so that the person has a better sense of being able to express the fullness of who they are. On this particular archetypal continuum, between experiencing 'split' identity or 'complementarity' of identities, the challenges and possibilities of exploring 'configurations' (Mearns, 1999), or 'plurality' (Samuels, 1989) of self gets constellated. The question remains, though, whether the individual who seeks their 'real' identity, or 'real' versions/aspects of self, and then expresses it, can also get caught by this process in ways that then dominate their sense of self?

Here, the debates around innate versus social constructivist identity formation (e.g. gender, Goss, 2010) bear consideration, alongside the important consideration that we each may construct our sense of who we are out of a deep-seated impetus to be 'ourselves'. So, the ongoing build of who this 'I' may be across a lifetime has the look of a house where the scaffolding is never completely taken down or fully falls away, as the interaction between these three influences is a work in progress which is never finally completed. Also, in shorthand: nature, society and soul (where 'soul-making' (Hillman, 1975), is something which seeks a wholeness that can only be worked toward but never 'completed'), can be looked at in many ways depending on one's standpoint – e.g. existential or spiritual.

Where the notions of social constructivism come into our thinking about identity formation, not to mention our sense of the ways in which being 'in therapy' can act as a crucible for the recasting of our perception of who we are or choose to be, it appears as if the scaffolding of our long-held beliefs about what makes us who we are is indeed something that can easily fall, say where it is described in social theory terms as stereotypes (e.g. about gender, culture, age or class) being exposed and dismantled (e.g. Connell, 2002). In the three main traditions of psychotherapy and counselling, such dismantling can be proposed in terms of culturally fixed conditions of worth dissolving (Merry, 2002) because of the offer of the person-centred core conditions, faulty beliefs about how to acceptably behave according to a prescribed identity being overcome through scrutinizing cognitions that sustain those beliefs and reality testing them to enable behaviour (Bandura, 1986) to change, through to tackling identifications that sustain old unconscious patterns of encultured behaviour by thought and feeling being worked through in the transference (Jacobs, 2006). In Jungian terms the notion of 'persona' (as the face or faces presented to the outside world by the ego) is also regarded as a way into helping a client peel off the layers that exist between the version of them who operates in response to the demands of life and their deeper self. This is seen as a way to get 'round the back' of ego and into its hidden 'shadow' side (Stein, 1998). From here deep links between individual and collective influences, including archetypal influences that cross cultural lines and set up polarities, including the tensions between the feminine and masculine (anima and animus) in the person's psyche can be formed and deep shifts can occur over time (ibid.). If an understanding is to be reached of the undoubted power of familial and social influences to generate a sense of who we are, which patterns behaviours and self-perceptions, and the way these can come to be felt to be at odds with 'who we really are', then it is also important to recognize the layers of familial and bodily based 'constitutional' factors which inform our sense of identity, as strongly implied by how different the personalities of siblings growing up in the same family can be. In respect to both areas of influence, how far can someone know who the real 'I' is and whether the changes they might have experienced in their sense of self and aspirations about their 'real' identity have truly brought them closer to it? This question reiterates the first one posed in the Introduction, and remains only partially answered at best, including the implications for how the taking of a new, 'other' or deepened identity affects relationships, as the subtleties and complexities inherent to individual personality and identity formation are very difficult to pin down. Nevertheless, the idea of the nature of self-development as one that is rooted in subjectivity suggests that identity is often a matter of perception, sometimes 'felt' perception and at other times 'thought' (or both).

The matter of whether the granting of 'permission' to become fully ourselves inwardly, or to take an identity that faces outside for others to become aware of and relate to – whether that permission is granted to ourselves or taken as a given from the social and public world in which we co-exist – is one I will next look at more closely in the context of the therapeutic space; considering the role of the therapist in facilitating the client's real encounter with themselves and what can arise helpfully or otherwise in pursuit of uncovering a 'real' sense of identity.

Behind the Selfie: the search for the I-I encounter in therapy.

The therapeutic encounter is between two people, psychotherapist or counsellor (for which I will use the shorthand of 'therapist') and client. However, for the client it is really about one person – them. Where the therapist plays a crucial part in facilitating in the client (for example) a feeling of being accepted for who they are, thus performing a vital reparative function (Clarkson, 2003) in respect to impoverished attachment relations to primary carers earlier in life, this can be seen as a relational pivot which enables the client to encounter this longed-for feeling in themselves. Once the therapy is over, the client can then draw on this experience to nurture both their self-acceptance, and their relational capacity toward others. So, whether describing the presence of deep connection between therapist and client in terms of 'relational depth' (Mearns and Cooper, 2005) or the constellation of the 'Analytic Third' (Ogden, 1994), what matters is what the client is left with and can take away and 'use' in order to consolidate some sense of core selfhood.

In this sense, while all relationships, including the therapeutic one, require the presence of another and reflect an archetypal need for meaningful connections with others in order to grow and flourish rather than wilt and die, I want to consider the way search for self, search for 'real' identity (or identities) in the therapeutic dyad is facilitated or not by the presence of the therapist, particularly in the light of the points arising about the contemporary prioritizing about 'finding and expressing identity'. I will use two fictionalized vignettes based loosely on my therapeutic practice to furnish and illustrate this discussion.

Crossing the river too soon?

In this example, representative of some work I have done with clients, I want to illustrate how therapy might throw up challenges around where a change of identity could get conflated with 'therapeutic change' and not enable the client to see themselves as much more than the new identity they have revealed to the world. I will reflect on my own part as therapist in working with this challenge and suggest how we might, as therapists, locate ourselves in a beneficent way to facilitate the client's process.

R was finding a rooted sense of self through leaving womanhood behind. The female body that had trapped him in what he described as a 'cage' was still his place of embodied habitation, as R had only recently declared their transgendered aspiration to partner, family and friends, but the step of sharing the painful hidden reality that had overshadowed childhood and early adulthood had been such a relief and fostered a new faith in his entitlement to be himself. I sat with this relief, and sense of liberation, which for a period he seemed to simply want to express to me and receive my empathy for, and validation of. I noticed in myself a pleasurable warmth and sense of privilege in being able to witness and acknowledge the client's sense of autonomy in having overcome the anxiety and fear about declaring to others around him that 'really I am a man'. I also noticed a sense of disconnect and a worry that we were both avoiding something … something about him being in a body that he did not want to be in, in its present form.

It seemed as if he noticed something about this at the end of a session when he said 'I identify as a man, but I am in a woman's body' and shook his head and left without us having a chance to explore this further. When he came for the next session I noticed a heightened level of anxiety in myself which seemed in part to be my own nagging concern that I had been too ready to be alongside his desire to be a man, based on what I saw as the importance of acknowledging the bravery and authenticity of the step he had taken, but partly out of what Withers (2015) highlights as a fear of psychopathologizing trans-sexual clients who are exploring the wish to undergo sex-reassignment surgery. The new alertness in both of us to the way in which the therapeutic 'boat' seemed to have been pushed by a tailwind of affirmation without a sense of where it was going, helped us to explore the tensions and painful complexities around the prospect of leaving his female body behind and help him locate his self in relation to where he was from as well as to where he was heading via the sex-reassignment surgery.

My learning from this clinical experience was two-fold: First, as may be obvious, it confirmed my understanding that who the person 'is', is not equivalent to the new expression of self, the new identity they feel impelled to declare and, in this case, even undergo profound physical changes to fulfil. Second, and in relation to this, 'identity', and a felt sense and perception of it, operates in between an instinctual, visceral, sense of what this 'is' to a person (in this case of being a man in a woman's body), and a kind of hard-won wisdom (which will vary in availability to a lesser or greater degree, and which therapy can help a person to get hold of) that there is more to 'me' than an identity or identities. From this can arise a wish and capacity to hold both together, one could say an archetypal continuum between certitude of identification with 'my identity' and a loose holding and playing with it. The therapist, by holding this continuum in awareness, can help create the container in which the client can locate a satisfactory relationship to it.

Agony Uncle

This second fictionalized example, which also reflects aspects of some client work from my practice, refers to the creation and sustaining of a 'false' personality on the internet which they heavily identify with but that also gives them the opportunity to express and explore aspects of self they had not lived out. P, an older man, lived by himself after losing his male partner to suicide a decade previously. Not surprisingly, this traumatic loss featured heavily in the therapeutic work done, including his perpetual worry that he had not done what he could for his partner and that he had 'not shown him I loved him enough'.

P, who was retired, spent much of his time as an online personality on social media, pretending he was a younger man giving relationship advice with the moniker 'Agony Uncle'. He found a lot of interest in this 'service', which he offered for free, but which gave him satisfaction in being able to provide advice even on aspects of relationships and family life he was not familiar with, or had only experienced earlier versions of, in what was now a fairly distant childhood. The character he created was authoritative in its tone, on occasion admonishing contributors to his forum for 'immoral behaviour' or for 'ducking the issue'. He noticed this approach seemed to generate more interest and so he had turned up the 'volume' in this respect, until he experienced a problem when a female contributor threatened to report him to the website provider – or even the police – for making comments which, she wrote, she found threatening.

This incident is what led P to come into therapy, saying that he 'knows I am doing this stuff on the internet because I'm very lonely and hate myself'. I experienced him initially as being out of touch with an authentic sense of identity, wondering if he had relied on his former partner to provide some sense of his own significance to himself. We worked on what it might be that led him to create an ostensibly 'unreal' version of himself online. He said that when he was 'Agony Uncle' he was able to forget his pain, but more than this he noticed something 'come to life in me'. He could not describe what this 'something' was but he was convinced 'this is more like the real me'. P expressed the wish to 'really be Agony Uncle', not because this would make for a 'completion' of who he was, but so that he could experience 'my own authority' more. This reflection led us to explore his experiences of authority and seemed to move him closer to grasping that feeling a quietly held but deep sense of his personal authority was very important to him, and this gave us a broad goal for our work together.

Reflecting on this example I can say that I initially mistook his quest for an online personality as an escape route only and mistakenly assumed our work would be about helping him face his grief and guilt and work it through. I also worried that this might even hold the risk of his reliance on the internet becoming pathological (Kuss and Griffiths, 2015). It turned out though that although he did need to grieve (and therapy provided the space for this), there was also grief and guilt about his loss of personal authority across most of his life (which one could say was a key part of the 'real' him) and for which he felt guilt at the sense of denial he had imposed on himself (and others) in not allowing this to come through.

In both cases, it helps to work on the premise that a living sense of identity springs from a deep place in the person but can get represented in ways that can seem tangential to, or even estranged from, this core need for expression. In this respect the role of therapy becomes to enable the 'I–thou' quality of the encounter to act as a stage toward the 'I–I' encounter with self, where the client recognizes the deeper call of self-identity, and then for the therapist to mediate between the outer expressions or identifications and this core sense of identity, helping the client locate themselves on the archetypal continuum described above – between a deeply aspired identity and the more partial, messy and semi-conscious attempts to find expression for this.

These examples help to support the hypothesis that when a person, whether in therapy or not, reveals a previously hidden 'real self', or reaches out for a new or alternative version of self, they may be unconsciously trying to transform their core self. One could argue such change can only be effected by really dropping down into the deeper aspects of self, and engaging with the more visceral and sometimes painful aspects of the individual's lived experience. This, in turn, then activates archetypal energies and influences, what Mitchell (2016) terms 'the Gears of Physis': deep-seated natural change, which can impact on neurologically wired unhelpful patterns of being, can then begin to move. It is also important to say, however, that a person who seeks to change their identity, or create an alternative one, is usually trying to take a step toward generating a genuinely renewed sense of self.

The quest for transformation in a trans-relational world

To conclude, I want to address the question of what wider implications may arise from the discussions about how real or not identity-based change might be, and how therapeutic work in this area throws up the possibility that there is a deeper wish for transformation at work behind the trends we are witnessing in the contemporary world. I use the term 'trans-relational' to refer to the way the world has become thoroughly interlinked, both in terms of the forces for global markets and media on a 'meta' scale – which acts as the backdrop to our consumption of many things, from food to entertainment – as well as on a 'micro' scale, where our individual daily lives are furnished by the possibility, through the internet and social media, for regular and easy contact with people across the world. This latter aspect also includes finding a sense of 'belonging' in the networks and forums online which can also lead to the activation of relational dynamics, from romance to bullying, which could previously only usually be experienced face to face. In this sense we seem to have unwittingly transcended the live interpersonal means for relationship, friendship, contact (though of course these still operate).

This 'trans-relational' development seems to point to a step change in human relations, including relationship to self. The 'Selfie' provides, as argued, a good symbol, as well as real representation of how we can 're-make' ourselves by capturing a picture of ourselves we would like others to see, and by a click of a button, being able to send it to those we want to see it ('this is the real me I want you to see').

However, though in a clear way, this is a 'step change'; I want to argue that it is a step change in terms of the mechanisms deployed to make it happen rather than in terms of a profound psychological change in 'being human'. From a Jungian perspective, deep-seated, archetypal influences retain their influence over time, and in this case, as implied earlier in this chapter, it is possible to read into the wish for identity change an archetypal yearning for transformation. To be clear, I am not wanting to argue that where someone wants to reveal their real and felt gender or sexuality identity they are unwittingly and solely doing this because of some unconscious wish for transformation which has an archetypal root. The wish to show or become who they really are is of course *real*. Nevertheless, I am arguing that this reflects a human capacity and aspiration for transformation at a deeper level, as does the seeking out of an identity change or presentation on the internet.

Cashford (2002), a Jungian writer, in her detailed and extensive study of the influence of the moon on how human beings and cultures have made sense of the life and the world they inhabit, came to conclude there are widely shared associations between the cycle of the moon and ideas and beliefs about death and rebirth. This includes the way the moon 'disappears' for three days and nights at the end of its cycle, influencing religious beliefs across cultures, from the descent of the Sumerian goddess Innana into the underworld and return from death to life, to the death, descent to hell and then resurrection of Jesus in Christianity. As she puts it:

> The Moon's cyclical death and rebirth, which used to be interpreted as promising rebirth after death for human beings, may now be read symbolically, as

> proposing a structure of transformation in which the individual dies to the old self and is reborn into a new mode of being.
>
> *Cashford, 2002, p. 357*

The relevance of this hard-won insight from careful study of a wide range of information across many cultures is that it speaks to the underlying yearning in the human psyche for transformation, which I am arguing in this chapter is subtly influencing the current trend for 'real' identity, and identity change, to drive individual aspiration. This influence does not dictate individual activity or usurp autonomy in any way, rather it quietly underpins individual agency for change. In this sense this is something to be worked with carefully, helping the client work through all the layers of what their identity/identities may mean for them, while also welcoming and honouring the deep wish for transformation.

References

Bandura, A. (1986). *Social Foundations of Thought and Action: A Social Cognitive Theory*. Saddle River, NJ: Prentice-Hall.

Cashford, J. (2002). *The Moon, Myth and Image*. New York: Four Walls, Eight Windows.

Clarkson, P. (2003). *The Therapeutic Relationship*. 2nd Ed. London: Whurr.

Connell, R. (2002). *Gender*. Cambridge: Polity.

Goss, P. (2010). *Men Women and Relationships: A Post-Jungian Approach*. Hove: Routledge.

Hillman, J. (1975). *Re-visioning Psychology*. New York: Harper & Row.

Jacobs, M. (2006). *The Presenting Past*. Maidenhead: Open University Press.

Jung, C. G. (1948/1968). Concerning the Archetypes, with Special Reference to the Anima Concept. In: H. Read, M. Fordham and G. Adler (eds) *The Archetypes and the Collective Unconscious, Complete Works*, Vol. 9, Part I (trans. R. F. C. Hull). London: Routledge & Kegan Paul.

Jung, C. G. (1951/1968). The Shadow. In: H. Read, M. Fordham and G. Adler (eds) *Aion, Complete Works*, Vol. 9, Part II (trans. R. F. C. Hull). London: Routledge & Kegan Paul.

Jung, C. G. (1960/1969). The Stages of Life. In: H. Read, M. Fordham and G. Adler (eds) *The Structure and Dynamics of the Psyche, Complete Works*, Vol. 8 (trans. R. F. C. Hull). London: Routledge & Kegan Paul.

Kuss, D. and Griffiths, M. (2015). *Internet Addiction in Psychotherapy*. London: Palgrave.

Mearns, D. (1999). Person-centred Therapy with Configurations of the Self. *Counselling*, 10(2), 125–130.

Mearns, D. and Cooper, M. (2006). *Working at Relational Depth*. London: Sage.

Merry, T. (2002). *Learning and Being in Person-Centred Counselling*. Ross-on-Wye: PCCS Books.

Mitchell, S. (2016). Gears of Physis: Sarah's Tale'. In: *The Prompt Dramatherapy Newsletter*. Cheltenham: BADTH Publications.

Ogden, T. (1994). The Analytic Third: Working with Intersubjective Clinical Facts. *International Journal of Psychoanalysis*, 75, 3–19.

Rogers, C. (1961/2004). *On Becoming a Person*. London: PCCS Books.

Rycroft, C. (1995). *A Critical Dictionary of Psychoanalysis*. London: Penguin.

Samuels, A. (1989). *The Plural Psyche*. Hove: Routledge.

Shakespeare, W. (1599/2005). *Hamlet* (Eds. R. Gibson and R. Andrews). Cambridge: Cambridge University Press.

Stein, M. (1998). *Jung's Map of the Soul: An Introduction*. Illinois: Open Court.

Van Deurzen, E. (2009). *Psychotherapy and the Quest for Happiness*. London: Sage.

Winnicott, D. W. (1965). *TheMaturational Processes and the Facilitating Environment*. London: Karnac.

Withers, R. (2015). The Seventh Penis: Towards Effective Psychoanalytic Work with Pre-surgical Transsexuals. *Journal of Analytical Psychology*, 60(3), 390–412.

PART II

Culture and personal context

5

CONTEXT, SOCIAL CLASS AND COUNSELLING

It's not all just psychology

Liz Ballinger

The aim of this chapter is to explore the continuing power of social class despite its dismissal as an outmoded concept. Following a brief look at terms used to describe class, I explore its continuing relevance, not only as a categorisation system that organises and describes patterns of social and economic inequality within societies, but as a causal phenomenon that underpins and perpetuates such inequalities over time, in terms of both opportunities and outcomes.

A number of concepts are utilised to explore its abiding power. Bourdieu's notions of economic, social, cultural and symbolic capital (e.g. Bourdieu, 1986, 1987, 1990) are applied to help develop an understanding of how inequalities are perpetuated intergenerationally. The subjective experience or 'psychic landscape' of class (Reay, 2005) is examined, utilising Bourdieu's notion of habitus to help elucidate the role of class in choice and meaning-making. The notion of 'free choice' is problematised and the parameter of choices placed within a vortex of individual habituses and histories, institutional habituses and structural inequality.

I argue that despite the social significance of class and its centrality to any pursuit of social justice, it has been accorded relatively little attention within the therapy world. I contend that this inattention matters and that any attempt to build a therapeutic system that can best meet the needs of all of its potential users needs to bring class in from the borderlands. The understandings that underpin a range of counselling approaches are challenged, in particular the valorisation of choice and personal empowerment. The relevance of psychological therapies in their current form is questioned and suggestions made for potential ways forward.

What is social class?

Any questioning of the importance of class inevitably raises the issue of what it actually is. Over time, different understandings have been applied and continue to be so. A thorough exploration of these is beyond the scope of this chapter but, in general, understandings have focused, with varying emphases, on three areas: lifestyles or social prestige; patterns of material inequalities; class consciousness and identity (Crompton, 2008). Material inequality dominates official categorisations of class, with occupation playing a central role. The National Statistics Socio-Economic Classification (NS-SEC) replaced the Registrar General's Scale as the official measure and socioeconomic status is the classification now widely used in class-related research. While it has evident limitations as a reflection of class in its entirety, it does facilitate measurement and connects with other salient factors such as income, acquired wealth and vulnerability to poverty. Rooted in the Registrar General's Scale, the terms 'working class' and 'middle class' still have popular currency, characterising notions of class identity and consciousness in particular (Evans & Mellon, 2015). Without wishing to sidestep the difficulties, I call on more than one term to describe class-based experiences and attributes throughout this chapter as appropriate.

The so-called 'death of class'

During the last quarter of the twentieth century, class was fast becoming viewed as a zombie concept, 'at best irrelevant, or at worst completely useless as a concept' (Crompton, 2008: xv). Its demise was attributed to the seismic economic and social changes of that period, marking what Beck (2000: 81) characterised as an epochal shift from 'first modernity' to 'second modernity':

> A new kind of capitalism, a new kind of economy, a new kind of global order, a new kind of politics and law, a new kind of society and personal life are in the making which both separately and in context are clearly distinct from earlier phases of social evolution.

The changes encompassed the globalisation of finance and industry, the expansion and liberalisation of international trade, the erosion of national regulatory powers and rapid technological development. Accompanying this in Britain and elsewhere was the decline of heavy industry and a wider shift away from manufacturing toward the service sector. Government intervention in the economy and society was rolled back under neo-liberalism, which rested on the belief that the best foundation for growth lay in the liberation of 'individual entrepreneurial freedoms and skills within an institutional framework characterised by strong private property rights, free markets and free trade' (Harvey, 2005: 2). Launched under 'Thatcherism', state support for ailing industries was withdrawn, trade union powers reduced and major national industries privatised. State involvement in housing provision was rolled back as 'right to buy' policies began the depletion of local authority housing stock.

As Beck (2000) observed, change extended to the social and cultural. Instability, fragmentation and fluidity became characterising features of society. 'Old' traditional communities, roles, values and solidarities were on the wane: individualist values and behaviour were on the rise. The decline of the traditional working class accompanied the decline of traditional industries such as steel, shipbuilding and coal. As work became less secure, its contribution to individual identity weakened (Sennett, 1998). The emphasis shifted from people as collective producers to people as individual consumers and, it is argued, lifestyle and taste increasingly superseded class as markers of social differentiation (Giddens, 1994). There was an identified shift from class politics to identity politics mirroring the rising significance of other sources of identity. New issue-based rather than class-based social movements were emerging (e.g. the peace movement and the environmental movement). Sources of inequality other than class (e.g. gender, race and sexuality) were becoming the focus of public and political attention.

The ongoing importance of class

While it was largely accepted that fundamental changes in lifestyles and class consciousness had occurred, some dissenters pointed to how its continued material power was being ignored. As early as 1991, Clegg and Emmison, were declaring that being for or against class was 'tantamount to being for or against the atmosphere' (1991: 37). While economic growth accompanied neoliberalism, there were clear winners and losers. Material inequality did not diminish: rather, it was on the increase. Britain gained the dubious distinction of becoming the third most unequal country in the western world (Wilkinson & Pickett, 2009). In 2006, the *annual* earnings of the average male were around half of the *weekly* earnings of chief executives of the top 100 stock exchange listed companies (Roberts, 2011). By 2012–2014, the richest 10% of households held 45% of the nation's wealth while the poorest half owned 8.7% (Office for National Statistics). Vulnerability to unemployment, underemployment and poverty were all patterned by socio-economic status.

As the statistics above imply, the turn of the century had not marked a reversal of such trends. From 1997, while the new Labour government introduced a range of measures that alleviated the situation of those on the lowest incomes, it made little impact on overall inequality (Hills, 2004). British governmental responses to the 2008 financial crisis were largely characterised by financial austerity, a strategy which Clark (2014: 12) argues 'could reasonably be caricatured as knocking down storm defences'. Economic hardship ensued, at its most pronounced among the most vulnerable sections of the population. Between 2010 and 2013, 33% of the population experienced relative poverty at least once, while nearly 8% were in persistent poverty throughout (Office for National Statistics). In-work poverty became more and more significant, reflecting the rising incidence of short-term and zero-hour work contracts, minimum wage levels, part-time work and underemployment. Three-quarters of workers do not receive the same pay month to month, with pay volatility most pronounced among the lowest paid (Tomlinson, 2018).

The economic divide had become a 'societal schism' (Clark, 2014) patterning opportunities as much as rewards. As before, social class of origin shapes both educational outcomes and occupational opportunities (Blanden et al., 2005). It is not just material opportunities that are affected: the chances of leading a long, physically and mentally healthy life are similarly impacted. Those in the strongest socioeconomic positions continue to have the best quality of health and longer lives; those in the weakest socioeconomic positions the worse health and the shorter lives (Benzeval et al., 2014). The social gradient in mental health means that across the UK both men and women in the poorest fifth of the population are twice as likely to be at risk of developing mental health problems as those on average incomes (Elliott, 2016).

As the mental health statistics demonstrate, class is lived out both internally and externally. There is what Reay (2005) termed a 'psychic landscape of class'. The so-called 'cultural turn' in sociology has led a range of authors to explore how social class continues to shape our sense of self, of others and of the world, as well as our emotional landscape (e.g. Hanley, 2016; McKenzie, 2015; Skeggs, 1997, 2004; Steedman, 1986). The importance of family history – or class born into – figures highly in these accounts and illuminates the sense of internal conflict that can accompany social mobility. The accounts vividly portray the abiding power of class for individuals and also its connection with a sense of justice. Steedman (1986) saw her own childhood as shaped by her mother's sense of longing for 'real things, real entities, things she materially lacked, things that a culture and a social system withheld from her' (Steedman, 1986: 6). This ties into Sayer's (2005) perception of the moral significance of class. Class patterns access not only to valued resources but to how we are valued by others and, by extension, our self-esteem. The intrapersonal and interpersonal transactions that accompany class, Sayer argues, are moral in nature. The related emotions such as pride, envy, respect, contempt, anger and shame can be understood as 'embodied evaluative judgments' of self and other (Sayer, 2005: 3). I am aware of such 'embodied evaluative judgments' within myself and their link to my past: 'I'm aware I was brought up with anger alongside shame. As I grew up it was mainly male working-class anger and female working-class shame I witnessed. I'm also aware that they both reside in me' (Ballinger, 2000).

There is a growing acceptance that while class has changed, it has not lost its power: indeed the unequal impact of the economic slump and austerity programmes in Britain has brought it back into the public eye. The move toward a recognition of the intersectionality of different sources of inequality has helped to bring class back into the equation. The intersection between class and age is an important area, with the effects of the slump falling disproportionately on the young, in particular the poorer young (Clark, 2014). The rise of Momentum, the 'people-powered, grassroots movement working to transform Britain in the interests of the many, not the few' (Momentum, 2018), could be seen as marking a resurgence of popular interest in class issues, particularly among the young. Both class and identity politics were evident in the vote to leave the EU, with a broad coalition of three groups dominating the leave vote – 'affluent eurosceptics', the 'older working class' and a smaller group of 'economically deprived, anti-immigration voters' (Swales, 2016: 2).

Bourdieu and class

The work of French sociologist Bourdieu has played an influential role in the emerging literature on class (e.g. Savage, 2015). His work would seem highly pertinent to the counselling world, given that its analysis encompasses both the external functioning and internal lived experience of class. For Bourdieu, classes are social groups distinguished by their conditions of existence and dispositions. The conditions of existence reflect ownership of, or access to, different forms of capital – economic (wealth, income, property, etc.), cultural (knowledge, skills, tastes, etc.), social (familial and social networks) and symbolic (prestige). Ownership of these different forms of capital brings privilege and opportunity for both the individual and their families and helps explain the barriers to social mobility. While economic capital remains foundational, Bourdieu emphasises the importance of social and cultural capital in the workings of the class system. Hanley (2016: xii–xiii) talks of social and cultural capital working on a 'compound-interest model: the more you have, the more you get'.

The barriers to mobility are further explained by Bourdieu's notions of habitus and symbolic violence, both of which further challenge the notion of free choice. Class is not just about ownership; it is about a way of being. The habitus of the group refers to the socialised norms that guide individual thinking, feeling, behaviour and practice. Habitus is 'society written into the body, into the biological individual' (Bourdieu, 1990: 63). It is embodied and embedded. As Kuhn (1995: 98) comments: 'Class is something beneath your clothes, under your skin, in your reflexes, at the very core of your being.' While our habitus can adapt and change, our early experiences are particularly powerful in shaping us – hence the significance of family history in the reports on the 'psychic landscape' of class.

Important to both the habitus and social mobility or, rather, its lack is symbolic violence, a term used by Bourdieu to describe the process by which patterns of dominance are legitimated, the status quo maintained. Symbolic violence refers to the process whereby the meanings and interest of dominant groups are accepted as legitimate and internalised by dominated groups. It 'is exerted for the most part … through the purely symbolic channels of communication and cognition … recognition or even feeling' (Bourdieu, 2001: 2). As Bourdieu argues, it necessitates 'consent to domination' within the habitus of dominated groups. Hanley (2016: xii) talks of how the status quo is maintained via 'the wall in the head where people set their own limits and restrict their own potential in accordance with their delimited social status'.

Bourdieu's analysis of the role of education is pertinent here. The well-documented educational underachievement of children from poorer backgrounds is explained by the workings of symbolic violence. The habituses of schools and universities reflect those of the dominant classes and act as primary vehicles for the infusion of their codes, values and predispositions (Reay, 2017). The ultimate result is the exclusion and marginalisation of dominated groups (Bourdieu & Passeron, 1977). Add to this the impact of living in a depressed area with few job opportunities and self-exclusion seems understandable. Jones (2016: 176) described the higher truancy rates among working-class children as reflecting 'a tragic lack of confidence on their part in the ability of education to be even remotely relevant to their lives'.

The power of economic, social and cultural capital, institutional and class habituses, and the workings of symbolic violence all challenge the notion of free choice. Of course, mobility occurs. Many of the authors cited here came from working-class backgrounds, including Bourdieu himself. As Hanley (2016) astutely observes, however, a class system needs both mobility and immobility to demonstrate its value or justice. Upward mobility demonstrates how people of merit can rise through its ranks: immobility thus demonstrates lack of merit; the system is justified. Given the huge influence of class born into and the mechanisms of class reproduction and symbolic domination in shaping people's fortunes, such claims would seem highly contestable. As Sayer (2005: 4) argues: 'Class lacks a moral justification.'

Class and counselling

I entered counsellor training in the 1990s. Looking back at my experiences through the lens of the 'death of class' (Paluski & Waters, 1996), I can see this reflected in its absence from my training experience. Although issues of power and status were explored, I recall only one session remotely connected to social class in the four years of certificate and diploma level training I undertook. Social inequality was not ignored – it just tended to be explored through other lenses. As Collini observed in 1994, of 'the frequently incanted quartet of race, class, gender and sexual orientation, there is no doubt that class has been the least fashionable' (p. 3). My personal experiences reflected this.

Referring to social studies, Lash (1990: 116) argued that the neglect of class was 'politically reprehensible in times of increased unemployment and social inequality'. Such a verdict is as apt – perhaps even more so – in 2018 as in 1990, and can be levelled equally at the therapy world. The lack of attention to class issues that I experienced as a trainee counsellor has continued. As a counselling tutor, I have experienced class as a difficult subject for many students, accompanied frequently by a 'loaded absence' in any discussion (Ryan, 2017: 103). In the final part of this chapter, I reflect on my sense of the major issues that class presents for therapy, and end by looking at how – or whether – a class-sensitive approach to therapy can be constructed. For ease of presentation I present them as separate issues but they need to be understood as intersecting parts of a whole. I incorporate here not only my views as well as those of others, but also some of my experiences as client, counsellor and tutor.

The limited potential of counselling to effect change

It might be taken as axiomatic that counsellors would wish to 'do good', to be part of a 'healing encounter'. A classic text boldly states that 'all counsellors seem to be imbued by sentiments of worthwhileness in giving personal service to others' (Halmos, 1965: 29). I have described elsewhere my involvement in counselling as an existential vote for kindness in human affairs (Ballinger, 2012). At the same time, I have described myself as a sceptical insider, and part of this scepticism centres on the purpose or aim of counselling and its consequences. As a range of commentators have observed, counselling and psychotherapy continue to root psychological distress within individual psychology rather than social circumstance. This somewhat simplistic perspective leads to a psychological reductionism (Pilgrim, 1997) that manifests in fault being sought within the client rather than explored within its socioeconomic context. Unlinking the individual from their context becomes a dominant norm (Layton, 2006). As a new practitioner working within the counselling service of an inner-city further education college, my growing sense of the economic and social basis of many of my clients' problems made 'doing good' seem unrealisable. As I wrote later:

> My clients often came to me with seemingly insoluble problems (to me and them) producing a mutual sense of powerlessness. I felt that my person-centred training had not prepared me for this experience. I perceived, albeit vaguely at this point, that what I needed was a theoretical base that embraced more fully the political and social dimensions of human existence. Mostly I felt personally inadequate.
>
> *Ballinger & Saxton, 2000: 3*

As I was learning experientially, the class gradient in mental health raises serious questions over therapy's relevance to disadvantaged members of society, pointing as it does to the close connection between mental wellbeing and external circumstance. This connection has become increasingly apparent with rising inequality from the 1980s, especially as it has brought with it reduced levels of mental and emotional wellbeing across the social spectrum (Wilkinson & Pickett, 2018). Generally, therapy's power to meaningfully address mental and emotional distress within society is called into question.

Moreover, the meaning counsellors attach to their work is raised. While Halmos (1965) linked the rise of counselling with an increasing disillusion with politics, he also argued the counsellor to be 'in favour of the kind of society whose arrangements will tend to reduce people's needs for his [*sic*] services' (p. 178). This is not immediately apparent. The lack of willingness on the part of therapists to identify with political ideas has been noted (e.g. Kearney, 1996; Winter & Hanley, 2015). Feltham points to the consequences of how 'a countercultural psychoanalysis or humanistic movement long ago became a professional juggernaut, small rebellious factions notwithstanding' (2015: 185). As a counselling tutor, I have witnessed the increasing focus among trainee counsellors on simply finding a job, an understandable response within the context of the high cost of training, the large number of qualified counsellors and the limited work opportunities available in either the statutory or third sector.

A related observation is that counsellors, myself included, can be guilty of political naivety. While individual counsellors might identify with a desire for a fairer society, the question is not just whether counselling can contribute to positive social change but whether it might be part of the problem. 'Contrary to person-centred claims to a "quiet revolution", might not most therapy constitute a rather conservative, indeed collusive, anti-revolutionary quietism?' (Feltham, 2015: 182–183). I have felt moral disquiet, for instance, at the thought that my counselling support for victims of abusive relationships might have helped them, ironically, to remain within the very relationships that were damaging them. While maintaining my primary commitment to my clients, I came to increasingly recognise that my institutional role as college counsellor was to conserve the wellbeing of that institution, to maintain the status quo, to be part of an 'anti-revolutionary quietism'. As a practitioner I came to understand how the criticism of social workers as society's 'sticking plaster' can be equally applied to therapy.

There is a final serious issue for counselling here. Even if you argue, as I ultimately do, that counselling has a potential place within the lives of people of lower socioeconomic status, there is an identified middle-class bias in the client base (e.g. Holman, 2014). A process of social exclusion would seem to be in action. Part of this is financial. Even though some practitioners offer sliding scales of payment, this does not fundamentally alter the exclusivity of private practice on price grounds. In the overstretched voluntary sector, itself facing substantial financial pressures and relying heavily on unpaid trainee counsellors, the frequent practice of asking for a financial contribution inevitably impacts on access. In the health sector, an important potential source of free therapy, central government rhetoric on increasing mental health resources has not translated into an evident expansion of provision. Moreover, there is a well-documented tendency for patients on lower incomes to be prescribed medication rather than be offered therapy, commonly linked to classism among referrers (Holman, 2014). Where therapy is accessed, what is on offer can be tightly circumscribed. Generally, shortage of accessible provision, waiting lists, limitations in choice of therapy, therapist and length of counselling can be common experiences for those lacking in economic wherewithal.

Working-class self-exclusion also plays a part or, to put it differently, the very notion of counselling works to exclude. As Trevithick (1998: 116) observed, the therapeutic world can be seen as 'worryingly out of touch with the needs, the strengths and struggles of working-class people'. This may well reflect its perception as a middle-class endeavour. A middle-class bias among counsellors and psychotherapists has been identified (e.g. Pilgrim, 1997). McLeod (1993) argues that even counsellors with working-class origins will have absorbed middle-class norms and values via professional training or higher education. Holman (2014) linked self-exclusion in part to a level of suspicion or aversion toward counselling and a favouring of more practical solutions over the verbalisation of emotions and introspection. Perhaps my early questioning of therapy's utility and my adoption of a sceptical insider position reflected *my* working-class background or habitus.

The counselling habitus and the workings of symbolic violence

The argument that counselling does not address the most powerful roots of mental distress can reflect not only its social blinkers but its very nature, its habitus. As with education, its habitus can be viewed as reflecting and perpetuating the codes and values of dominant classes and actually contributing to, rather than addressing, the exclusion and marginalisation of dominated groups. As education, it can be the purveyor of symbolic violence. This might feel like a difficult piece of analysis for counsellors to swallow, but I believe it is important to engage with.

First, its emphasis on an individual psyche unshaped by social forces and relationships mirrors neoliberal valorising of 'the entrepreneurial self, free of any social context, where all mental health issues are seen only as matters of individual deficits, and the impacts of social circumstance and policy are given no recognition' (Ryan, 2017: 183). This mirroring of wider ideology makes counselling potentially one of its conduits. Therapeutic goals such as autonomy, self-actualisation and personal empowerment sideline the constraints on individual power, choice and potential that emanate from class position. The 'surplus powerlessness' that Lerner (1991) identified among working-class clients may easily be identified by therapists as a reflection of individual deficit rather than social circumstance. Carl Rogers (1961) talked of the limited potential of therapeutic success with clients who have difficulty accessing and verbalising emotions and who see the source of their problems as external to self. There is no analysis provided of how this might reflect a working-class habitus or an external reality. Neither is there any acknowledgement of how the middle-class speech patterns and vocabulary of therapists might impact on the client's ease and ability to verbalise their own feelings. In Balmforth's (2006) research, working-class clients talked of their sense of inferiority and discomfort, of 'feeling unable to be fully self' when working with a middle-class therapist (p. 219). Generally Rogers' focus is on the limitations of clients rather than the therapy on offer. The potential is evident for working-class people to have the shaming experience of feeling negatively judged as inadequate and disempowered (Sayer, 2005).

The critique above can be contextualised within a larger one – that of the unreflexive nature of counselling and, by extension, counsellors. One aspect of reflexivity is development of consciousness of the ways that values, interests, beliefs, political commitments and ideologies shape practices and their impact. Ryan (2017) points to the lack of a reflexive position within psychoanalysis, and this criticism can be extended to other therapeutic approaches. This lack of reflexivity extends to its practitioners – a criticism I would attach to myself in my earlier years as a counsellor. As in counselling practice, the emphasis in training is on developing self-awareness rather than social awareness, on pursuing self-actualisation rather than social justice. Practitioners are not generally encouraged to question the underlying ideological forces that shape counselling and its outcomes or how their own political beliefs might play out in the counselling process. As Kearney (1996) argues, we all hold political models in our head, regardless of whether or not we identify ourselves as political. Lack of awareness of them may mean we fail to take responsibility for the consequences of their enactment. Class-related power issues remain under-explored; classism remains unacknowledged; the crystallisation of economic, social and cultural capital that shapes its very nature goes unquestioned. Basically, a lack of critical analysis characterised my training in both the university and private sector, a lack that Feltham (2015) depicts as a general phenomenon.

What would a class-sensitive approach to counselling look like?

The easy answer is to argue that the construction of a class-sensitive approach to counselling calls for the addressing of the issues sketched above. Any such approach would incorporate ways of lowering barriers to access for working-class clients and of drawing in therapists from across the social spectrum. Training would embrace more critical thinking, incorporate sociological understandings and promote class awareness. The class base of values and language systems and their impact would be highlighted. Classism would take its rightful place among areas of discrimination and prejudice to be addressed. The potential importance of extending therapeutic exploration of the causes of distress to the social and economic spheres would be examined.

Critical thinking would extend to the questioning of the goals of counselling alongside its impacts. The impact of becoming a 'professional juggernaut' would become part of this critical questioning. Has the striving to become more embedded and accepted as a profession led to our involvement in the 'medicalisation of misery' and indeed to the drive to become accepted as the treatment of choice for a range of mental health issues? Does not that inevitably lead us into siding with the notion that lack of wellbeing is to be addressed via the individual psyche rather the workings of a toxic society? Does it not reinforce our status as a socially conservative agency?

Concluding thoughts

While much of what I have written here is critical of the therapeutic world, it has not led me to leave it. I do believe that individual counsellors can attempt to address such issues in their practice. They can incorporate class awareness into their understanding of self, clients and their relational dynamics, alongside their thinking about appropriate therapeutic settings, approaches, boundaries, goals and processes. They can think about how to widen access, address power issues, provide avenues to other forms of support and avoid pathologisation. Underpinning all of this is a necessary individual commitment to reflexivity and critical thinking.

Speaking personally, I have chosen to work within agencies where counselling is free at the point of access and where long-term therapy is available to those who want it. I have provided free or very low-cost counselling and counselling supervision to help enable counsellors from working-class backgrounds to similarly practise. I also recognise that this reflects my material ability to do so. While the person-centred core conditions continue to underpin my practice, I have taken from other theoretical bases to help me think more effectively about my work. One source has been feminist theory with its understanding of the relationship between internal distress and external circumstance. As it argues 'the personal is political'. Another source has been existential theory. Its notion of situated freedom has been particularly important to me, referring to the way that our choices are conditioned and constrained by our life circumstances. I have incorporated ongoing critical thinking into my way of being as a counsellor. I have learnt that I can burden clients with an agenda for change when their focus is on survival. I have also learnt that effective help for some clients involves practical help and a willingness to have flexible boundaries. I came to understand my job as listening to the unlistened to – be it people in their entirety or their secrets and pains. I have concluded that counselling means different things to different people and that is okay.

On a final note, while I indeed remain in counselling as an existential vote for human kindness, I do not regard it as the answer to all human ills and I suspect attempts to portray it as such. Like Feltham (2015: 184), I can feel like a 'downbeat minority in the world of therapeutic optimism'. I cannot know of the wider or long-term impact of my work as counsellor on client wellbeing. My personal experience of long-term therapy has been the gaining of insight, some of it very important to me, but of no fundamental shift in my sense of wellbeing, certainly not happiness. I can chart that much more easily to the quality of my relationships, my economic fortunes, the vicissitudes of my working life, the respect accorded to me or its lack, the losses of those close to me. While I think counselling has something to offer and indeed argue passionately for greater therapeutic provision for working-class people, this sits alongside my knowledge that it cannot cure the human condition or a toxic environment. I find myself agreeing with Smail's comment that perhaps we need to acknowledge that 'our principal and most potent function lies in accepting people as they are and providing solidarity in the face of tragedy' (1997: 169).

References

Ballinger, L. (2000) *Power and Oppression*. Presentation given at Nottingham Trent University.

Ballinger, L. (2012) *The Role of the Counsellor Trainer: The Trainer Perspective*. Unpublished PhD thesis. University of Manchester.

Ballinger, L. & Saxton, D. (2000) *A Co-operative Inquiry into Counselling and Class*. Unpublished MA dissertation. Nottingham Trent University.

Balmforth, J. (2006) Clients' experiences of how perceived differences in social class between counsellor and client affect the counselling relationship. In: G. Proctor, M. Cooper, P. Sanders & B. Malcolm (eds) *Politicizing the Person-Centred Approach: An agenda for social change*. Ross-on-Wye: PCCS Books (pp. 215–224).

Beck, U. (2000) The cosmopolitan perspective: sociology of the second age of modernity. *British Journal of Sociology*, 51(1), pp. 79–106.

Benzeval, M., Bond, L., Campbell, M., Egan, M., Lorenc, T., Petticrew, M. & Popham, F. (2014) *How Does Money Influence Health*? York: Joseph Rowntree Foundation.

Blanden, J., Gregg, P. & Machin, S. (2005) *Intergenerational Mobility in Europe and South America*. London: Centre for Economic Performance, London School of Economics.

Bourdieu, P. (1986) *Distinction: A Social Critique of the Judgement of Taste*. London: Routledge.

Bourdieu, P. (1987) What makes a social class? On the theoretical and practical existence of groups. *Berkeley Journal of Sociology*, 32, pp. 1–17.

Bourdieu, P. (1990) *In Other Words*. Stanford, CA: Stanford University Press.

Bourdieu, P. (2001) *Masculine Domination*. Cambridge: Polity Press.

Bourdieu, P. and Passeron, J.-C. (1977) *Reproduction in Education, Society and Culture*. London: Sage.

Clark, T. (2014) *Hard Times: The Divisive Toll of the Economic Slump*. London: Yale University Press.

Clegg, S. & Emmison, M. (1991) Classical and contemporary sociological debates. In: J. Baxter, M. Emmison & J. Western (eds) *Class Analysis and Contemporary Australia*. Melbourne: Macmillan (pp. 23–37).

Collini, S. (1994) Escape from DWEMsville. *Times Literary Supplement*, May 27.

Crompton, R. (2008) *Class and Stratification* (3rd edition). Cambridge: Polity Press.

Elliott, I. (2016) *Poverty and Mental Health: A Review to Inform the Joseph Rowntree Foundation's Anti-poverty Strategy*. London: Mental Health Foundation.

Evans, G. & Mellon, H. (2015) Social Class. *British Social Attitudes*, 33, pp. 1–19.

Feltham, C. (2015) Critical priorities for the psychotherapy and counselling community. In: D. Loewenthal (ed.) *Critical Psychotherapy, Psychoanalysis and Counselling: Implications for Practice*. Basingstoke: Palgrave Macmillan (pp. 175–188).

Giddens, A. (1994) *Beyond Left and Right: The Future of Radical Politics*. Cambridge: Polity Press.

Halmos, P. (1965) *The Faith of the Counsellors*. London: Constable.

Hanley, L. (2016) *Respectable: The Experience of Class*. London: Allen Lane.

Harvey, D. (2005) *A Brief History of Neoliberalism*. Oxford: Oxford University Press.

Hills, J. (2004) *Inequality and the State*. Oxford: Oxford University Press.

Holman, D. (2014) 'What help can you get talking to somebody?' Explaining class differences in the use of talking treatments. *Sociology of Health and Illness*, 36(4), pp. 531–548.

Jones, O. (2016) *Chavs: The Demonization of the Working Class*. London: Verso.

Kearney, A. (1996) *Counselling, Class and Politics: Undeclared Influences in Therapy*. Ross-on-Wye: PCCS Books.

Kuhn, A. (1995) *Family Secrets: Acts of Memory and Imagination*. London: Verso.

Lash, S. (1990) *Sociology of Postmodernism*. London: Routledge.

Layton, L. (2006) Attacks on linking. In: L. Layton, N. Hollander & S. Gutwill (eds) *Psychoanalysis, Class and Politics: Encounters in the clinical setting*. London: Routledge (pp. 107–117).

Lerner, M. (1991) *Surplus Powerlessness: The Psychodynamics of Everyday Life – and the Psychology of Individual and Social Transformation*. Atlantic Highlands, NJ: Humanities Press International.

McKenzie, L. (2015) *Getting By: Estates, Class and Culture in Austerity Britain*. Bristol: Policy Press.

Momentum (2018) Available at https://peoplesmomentum.com (accessed 2 October 2018).

Office for National Statistics (2015) *Wealth in Great Britain Wave 4: 2012–2014*. Available online at www.ons.gov.uk (accessed 31 August 2019).

Office for National Statistics (2016) *Persistent Poverty in the UK and the EU: 2014*. Available online at www.ons.gov.uk (accessed 31 August 2019).

Paluski, J. & Waters, M. (1996) *The Death of Class*. London: Sage.

Pilgrim, D. (1997) *Psychotherapy & Society*. London: Sage.

Reay, D. (2005) Beyond consciousness? The psychic landscape of social class. *Sociology*, 39(5), pp. 911–928.

Reay, D. (2017) *Miseducation: Inequality, Education and the Working Classes*. Bristol: Policy Press.

Roberts, K. (2011) *Class in Contemporary Britain* (2nd edition). London: Palgrave Macmillan.

Rogers, C. R. (1961) *On Becoming a Person*. London: Constable.

Ryan, J. (2017) *Class and Psychoanalysis*. London: Routledge.

Savage, M. (2015) *Social Class in the Twenty-First Century*. London: Penguin Books.

Sayer, A. (2005) *The Moral Significance of Class*. Cambridge: Cambridge University Press.

Sennett, R. (1998) *The Corrosion of Character: The Personal Consequences of Work in the New Capitalism*. London: W.W. Norton.

Skeggs, B. (1997) *Formations of Class and Gender: Becoming Respectable*. London: Sage.

Skeggs, B. (2004) *Class, Self, Culture*. London: Routledge.

Smail, D. (1997) Psychotherapy and tragedy. In: R. House & N. Totton (eds) *Implausible Professions. Arguments for Pluralism and Autonomy in Psychotherapy and Counselling*. Ross-on-Wye: PCCS Books (pp. 159–170).

Steedman, C. (1986) *Landscape for a Good Woman*. London: Virago.

Swales, K. (2016) *Understanding the Leave Vote*. London: NatCen Social Research.

Tomlinson, D. (2018) Irregular payments: Assessing the breadth and depth of month to month earnings volatility. *Resolution Foundation*. Available online at www.resolutionfoundation.org/publications/irregular-payments (accessed 15 October 2018).

Trevithick, P. (1998) Psychotherapy and working class women. In: I. Bruna Seu & M. Colleen Heenan (eds) *Feminism and Psychotherapy: Reflections on Contemporary Theories and Practice*. London: Sage (pp. 115–134).

Wilkinson, R. & Pickett, K. (2009) *The Spirit Level: Why Equality is Better for Everyone*. London: Penguin.

Wilkinson, R. & Pickett, K. (2018) *The Inner Level: How More Equal Societies Reduce Stress, Restore Sanity and Improve Everyone's Wellbeing*. London: Penguin.

Winter, L. & Hanley, T. (2015) "Unless everyone's covert guerilla-like social justice practitioners…": A preliminary study exploring social justice in UK counselling psychology. *Counselling Psychology Review*, 30 (2), pp. 32–46.

6

CONFIDENCE WITH DIFFICULT CONVERSATIONS

The need to explore taboo subjects in particular relation to the sexual abuse of children

Barry O'Sullivan

Undertaking a difficult conversation, such as that between teacher and pupil, employer and employee, parent and child, between friends, or between long-term partners, requires confidence and training in order to change behaviour effectively. This is especially true when the subject is a taboo such as the sexual abuse of children. This chapter explores the various dynamics that can exist within the context of having the confidence to hold difficult conversations and is based on my training as a priest and counsellor, my experiences in child safeguarding in the Roman Catholic Church and my doctoral research into the effects of clergy child sexual abuse on non-offending priests (O'Sullivan, 2018).

Conversations, difficult or otherwise, are vital to understanding. Rorty (1979) argues that conversation may be conceived epistemologically as a basic mode of knowing. The basis of our knowledge is a matter of conversation between two people in a way that significantly differs from the knowledge gained from interaction with a non-human reality. It is "the ultimate context within which knowledge is understood" (Rorty, 1979). Shotter goes further by stating:

> For conversation is not just *one* of our many activities in *the* world. On the contrary, we constitute both ourselves and our worlds in our conversation activity. For us they are foundational. They constitute the usually ignored background within which our lives are rooted.
>
> *Shotter, 1993, p. vi*

If conversations are such an integral part of our experience and interpretation of reality as we perceive it, then the concept of difficult conversations becomes even more important. The reluctance or failure to engage in conversations that we find difficult might mean that we miss the opportunity to engage with an aspect of reality that is challenging. It might be the key to acknowledging and experiencing a reality without which we will remain at least in part in the dark, and while protected from the challenge the reality might be that we remain couched in ignorance.

Difficult conversations, in all their forms but especially those about taboos, raise many issues including whether the other person(s) should be confronted with interpretations of themselves, especially if they have not asked for them and may not appreciate exploring these areas. Also when difficult issues are raised it will often mean that inherent in the dialogue is disagreement. This, in turn, raises the question of the power dynamic between those having the conversation and, by implication, whose interpretation of reality informs the outcome. When broaching any subject that will lead to a difficult conversation it is important to consider who initiated the dialogue and whether one of the parties may be asked for interpretations leading to fundamental challenges that may undermine the way they see themselves and their world. This chapter explores these and other implications of having difficult conversations within the particular context of training individuals and groups to deal with difficult taboo subjects such as the sexual abuse of children. This is an integral part of safeguarding training in the Roman Catholic Church to deal with and prevent the sexual abuse of children and to assist priests in their ministry with children. In effect, this chapter explores what we should do when we do not know what to do.

Learning first-hand

From 1995 to 1999, while working as a prison chaplain, I trained to be a tutor on the Sex Offender Treatment Programme which was run by the Prison Service in 28 prisons throughout England and Wales. Due to the sensitive and sometimes gruesome content of the disclosures by the inmates in the programme, an integral part of our training as tutors was to foster an insight and understanding of taboos with special reference to taboos within ourselves. On the first day of the tutors' course, all the participants were informed that if there was a road we were not prepared to travel down then we should leave the course immediately. The tutor went on to explain that due to the nature of the extraordinarily sensitive information to which we would be exposed, any hesitancy to deal with the subject material would neutralise the process. In other words, if a tutor found something particularly repugnant in an inmate's detailed account of his offences, the inmate would pick that up and exploit it. For four years I was a tutor on this programme and while it was a very challenging and demanding role, it gave me invaluable experience and enabled me to lay a foundation on which to build my work in child protection and the promotion of the welfare of the child. Anyone working in safeguarding must be both willing and able to walk a road down which a child has been taken, especially when that journey has led to horrific abuse. Victims are much more likely to disclose what has happened to them and begin their healing process if the person they are disclosing to does not flinch when hearing about such atrocities.

The taboo of sexual abuse within Roman Catholic communities in England and Wales used to be an issue we learned to stay away from, to pretend was not there or was not relevant. Failing to engage with this taboo facing our communities only served to sustain it and impair our ability to both acknowledge and deal with it. First as a Safeguarding Co-ordinator within the Roman Catholic Church and in my subsequent work in this area I witnessed the threat of this particular taboo, and the "not knowing what to do" that came with it, force some priests to freeze into a seemingly permanent paralysed state when it came to their ministry with children. The whole area of child abuse within this particular community prompted all kinds of alarm bells and red flags. For some priests it undermined their confidence in their own competence and they avoided training in an area that made them feel most uncomfortable. Due to the taboo nature of child sexual abuse, some clergy would not engage in conversations, exploration or training in this area, even though they had previously expressed a willingness to do so. Ironically, despite this I never ceased to be surprised by the fact that when I was alone with a fellow priest or with a small group of priests the conversation invariably came round to child abuse and my connected role within my diocese. This indicated to me that although the subject of child protection caused dismay particularly among priests, paradoxically, it was accompanied by an insatiable curiosity. It is this curiosity which I sought to exploit to encourage engagement in training that would involve the necessity of daring to have difficult conversations. There was a tendency to ignore, deny or simply refuse to discuss the issue officially and sadly some clergy preferred to labour under the burden of not knowing rather than to deal with a taboo subject which has had a detrimental effect on their overall ministry as priests. My subsequent doctoral qualitative research into the effects of the child sex abuse scandals on non-offending priests (O'Sullivan, 2018) revealed eight broad areas of psychological concern, superordinate themes that continued to seriously affect how they viewed other priests, their confidence in themselves as priests, their perception of their role in ministering to children and their faith in the establishment they served. They constituted a previously unrecognised group of secondary victims whom the Catholic Church, despite being the fount of their religious and moral lives and their employer, was not addressing. One of the superordinate themes uncovered in my research, betrayal, bridged both dimensions of the crisis as priests struggled to deal with brother priests who had betrayed them and with the Church which was both a victim and a perpetrator of betrayal.

Priests, like other professionals, are prone to the temptation of choosing not to explore taboo subjects, especially when they find it difficult to see any solutions. The danger is that this mindset simply serves to avoid the steps that need to be taken to find an instructive and useful way out of an impasse.

The basis of a difficult conversation

Before a conversation, difficult or otherwise, takes place it is important to bear in mind Rogerian principles of counselling to uphold the intrinsic dignity of the people who are engaging in the conversations. As Rogers (1940) reminds us, before a person can receive help from a therapist or a counsellor it is essential that certain basic or core conditions are met. Thorne (1992, p. 126) argues that it is not too simplistic to "affirm that the whole conceptual framework of Carl Rogers rests on his profound experience that human beings become increasingly trustworthy once they feel at a deep level that their subjective experience is both respected and progressively understood". Notions of wholeness overlap with what Carol Rogers describes as congruence or "realness"; and the attitude embodied and conveyed by educators may be accepting and valuing of the other (Rogers, 1952).

This principle can also be applied in the context of a conversation and is especially true in difficult conversations. In my qualitative research with six non-offending priests (O'Sullivan, 2018), I sought to adhere to this and Rogers' other principles and I am convinced that this enabled me to elicit real reactions from them to the difficult taboo subjects we discussed. When dealing with difficulties it is important to ascertain whether there is any dissatisfaction with a given topic and whether adjustment and a fundamental need for enquiry that might lead to change will be welcome. The fact that it might or might not be welcome is important information, but it should not be the determining factor as to whether the conversation should take place. It can be difficult to be faithful to Rogers' core principles whose purpose is to release and strengthen the individual rather than intervene in his or her life. The tension arises when an intervention is deemed necessary by a third party with clear instructions to challenge and enlighten individuals who have neither asked for nor will welcome the intervention and will resent the challenge. This is especially true when dealing with taboo subjects and the difficult conversations they entail. This also has serious implications for the importance of the therapeutic alliance between the therapist/client, or trainer/trainees, such as those I have undertaken as a Church Safeguarding Co-ordinator responsible for training. It is necessary to consider how effective an intervention will be if it results in the fracture of a therapeutic alliance, especially one that is already well-established. Consideration needs to be given as to whether taboo subjects should be discussed if the conversation will result ultimately in alienation between parties. This difficulty in turn raises the question of who sets the agenda, who sets the pace at which things will be discussed, who decides when the discussion is over, and who interprets the interaction.

For any in-depth conversation to take place it is important that a degree of rapport is established and that there should be a genuine interest in the individual and a respect for what that person brings to the dynamic. These principles can sometimes be compromised in the context of training, especially when that training involves conversations which are neither asked for nor welcomed. During training, and again this is especially true with difficult topics and taboos, the dynamic can be drastically different from that which exists between a therapist and a client who is simply being encouraged to take responsibility for their choices. During training, the trainer can be tasked with taking people down avenues they do not wish to explore but which must be encountered if the desired insight and subsequent change is to take place. I am conscious that this challenges the notion that this dynamic is a conversation, difficult or otherwise. It is extraordinarily difficult to balance the give and take that should occur before, during and after difficult conversations. It raises the question of how best to encourage expression and how interpretations may be made during a conversation. Rogers (1959) reminds us that individuals have within themselves vast resources of self-understanding and for altering their concepts of themselves. In the context of a conversation between individuals, Rogers argues that three conditions must be present to facilitate the development of a person. The first element he calls genuineness or congruence, i.e. the more the therapist is himself or herself the greater the likelihood that the client will change. This can be applied to the dynamic of difficult conversations because "there is a close matching, or congruence, between what is being experienced, what is present in awareness, and what is expressed to the client" (Rogers, 1959, p. 127).

Rogers' second element is "unconditional positive regard" in which the therapist experiences a positive attitude to whoever the client is at that moment, thus making therapeutic movement or change more likely. Unconditional positive regard is an integral part of any difficult conversation, since it gives permission for the participants to recognise what is going on at any given time, be that confusion, resentment, fear, anger, relief or enlightenment. This approach is fruitful not least because it encourages the participants in a conversation to value each other in their totality rather than in a conditional way.

Rogers' third core condition in any relationship is "empathic understanding" through which the therapist senses the feelings and personal meanings that the client is experiencing and communicates this understanding to the client. Integral to Rogerian therapy is sensitive, active listening which he regards as the most potent force for change as people feel they are being accepted and prized and are worthy to be listened to. This, in turn, enables a person to become what Rogers describes as more real and more genuine. This realness and genuineness are essential components of any worthwhile conversation and especially so in difficult conversations and discussion of taboos. In the particular context of training and by implication learning, participants should to some extent perceive that these core principles exist.

McLeod (2001) stresses the importance of encouraging participants in conversations to talk about their experiences and opinions in ways that are complete, honest and authentic. This has implications not only for difficult conversations but also for the dynamics that exist within the training arena. It is particularly important to be mindful of the extent to which an individual or a group is not only given permission to participate but encouraged to do so in an honest and open manner. This, as noted by Rogers, will be more likely if his core conditions are an integral part of the interaction. McLeod goes on to note that when attempting to discuss difficult topics it can be extremely upsetting and intrusive when done badly. However, he also notes that being interviewed can be cathartic and liberating when done well, since the effects of a well-conducted conversation can give the participants new insights. During a conversation, difficulties may arise when entering into new aspects of an issue, so consideration should be given as to who has control of the time limits and at which point either party closes down the interaction. For this reason McLeod (2001) suggests the adoption of a "process consent" procedure which, he argues, will deal with the immediate moral dilemmas arising from the intensity of a conversation. The Ethical Guidelines published by the British Association for Counselling and Psychotherapy (2018) clearly outline a consent process consistent with good practice and basic human and civil rights. They call for consent to be, among other criteria, based on full written information, freely given and open to modification or withdrawal particularly as circumstances change.

In the context of a conversation, be it difficult or otherwise, it is relatively straightforward to establish whether consent has been granted. However, in some contexts it can be argued that the assumption should be made that consent should not be assumed and, in fact, the assumption should be that consent has been withheld. This difficulty presents itself when training or difficult conversations become mandatory and, as noted above, it has serious implications for the dynamic and the alliance forged between trainer and trainee.

Overcoming obstacles

Training, by implication, will at least in part involve the imparting of information that might be both new and potentially unwelcome to the trainees. Working on the assumption that at least in part the purpose of the new information is to elicit change, Mearns, Thorne and McLeod (2013) suggest five elements that denote a person's readiness for change. They argue that while none of these would make change impossible, their presence or absence may lengthen or shorten the process. These elements include: (1) indecision about wanting to change; (2) general lack of trust for others; (3) unwillingness to take responsibility for self in life; (4) unwillingness to take responsibility in the changing process; and (5) unwillingness to recognise and explore feelings about change.

Mearns, Thorne and McLeod (2013) go on to explain that the most difficult thing to predict in the changing process is its speed. This can raise particular difficulties if a trainer is attempting to implement a changed way of thinking among the trainees, because individual participants will be in their own place moving at their own speed. This, in turn, can lead either to the group as a whole or individuals within the group being "stuck" in a changing process. Further difficulties arise because people can be stuck for different reasons, such as an inability to grasp a concept, or an unwillingness or unreadiness to be confronted with issues which they perceive will elicit a change with which they are not prepared to engage. Sometimes people can be stuck for very genuine reasons and the "stuckness" is valuable information in itself. But it takes more than a few sessions or training hours to change how someone feels or thinks about an issue and the more so when that issue is particularly sensitive. While it may be tempting, not least because of time constraints, to press on and elicit change, too much change too fast may derail the whole process. Mearns, Thorne and McLeod (2013) suggest five questions to ask to reveal the stage of "stuckness" during the changing process:

1. Are we indeed stuck, or am I misperceiving the process through my own impatience, or perhaps because I expect the client to move in different directions from what is happening just now?
2. How does my client perceive the process at this time?

If we are stuck:

3. What is the source of our stuckness?
4. How far is it important to our process at this time that we are stuck?
5. How might we move on?

These questions are integral to give people the confidence to have difficult conversations. "Stuckness" can result when people gain something but are reluctant for whatever reason to risk going further. Also participants, both consciously and unconsciously, may have well-developed defence mechanisms that enable them to either deny or minimise a motivator for change. Sometimes people can get stuck because the initial insight has been too rapid and too profound. It is as though so much progress has been made that it is necessary to pause to process what has happened. Mearns, Thorne and McLeod (2013) note "stuckness" can also occur when a person has experienced significant movement in perception or insight and realises that there is no going back, while at the same time they have also worked out that to go on may lead to considerable unalterable and unwelcome life changes. In such circumstances it is imperative that a person should be encouraged to pause, if for no other reason than to gather energy and motivation to deal with the difficult issues that will ensue.

Given that it is so important that the person-centred counsellor be sensitive to any "stuckness", the question arises as to how one assesses the "stuckness" when attempting to address sensitive issues with a group of people. Any challenge that leads to dramatic change within the context of difficult conversations should make allowance for the fact that, in the longer term, dramatic insights will only facilitate change insofar as the person or people challenged to change can integrate the changes, the process of which will invariably take longer than the newly discovered insight. Mearns, Thorne and McLeod (2013) also point out that "stuckness" in the process of change and challenging can also originate in the therapist/trainer. For the therapist/trainer the pace at which challenges are made is vital, so consideration should be given to the implications of either pushing things through too hurriedly or the danger of going so slowly as to lose the motivation of the participants. It is also worth considering the therapist/trainer's own insight into the subject, especially when that subject is a cultural taboo and even more importantly when the client/trainer is a member of the society or community in which that particular issue is taboo. I was to consider this issue carefully in my semi-structured research interviews with my six fellow priests. I am convinced it led to a greater depth of analysis and lent greater weight to the integrity of the data. As a non-offending Roman Catholic priest myself, I was interested to explore the view of other priests who lacked both the experience of being involved in this specialised work and the time to research the matter.

Dealing with taboos

Whether we are aware of it or not, we decide what topics are to be ignored, denied, discounted or examined at our peril. Quite often topics that are taboo receive only superficial treatment, perhaps because they provoke anxiety, discomfort and confusion. Taboo subjects, by their very nature, can be threatening and for many people, therefore, are to be avoided. However, some taboo subjects such as the sexual abuse of children by some in the clergy ought to be explored, not least because they encourage a mindful awareness of the complex, messy situations that occur in real life, and of how we respond to them. Taboo subjects if unaired and unexplored, will continue to have a toxic effect on individuals, groups, communities and even institutions, as has been the case with the child sexual abuse scandals in the Roman Catholic Church.

The readiness to question must not only encompass myths, taboos and uncomfortable topics, but also our own presumptions and our ways of thinking about these issues and "taken for granted" certainties. We need to begin the process of challenging areas where our thinking has become somewhat lazy and confused. This must be part of a life-long strategy to constantly challenge and be open, especially about subjects that we find most uncomfortable.

When one attempts to discuss a particular taboo, a common response is silence. Although group and individual silences can be constructive in some instances, there are silences that are not constructive and can lead to difficulties. These silences can produce negative effects on the group and its members. Techniques for dealing with them run the gamut from raising a diversionary topic to reduce anxiety, to asking group members to share their thoughts about what the silence means. A number of writers mention that silence is most often caused by members being frightened and uncomfortable in the presence of the therapist. Some silences can be exhausting as the energy required to sustain them can be greater than the energy required to participate (Lewis, 1977).

Troubling silences can present difficulties for the group, the leader and for individual members. Sometimes a group silence can be reflective, such as can occur after a meaningful or thoughtful exchange. However, tense and hostile group silence is more troubling and often reflects intense and possibly repressed emotions. This can be of particular concern when a group remains silent even after the trainer has invited them to acknowledge and speak about the silence. According to Brown (2008), possible reasons for group silence include: increased anxiety, the inability of group members to comprehend what is taking place, general hostility or other strong unresolved emotions, and the mention of taboo topics. Difficult conversations will invariably involve a measure of discomfort, but this is not a reason to avoid them. Sometimes discomfort and tension can lead to a new awareness and insight. The difficulty lies in striking a balance between challenging attitudes and behaviours and leaving individuals or a group feeling totally overwhelmed. If individual members within a group simply refuse to speak there is very little that a trainer or other facilitator can do to make them discuss something they do not want to discuss. One strategy is to change the topic in the hope of temporarily relieving the tension. However, this is only a short-term remedy and does nothing to address the underlying problem. When an individual group member, or indeed the group as a whole, feels threatened it is imperative to be mindful of the very delicate balance between fostering insight and causing the taboo to be even further ingrained. While it can be extremely frustrating when a group retreats into silence, no matter how strongly the facilitator feels about a given topic, whatever the taboo, individual group members and whole groups retain the right either not to engage or to disengage at any time during the process. Taboos within the individual, a group or a particular culture are there for a reason and no matter how passionate a facilitator or researcher feels about a given subject, it is imperative to respect the right of people not to be challenged and, if they so choose, to maintain any particular taboo with all it entails.

When addressing any taboo it is important to acknowledge the primary accompanying emotion, which is invariably shame. In itself, shame is neither good nor bad since it is a normal human emotion. In fact, it is necessary to be able to feel shame because sometimes it can be indicative of an action or train of thought that is inappropriate. Shame can sometimes serve to remind us of our boundaries. However, once a taboo is introduced the type of shame experienced is likely to be toxic. Kaufman (1992, p. 60) describes toxic shame:

> Shame is the affect which is the source of many complex and disturbing inner states: depression, alienation, self-doubt, isolating loneliness, paranoid and schizoid phenomena, compulsive disorders, splitting of the self, perfectionism, a deep sense of inferiority, inadequacy or failure, the so-called borderline conditions and disorders of narcissism.

Sexual abuse often triggers a particularly pervasive form of shame. Working as a counsellor with victims of sexual abuse for more than ten years, I witnessed first-hand the type of toxic shame experienced by victims. This shame is compounded in that victims stated that the greatest shame was not the actual sexual abuse but the fact that the sexual abuse was often pleasurable not only on a physiological level but also, perhaps more damagingly, from a psychological and emotional perspective. The attention they received and the feelings that accompanied being treated as "special" were a source of both comfort and pleasure. Even after a considerable amount of therapy, most were plagued with the belief and ensuing guilt that they were actually compliant in the abuse. Only after further in-depth therapy were victims able to appreciate that any pleasure was in fact part of an elaborate grooming process adopted by perpetrators. The 2018 Interim Report of the United Kingdom Independent Inquiry into Child Sexual Abuse (IICSA) provides the latest and perhaps the broadest and most comprehensive confirmation of this process.

Toxic shame seems to be an integral part of the shame that accompanies sexual abuse, especially so when confronting the taboo of child sexual abuse in society. Fortunately society, certainly within the Western world, has begun to acknowledge and to explore this particular taboo and its devastating effect on all members of society. Difficult conversations about this subject are therefore becoming much more common, and in certain circumstances under the UK Children Acts of 1989 and 2004 they are even mandatory.

Difficult conversations: one-to-one

In my doctoral research (O'Sullivan, 2018), I experienced instances of the six priests I interviewed struggling to overcome the obstacles thrown up by a difficult conversation about an extremely difficult taboo. However, the priests saw value in being able to talk about their issues, reinforcing the importance of creating opportunities to engage in difficult conversations.

Priests, unlike other professionals, are not required to undertake continuing professional development, regular professional supervision or any performance assessment. Spiritual directors and regular attendance at the Sacrament of Reconciliation (confession) are at the discretion of each priest. In my experience, many therefore live and work alone, often with little effective peer support or with only superficial peer relationships which can neither affirm nor challenge their ministerial practice or their way of living. Isolation can be profoundly detrimental to a person.

My experience with my six interviewees has led to my concluding that Mearns, Thorne and McLeod's (2013) five questions on "stuckness" in therapy, outlined above, are integral when seeking to define what gives people the confidence to have difficult conversations. Feelings on the part of the six priests of shame, isolation, humiliation and betrayal persist and need to be addressed by the Church and by them as individual priests. There was much evidence in my findings of the necessity to pause in order for the priests to process what had happened as they reported continuing shock, a loss of their core identities as priests, disillusionment and a loss of their reference point.

There were signs of another source of "stuckness", the realisation that there was no going back and they were heading toward considerable unalterable life changes. The interviewees reported feeling overwhelmed by the process. While there was no resistance to the changes in child protection and their role and position in the Church, they repeatedly expressed a realisation that they were having trouble adapting and the Church was not providing help.

Willingness to question must include not just taboos but also presumptions and ways of thinking about these issues and "taken for granted" certainties. It is necessary to begin challenging areas where thinking has become somewhat lazy and confused. This must be part of a life-long strategy to constantly challenge and be open, especially about uncomfortable subjects. The responses of the six priests indicate this may be a problem among priests in general and one that the Church is not recognising or addressing.

Structures to respond to the taboo

Since sexual abuse in the United Kingdom continues to be alarmingly prevalent in both secular and spiritual communities, there has been a concerted effort by governments across the United Kingdom to link legislation pertaining to sexual abuse with the work done by non-government organisations, including faith communities.

Individual agencies have developed intricate and robust safeguarding policies for children, and are cooperating in a concerted effort to weave these policies into an integrated multi-agency response such as that developed by the Manchester Safeguarding Children Board. The Board explicitly cites the need for people to be confident, not only in their ability, but in other people's roles and responsibilities, sharing information across agencies (MSBC, 2007).

Local Education Authorities have been at the forefront of developing child protection policies and responding effectively to disclosures. Failure to comply with the exacting standards of safeguarding can result in schools being put into special measures. Whilethis puts both staff and governing body under a degree of stress, it emphasises the fact that Local Education Authorities regard safeguarding of children as a non-negotiable requirement under law.

Faith communities have either had to introduce or renegotiate safeguarding policies for children. The Church of England is an example of a faith community's aspirations to revisit policies and procedures in this arena. It cites the need for careful selection and training of both ordained and lay ministers, and the importance of safe recruiting (Church of England, House of Bishops, 2004). This inevitably entails difficult conversations about taboos. In a similar way to other faith communities with which it works through the Churches' Child Protection Advisory Service, its policy explicitly states the need for full cooperation with statutory agencies during an investigation of any harm to a child. Somewhat controversially, both the Church of England and the Roman Catholic Church in England and Wales also have a policy to care for and supervise any member of the Church, whether ordained or lay, known to have offended against a child. These developments also involve difficult conversations.

For too long, people, again especially the clergy, have made a fundamental error in refusing to engage with children because they mistakenly believed that child protection policies did not allow it, and they reported a fear of being in breach of these policies. The error lies in the sad reality that they are confusing child protection with self-preservation. They refuse to engage with children, and refuse to acknowledge and understand the vast sea change that has taken place within our communities with regard to the taboo that is child abuse. This is more than likely one of the results of the refusal or inability to undertake a difficult conversation about a taboo.

The Catholic Church in England and Wales has been credited with being among organisations with the highest standards of child protection policies and procedures in the country (Sullivan, 2009). The Church has taken considerable strides toward the goal of confronting this difficult subject. It introduced new national safeguarding structures from 2008 as a result of two special commissions led by Lord Nolan and Baroness Cumberlege, respectively.

Given that there is now a national, co-ordinated response embedded in legislation, it is necessary to explore the practical implications for, in my case, how faith communities within the Roman Catholic tradition are willing and able to engage in difficult conversations about the taboo of sexual abuse and its effects on individuals, groups and whole congregations. They have been urged to do so by the Vatican, most recently in the "Letter of His Holiness Pope Francis to the People of God" on 20 August 2018. Sadly, this issue is not going away, as is shown in the IICSA (2017) research report on abuse in the Catholic and Anglican Churches. Elsewhere, in 2018, a Pennsylvania grand jury found historic abuse by more than 300 clergy, an Australian archbishop resigned after being convicted of concealing child sex abuse, a former Vatican diplomat was sentenced to five years in prison for child pornography offences, and 34 Roman Catholic bishops in Chile offered to resign over a child sex scandal and cover-up. Clearly, many more difficult conversations are urgently needed throughout the Roman Catholic Church.

Conclusion

Trying to instil the confidence to have difficult conversations does lead to a quandary. It is difficult to identify clearly how difficult conversations and training about taboo subjects can be successfully achieved if a conversation or a training module is mandatory. Can change, other than superficial change, ever take place in the absence of a substantial therapeutic alliance and adherence to the Rogerian core conditions?

However, while having the confidence to have difficult conversations is, by definition, challenging, it is not impossible. Robust and detailed training modules following Rogerian core principles to address the difficult taboo of sexual abuse, such as those developed for Catholic parishes in the north of England, can help to build the confidence and skills required to have conversations that both parties for different reasons might find difficult. Such training modules, with supporting resource material, are an initial attempt to facilitate discussion about a thorny issue, but an issue about which conversations must be had. While conversations about this taboo are, and perhaps always will be, particularly difficult, they are imperative to safeguard the welfare of children so individuals, groups and institutions do not stay stuck in old patterns of self-denial.

But courses and resource material are only part of a response to enable the taboo of child sexual abuse to be an integral part of the dialogue within the Catholic and other faith communities. The ability to effectively conduct difficult discussions underpins all these measures. Difficult conversations will always be seriously impaired and might, in fact, prove counter-productive if participants' self-worth and intrinsic dignity are not integral to the process. Considerable effort is therefore required at the preparatory stages of a difficult conversation or training, including considering whether it should be mandatory, in order that those involved acknowledge, engage in and have the confidence to begin a difficult conversation about the taboo of child sexual abuse.

The Vatican could – and many have argued should – play a strong leadership role in raising consciousness around the world about the evil of child sexual abuse and supporting rigorous steps in prevention and treatment. It could be a potent force in assisting the Church throughout the world to face the reality of sexual abuse, sometimes by its own clergy, with honesty and openness by encouraging and facilitating difficult conversations to shed light on this particular taboo.

Useful sources

United Kingdom policies

Department for Children, Schools and Families (2003). *Every Child Matters*. Norwich: HMSO Cmd 5860.

Department for Education (2018). *Working Together to Safeguard Children*. London: HMG. Available at: https://assets.publishing.service.gov.uk/government/uploads/system/uploads/attachment_data/file/722305/Working_Together_to_Safeguard_Children_-_Guide.pdf.

Books, articles and other documents

Church of England, Manchester Diocese (2009). *Handbook of Policies and Procedures*. Manchester: Church of England. Available at: www.manchester.anglican.org/upload/userfiles/file/pdf/Children/Safeguarding%20Children%202009.pdf.

Cumberlege Commision. (2007). *Safeguarding with Confidence: Keeping Children and Vulnerable Adults Safe in the Catholic Church*. London: Incorporated Catholic Truth Society.

Independent Inquiry into Child Sexual Abuse (IICSA) (2018). *Interim Report*. London: IICSA. Available at: www.iicsa.org.uk/reports.

IICSA (2017). *Child Sexual Abuse Within the Catholic and Anglican Churches: A Rapid Evidence Assessment*. London: IICSA. Available at: www.iicsa.org.uk/key-documents/3361/view/iicsa-rea-child-sexual-abuse-anglican-catholic-churches-nov-2017.pdf.

Kvale, S. (1999). "The psychological interview as qualitative research". *Qualitative Inquiry*, 5:1, pp. 87–113.

Nolan Committee. (2001). *The Final Report*. Available at: www.cathcom.org/mysharedaccounts/cumberlege/finalnolan4.htm.

Peter, T. (2009). "Exploring taboos comparing male- and female-perpetrated child sexual abuse". *Journal of Interpersonal Violence*, 24:7, pp. 1111–1128. Available at: http://jiv.sagepub.com.

Pope, K.S., Sonne, J.L, and Greene, B. (2006). *Questioning Myths, Taboos, Secrets and Uncomfortable Topics, What Therapists Don't Talk About and Why: Understanding Taboos that Hurt Us and Our Clients*. Washington, DC: American Psychological Association.

Rogers, C.R. (1980). *A Way of Being*. Boston, MA: Houghton Mifflin.

Rossetti, S.J. (1990). *Slayer of the Soul: Child Sexual Abuse and the Catholic Church*. New London, CT: Twenty-third Publications.

Rossetti, S.J. (1996). *A Tragic Grace: The Catholic Church and Child Sexual Abuse*. Collegeville, MN: The Liturgical Press.

Shulman, L. (2002). "Learning to talk about taboo subjects: A lifelong professional challenge". *Social Work with Groups*, 25:1–2, pp. 139–150.

References

British Association for Counselling and Psychotherapy (2018). *Ethical Framework for the Counselling Professions*. Available at: www.bacp.co.uk/events-and-resources/ethics-and-standards/ethical-framework-for-the-counselling-professions/.

Brown, N. (2008). "Troubling silences in therapy groups". *Journal of Contemporary Psychotherapy*, 38:2, pp. 81–85.

Church of England, House of Bishops (2004). *Protecting All God's Children*. London: Church House Publishing.

Kaufman, G. (1992). *Shame: The Power of Caring*. Cambridge, MA: Schenkman Books.

Lewis, B.F. (1977). "Group silences". *Small Group Research*, 8:1, pp. 109–120.

Manchester Safeguarding Children Board (2007). *Safeguarding Children Procedures*. Manchester: MSCB.

McLeod, J. (2001). *Qualitative Research in Counselling and Psychotherapy*. 1st edn. London: Sage Publications.

Mearns, D., Thorne, B. and McLeod, J. (2013). *Person-Centred Counselling in Action*. 4th edn. London: Sage Publications.

O'Sullivan, B. (2018). *The Burden of Betrayal: Non-offending Priests and the Clergy Child Sexual Abuse Scandals*. Leominster: Gracewing.

Rogers, C.R. (1940). "The process of therapy". *Journal of Consulting & Clinical Psychology*, 4:5, pp. 161–164.

Rogers, C.R. (1952). *Client-Centred Counselling*. Boston, MA: Houghton Mifflin.

Rogers, C.R. (1959). *Counselling and Psychotherapy: Newer Concepts in Practice*. Boston, MA: Houghton Mifflin.

Rorty, R. (1979). *Philosophy and the Mirror of Nature*. Princeton, NJ: Princeton University Press.

Shotter, J. (1993). *Conversational Realities*. Thousand Oaks, CA: Sage Publications.

Sullivan, J. (2009). "Child Exploitation Online Protection". CEOP Conference Papers, March 2009.

Thorne, B. (1992). *Carl Rogers*. London: Sage Publications.

7

CULTURE AS A RESOURCE IN THE CREATION OF MEANING

Part One

George MacDonald

Introduction

This chapter and the next seek to develop a metacultural approach to the understanding of subjectivity. They turn back upon itself the normal view of culture as a passive and often negative influence, to view individuals through the lens of their cultural life. This supplements rather than replaces traditional approaches, since an understanding of the common usages of cultural categories is the foundation on which a metaculture understanding is built. Some readers may be offended by my failure to refer more extensively to specific dimensions such as gender, race and religion. This is deliberate and is not an indication of culture blindness.

I believe that, in our postmodern, postcolonial world, individuals are increasingly freed but frequently compelled to use culture as an expression of individuality, and a way of relating. It is not a free for all, or a Utopian fairy-tale. There are personal challenges, and a high price is often paid by those that ignore dominant aspects of cultural imperatives or seek to appropriate the culture of others. The approach can be used in therapy to simply wonder why a client or patient has made choices; and it provides a way of thinking about social phenomena such as fundamentalism, radicalisation and betrayal. The chapter is based on my doctoral thesis (MacDonald, 2015), which was conducted in the context of my role as a counsellor and psychotherapist. However, it also extends into the world of everyday life. In the context of therapy it is not a new approach, but a potential addition to existing modalities that fits well with psychodynamic, humanistic and cognitive-behavioural approaches. I begin by considering the ideas of culture and metaculture. Then I sketch out a psychoanalytic and group analytic theory of culture and describe three foundational ideas that underlie the approach. After this, in the next chapter, I give an overview of the findings of my research and move on to look at case examples from 'real life' and clinical practice that illustrate the ideas in action. Finally, I reflect on these and draw conclusions about the utility and application of the approach.

What is culture?

Culture is beset by definitional difficulties (Kroeber & Kluckhohn, 1963; Williams, 1983) and I have found that a fixed definition is neither possible nor helpful. Mulhearn (2000: xiv) regards it as a topic. For him this is 'an established object of discussion with established terms of treatment'. A topic is therefore always already a convention, with a defined relationship between those who participate in it. Mulhearn suggests that successful topics, such as culture, can achieve the status of commonplaces, which in the words of Bourdieu (1993: 168) are 'those places in discourse in which an entire group meets and recognizes itself'. This resonates with the psychoanalytic account of nationality provided by Žižek (1993: 201), who argues that 'the element that holds a community together cannot be reduced to the point of symbolic identification', and that the bond between members involves a shared relationship toward a 'thing'. This 'thing' cannot be defined except in contradictory terms and can only be understood by 'us'. Mulhearn's approach frees us from the need to impose cultural categories, which is otherwise incompatible with a phenomenological epistemology, and can be seen as cultural imperialism (Tomlinson, 1991) or racialisation (Dalal, 2002). Culture is always associated with a group of people, a sense of belonging and a basis for relating. At a macro level it surrounds us, and is present before our birth (Le Roy, 2000); while at a micro level it is personal (Dalal, 2006; Moodley & Palmer, 2006), and influenced by the many groups to which we belong. In addition to the accident of birth there are contributions from biology, environment, life events, and the progress of the human lifecycle. The main dimensions include: 'race', gender, class, sexual orientation, (dis)ability, religion, age, socioeconomic group and language (Ivey, Ivey, & Simek-Morgan, 1980; Moodley, 2007). Further contributions arise from environmental factors, such as: rural versus urban, totalitarian versus democratic, or competitive versus uncompetitive; participation in discretionary activities such as sports or politics; membership of groups; or identification with ideas or forms of artistic expression. Under normal circumstances, it is unconscious and individuals become aware of their culture only when they find themselves in a strange context (Le Roy, 2000). It is impossible to capture the almost infinite and shifting hierarchical distinctions, and factors such as: intersectionality (Burman, 2004), contextuality (Ewing, 1990), or the way in which dimensions come to stand in for each other (McClintock, 1995). It has characteristics of a kaleidoscope, in which the individual pieces move around, forming complex, ever changing patterns that defy classification. While it might be useful to examine and describe individual pieces, the overall pattern is more than the sum of its parts. It requires interpretation by the observer, and attempts to focus on one piece serve to defocus the others (Lewis, 2000).

In psychoanalytic terms, modern culture is over-determined (Hall, 1996). This contains within it the ideas that a formation can result from multiple causes, that a cause can give rise to multiple formations, and that the process goes on at multiple levels of interpretation (Laplanche & Pontalis, 1973). In social constructionist terms (Burr, 2015) it corresponds to the idea that each individual has access to a multiplicity of competing discourses between which they can choose, and within which they can accept or resist being interpolated or called into place as subjects (Althusser, 2001 [1970]).

My rejection of a fixed definition of culture raises difficulties. However, it is a necessary step in attempting to enter the world of an individual – accepting that the picture produced is an inevitable co-construction between observer and observed. It seems to me that these co-constructions have equal, if not greater, value than an analysis expressed in terms of specific pre-determined dimensions; that can lead to unhelpful stereotyping, reluctance to challenge and paralysing political correctness (Dalal, 2012).

What is metaculture?

One useful concept is that of metaculture. Like culture, this has many definitions, most of which stress aspects of universality, commonality and generality across cultures. The word does not appear in more traditional dictionaries. Wiktionary defines it as 'all the universal concepts that are present in all cultures', while other definitions see it as more of a process of building a taxonomy. Tiryakian (1996: 102) understands it as 'a set of beliefs, generated in the distant past and renewed by succeeding generations of actors'. For him, this process constitutes an operating system of civilisation, which is supported by Urban (2001) who uses it to explain the process by which culture is propagated across the world.

The idea of metaculture supports the search for the universal, and those things that are common to some or all of mankind. Mulhearn (2000) uses the word interchangeably with metacultural discourse, and for him it means discourse in which culture addresses its own generality and conditions of existence. I will be using it to refer to a deeper level of understanding of the origins and use of culture. While I do not wish to argue that there are universal constants, metaculture encapsulates a search for understanding and meaning that attempts to make sense of culture at a different or higher level.

Psychoanalytic and group analytic theory of culture

Within the scope of this chapter it is not possible to give a comprehensive account of theories of culture. I will, therefore, sidestep certain theoretical and philosophical difficulties to focus on some basic ideas from psychoanalysis and group analysis that should also make sense to less psychoanalytically oriented readers.

Freud (1913) built his theory of culture on the drives, the Oedipus complex (1905), the incest taboo and the rule of exogamy. It is a universalist definition that

I have not found to be especially helpful. Instead, I start with Winnicott, an early member of the British Independent School (Kohon, 1986; Stewart, 2003). He saw culture as a transitional phenomenon located in the potential space between the individual and the environment (Winnicott, 2005 [1971]). In simple terms, it was an adult development of the transitional object (Winnicott, 1953), but one that the individual was actively involved in creating. He saw culture as a space in which 'play' could take place, and because the space was neither biologically determined nor common property, it was the root of individuality. He states that:

> The potential space between baby and mother, between child and family, between individual and society or the world depends on experience which leads to trust. It can be looked on as sacred to the individual in that it is here that the individual experiences creative living.
>
> *Winnicott, 2005 [1971], p. 135*

He saw the ability to develop this cultural world as dependent on the safety and security experienced in childhood and defined the primary culture as the early mother–infant relationship. The progress from this early state, through physical transitional objects, to a more abstract cultural world was a natural process of growth and development that continued throughout life.

Transitional phenomena are frequently sources of soothing, and Winnicott saw them as symbols for a part object such as the breast (Winnicott, 2005 [1971]). However, they were not substitutes for good external or internal objects. The infant could only employ early transitional objects 'when the internal object is alive, and real, and good enough' (2005 [1971]: 13). In addition, their role was not always benign, and the relationship could be one of hate as well as love:

> At that point my subject widens out into that of play, and of artistic creativity and appreciation, and of religious feeling, and of dreaming … and also of fetishism, lying and stealing, the origin and loss of affectionate feeling, drug addiction, the talisman of obsessional rituals, etc.
>
> *Winnicott, 2005 [1971], p. 7*

I think Winnicott provides a clear view of what I will later call a personal culture. It is a definition that recognises the importance of personal factors on the one hand, and social influences on the other; and it sees cultural life as a unique, evolving personal creation. He provides a good summary of these ideas: When one speaks of a man, one speaks of him along with the summation of his cultural experiences. The whole forms a unit.

I have used the term cultural experience as an extension of the idea of transitional phenomena and of play without being certain that I can define the word 'culture'. The accent indeed is on experience. In using the word culture, I am thinking of the inherited tradition. I am thinking of something that is the common pool of humanity, into which individuals and groups of people may contribute, and from which we may all draw if we have somewhere to put what we find (Winnicott, 2005 [1971], p. 133).

Culture and growth

Winnicott (2005 [1971], p. 135) states that '[f]or every individual the use of this space is determined by life experiences that take place in the early stages of the individual's existence'. An infant begins this process when it develops the ability to symbolise, which usually happens at six months to a year or later, indicated by the adoption of the first transitional or 'not-me' object. For Winnicott, child development was a movement from dependence toward independence. He wrote that: 'Independence is never absolute. The healthy individual does not become isolated, but becomes related to the environment in such a way that the individual and the environment can be said to be interdependent' (Winnicott, 1965 [1963], p. 84).

This process is initially managed by the attunement and behaviour of the 'good enough mother' (Winnicott, 1965 [1960]). If the mother is absent for an extended period, the baby can be traumatised, and permanent damage done; while shorter absences create anxiety that must be managed (also illuminated by Freud (2001 [1920]) in *Beyond the Pleasure Principle*). Here, Winnicott develops the idea of the repetition compulsion, which is now viewed as a neurotic defence (Wolf, Gerlach, & Merkle, 2014). He illustrates the process with the example of a game played by an 18-month-old child, thought to be his grandson, Ernst. In this, the child plays with a cotton reel on the end of a string. The child repeatedly throws the reel away uttering a word that is assumed to be '*fort*' in German or 'gone' in English. Then he reels it back, hailing its reappearance with a joyful '*da*' or 'there'.

> The interpretation of the game then became obvious. It was related to the child's cultural achievement – the instinctual renunciation (that is the renunciation of instinctual satisfaction) which he had made in allowing his mother to go away without protesting. He compensated himself for this, as it were, by himself staging the disappearance and return of the objects within his reach.
>
> *Freud, 2001 [1920], p. 5*

To some extent the objective of the game was the pleasure of the joyful reunion; but the departure was also included. Freud speculated that the boy was attempting to move from a passive to an active state, in which he had mastery of the situation. He described the same boy a year later angrily throwing toys away, while exclaiming (in German) 'go to the front'. This was at a time when his absent father was away fighting, leaving the child in sole possession of his mother (2001 [1920], p. 16). The '*fort da*' game is a repetitive ritual involving a transitional object, and it is plausible to speculate that increasingly sophisticated versions of this 'non-climactic game' will continue into adulthood, in the transitional space of culture.

Another aspect of the process of growth is described by Bowlby (1988, 1997). This concerns a toddler, who at the age of one or two years leaves its mother's side for longer and more adventurous periods of exploration but needs periodically to return. As the child grows, it becomes increasingly able to internalise the mother, so that longer periods of absence can be tolerated. It seems to me that this pattern of exploration and return to safety continues into adulthood in the cultural world.

Group analysis

The psychoanalytic theory of culture can be enriched by a contribution from Foulksian Group Analysis (Barnes, Ernst, & Hyde, 1999; Behr & Hearst, 2005; Foulkes, 1975; Foulkes & Anthony, 1965). As well as mainstream psychoanalysis, its founder Foulkes was influenced by a variety of writers including Elias (1991, 2000) and other members of the Frankfurt School. He, and subsequent group analysts, have made valuable contributions to the topic of culture. Group analysis contains many concepts that are relevant to culture, including the social unconscious (Dalal, 2001; Hopper, 2003), the foundation matrix (Foulkes, 1966) and the primordial level (Foulkes, 1964). However, I think the most important contribution is the recognition of the group-as-a-whole (Foulkes, 1964), which contains within it the idea that every group has a culture (Foulkes, 1990 [1975]), and that individuals are influenced by all groups to which they belong (Le Roy, 2000; Roberts, 1982).

Le Roy (2000) provides a view of culture, rooted in the work of the French psychoanalysts René Kaës (1979, 1987a, 1987b) and Jean Claude Rouchy (1982, 1983, 1987, 1995). He argues that the psychic functions of culture are to contain the undifferentiated and syncretic aspects of the individual psyche and to promote structuralisation through its introduction into a series of symbolic orders. Culture is used proactively to avoid the psychotic anxieties resulting from failed introjections and is frequently used as a defence. To put it another way, primary and secondary belonging groups such as family, village, ethnic group or country can act as repositories for the psychotic parts of the self, and loss of this containment is perceived as traumatic. The individual will seek replacements for these in the form of membership of other groups. Dalal (2006) builds on this to provide a pragmatic view of culture that is personal and contextual, and in which an individual simultaneously inhabits multiple, contesting and overlapping cultural frames. He balances this with ideas from Elias (1991; 2000) that portray culture as the institutionalisation of systems of oppression.

In summary, culture as a transitional phenomenon, the repetition compulsion and a model of growth provide a somewhat simplistic but useful starting point for a theory of culture that is enhanced by the group analytic concept of the group-as-a-whole.

Three foundational ideas

Three foundational ideas are employed in this chapter and the next: *cultural identity*; *culture as a resource*; and *personal culture*. It seems to me that these help us to hold in mind both the personal and the social.

Cultural identity

The concept of cultural identity is central, and it is widely discussed in philosophy, psychology and psychoanalysis. The philosopher Taylor (1989: 3) regards identity as the 'notion of what it is to be a human agent, a person, or a self'. Argyle (1969: 370) gives a traditional view of the development of a unified identity in adolescence, when prompted by the 'growth spurt and development of sexual maturity' a young person makes important decisions about matters such as vocation, politics and religion and strives for what Lecky (1945) called self-consistency. Erikson (1963) believed that humans go through a genetically determined sequence of psychosocial stages and that each stage involves a struggle between two conflicting personality outcomes, one that is positive or adaptive and the other negative or maladaptive. He proposed that there was an identity crisis in late adolescence and that the developmental task of that stage was to establish the ego-identity.

These views suggest that identity is determined at the completion of adolescence, and that it is relatively fixed and stable. This is questioned by Goffman's (1971) dramaturgical approach and by social constructionism (Burr, 2015). More transient alternatives are also enabled by psychoanalytic processes such as identification and projection. The problems of theorising the link between social and personal and the irreconcilable differences between the perspectives of social constructionism, phenomenology and psychoanalysis are widely acknowledged (Burkitt, 1991; du Gay, Evans, & Redman, 2000; Stevens, 1996). However, I believe that it is necessary to engage with these issues to address the significance of cultural identity even if, as du Gay et al. (2000: 3) point out, there are good reasons why a 'rapprochement' is problematic.

My favoured approach was suggested by the sociologist Hall (1996), who argued that the interpellation of individuals as subjects (Althusser, 2001 [1970]; Edley, 2001; Harré & van Langenhove, 1999) was a psychic mechanism. He related identity to identification: a concept that 'is drawing meaning from both the discursive and the psychoanalytic repertoire, without being limited to either' (Hall, 1996: 2). The definition of identity that he offered was:

> [T]he meeting point, the point of suture, between on the one hand the discourses and practices which attempt to 'interpolate', speak to us or hail us into place as the social subjects of particular discourses, and on the other hand, the processes which produce subjectivities, which construct us as subjects which can be 'spoken'. Identities are thus points of temporary attachment to the subject positions which discursive practices construct for us.
>
> *Hall, 1996, p. 2*

The concept of suture was first suggested by Miller (1978), a follower of Lacan, and is 'that moment in which the subject inserts itself into the symbolic register in the guise of a signifier, and in so doing gains meaning at the expense of being' (Silverman, 1983, p. 99). Miller (1978, p. 2) states that 'suture names the relation of the subject to its chain of disclosure … it figures there as the element which is lacking, in the form of a stand-in'. This approach makes possible a cultural identity that is multiple, inconsistent, contextual and malleable.

It is not an easy concept to grasp and is one with which I have struggled. It seems impossibly vague or unclear, and reluctance to adopt the term probably reflects this. It has been used most extensively in the fields of semiotics and film studies (Silverman, 1996). However, I have found that it begins to make sense when used in a concrete way. It is no more than a type of interpretation that speculates on the link between a preference for a discourse or a subject position within a discourse and events from earlier life or internalised object relations. Interpretation is the substance of psychoanalytically oriented therapy, and here subject positions in a discourse come to participate in psychoanalytic processes as objects, which is an extension of the psychoanalytic understanding of the world, but one that is already employed in fields such as management science (Huffington, Armstrong, Halton, Hoyle, & Pooley, 2004; Obholzer & Roberts, 1994).

Culture as a resource

This idea arose spontaneously out of earlier study (MacDonald, 2007), and from incidental uses of the words that I found (e.g. Burman, 2004). There are many definitions of resource in common usage, and two are representative:

1 A stock or supply of money, materials, staff, and other assets that can be drawn on by a person or organisation in order to function effectively.
2 An action or strategy that may be adopted in adverse circumstances.

(www.oxforddictionaries.com/definition/english/resource)

My usage is closer to the second definition, although I would like to move it toward the first. My best attempt at a definition is 'any external object, phenomenon, practice or discourse that is used to define identity, manage distress or achieve a conscious or unconscious objective'. Cultural resources are real or discursive constructions that originate in the outer world, but are usually made personal through the psychoanalytic process of introjection and the social constructionist process of internalisation (Berger & Luckmann, 1966). Linguistically they are signifiers (Saussure, 1916) that can participate in a chain of signification (Lacan, 2006). Recognisable examples include cultural traumas (Alexander, Eyerman, Giesen, Smelser, & Sztompka, 2004), cultural stereotypes (Jahoda, 1978), and a variety of figures from literature, myth and folklore. Phenomena such as a disease like AIDS (Sontag, 1991) or practices such as female genital mutilation (Gibeau, 1998) can also, in some contexts, be thought of as cultural resources.

In psychoanalysis, the word resource is seldom used in this way; probably because of the focus on the internal world, and because it resides in a 'no man's land' between drives or instincts and object seeking. There are some random examples, and the mechanism can be seen at work in most psychoanalytic processes and defences.

The idea appears more directly in social constructionism and discourse analysis, where terms such as discursive resource (Potter & Wetherell, 1987; Taylor, 2006), interpretive resource (Wetherell, 2001) and, more generally, language as resource (Wetherell, Taylor, & Yates, 2001) are in wide use. This makes sense, because the performative processes involved operate largely through the medium of discourse. It is in terms of agency, intentionality and metaphoric or metronymic significance that the psychoanalytic view comes into effect.

Personal culture

Internet searches yield a bewildering array of usages of the term personal culture. At one extreme it is simply identity, and includes diverse aspects such as personal standards, self-discipline and politics. At the other extreme it is the sum of influences on and choices made by an individual. My usage is somewhat different and lies between these. Cultural identity provides a linkage between social and personal, and its volatility admits a culture that is multiple, fragmented, inconsistent, contextual and changeable. However, the experience of analysing data provides evidence for the existence of a more stable concept that sums up the totality of the discourses, subject positions and cultural resources habitually employed by an individual in the formation and reformation of cultural identities. Certain psychoanalysts, and group analysts such as Dalal (2006) acknowledge the idea, and it can be seen in the work of psychological anthropologists such as Ewing (1990, 1992, 1997) and Stewart (1991, 1996, 2007). It is implied in the social constructionist idea of interpretive repertoires, and is implicit in much psychoanalytic writing, hidden behind ideas like the self (Masterson, 1985).

Putting aside the evidence for its existence, it seems fairly apparent that there is a need for an executive process that operates over time to: reduce gross inconsistency; provide reality testing (Freud, 2001 [1920]); and introduce a moral dimension. In terms of Freud's (1961 [1923]) structural model of the psyche, this would reside within the ego and operate through the secondary process of thinking described by Bion (1962). The cultural identities that can be adopted are, by their very nature, volatile and transient; and psychic processes operate to achieve an illusion of wholeness (Ewing, 1990). However, without some form of executive process, albeit one that is frequently stalled or ineffective, individuals will be trapped in unhelpful, irrational or unacceptable positions. At the level of a group or society, this can lead to extreme or radical views, fundamentalism and inappropriate expressions of opinion.

A deeper discussion of this topic would be a significant undertaking that would plumb psychoanalytic, discursive and philosophical depths. It would touch on Foucault's (1991) regimes of truth and many other topics. For the time being, I simply wish to register the fact that something of the sort is needed, as Stewart puts it, 'to inhibit a slippage between sign and meaning' (Molino, 2004: 150) and make social life possible.

Conclusion

In this chapter I have explored various understandings of culture as applicable to the theory and practice of psychotherapy and counselling and how it can be used. In the next chapter I will draw on my recent doctoral research (MacDonald, 2015) and some case examples to examine the ways in which people are able to draw on culture as a positive resource.

References

Alexander, J. C., Eyerman, R., Giesen, B., Smelser, N. J., & Sztompka, P. (2004) *Cultural trauma and collective identity*. London: University of California Press.

Althusser, L. (2001 [1970]) Ideology and ideological state apparatuses: Notes towards and investigation. In L. Althusser (Ed.) *Lenin and philosophy and other essays* (pp. 85–132). New York: Monthly Review Press.

Argyle, M. (1969) *Social interaction*. London: Tavistock.

Barnes, B., Ernst, S., & Hyde, K. (1999) *An introduction to groupwork*. Basingstoke: Palgrave Macmillan.

Behr, H., & Hearst, L. (2005) *Group-analytic psychotherapy: A meeting of minds*. London: Whurr.

Berger, P. L., & Luckmann, T. (1966) *The social construction of reality: A treatise on the sociology of knowledge*. London: Penguin.

Bion, W. R. (1962) The psycho-analytic study of thinking: A theory in the making. *International Journal of Psycho-analysis*, 43, pp. 306–310.

Bourdieu, P. (1993) Editor's introduction: Pierre Bourdieu on art, literature and culture. In P. Bourdieu (Ed.) *The field of cultural production* (pp. 1–23). Cambridge: Polity Press.

Bowlby, J. (1988) *A secure base*. New York: Basic Books.

Bowlby, J. (1997) *Attachment and loss: Attachment* (Vol. 1). London: Pimlico.

Burkitt, I. (1991) *Social selves: Theories of the social formation of personality*. London: Sage.

Burman, E. (2004) From difference to intersectionality: Challenges and resources. *European Journal of Psychotherapy, Counselling & Health*, 6(4), pp. 293–308.

Burr, V. (2015) *Social constructionism* (3rd ed.) Hove: Routledge.

Dalal, F. (2001) The social unconscious: A post Foulksian perspective. *Group Analysis*, 34(4), pp. 539–555.

Dalal, F. (2002) *Race, colour and the processes of racialization: New perspectives from group analysis, psychoanalysis and sociology*. Hove: Brunner-Routledge.

Dalal, F. (2006) Culturalism in multicultural therapy: Critical perspectives in multicultural practice. In R. Moodley & S. Palmer (Eds) *Race, culture and psychotherapy: Cultural perspectives in multicultural practice* (pp. 36–45). Hove: Routledge.

Dalal, F. (2012) *Thought paralysis: The virtues of discrimination*. London: Karnac.

Du Gay, P., Evans, J., & Redman, P. (Eds) (2000) *Identity: A reader*. London: Sage.

Edley, N. (2001) Analysing masculinity: Interpretive repertoires, ideological dilemmas and sunbect positions. In M. Wetherell, S. Taylor, & S. J. Yates (Eds) *Discourse as data: A guide for analysis* (pp. 189–228). London: Sage.

Elias, N. (1991) *The society of individuals*. London: Continuum.

Elias, N. (2000) *The civilizing process* (revised ed.). Oxford: Blackwell.

Erikson, E. H. (1963) *Childhood and society* (2nd ed.). New York: Norton.

Ewing, K. P. (1990) The illusion of wholeness: Culture, self, and the experience of inconsistency. *Ethos*, 18(3), pp. 251–278. doi: http://dx.doi.org/10.1525/eth.1990.18.3.02a00020

Ewing, K. P. (1992) Is psychoanalysis relevant for anthropology? In T. Schwartz, G. M. White & C. Lutz (Eds) *New directions in psychological anthropology* (pp. 251–268). Cambridge: Cambridge University Press.

Ewing, K. P. (1997) *Arguing sainthood: Modernity, psychoanalysis, and Islam.* Durham, NC: Duke University Press.

Foucault, M. (1991) *Discipline and punish: The birth of the prison.* Harmondsworth: Penguin.

Foulkes, S. H. (1964) *Therapeutic group analysis.* London: George Allen and Unwin.

Foulkes, S. H. (1966) Some basic concepts in group psychotherapy. In J. L. Moreno (Ed.) *The international handbook of group psychotherapy* (pp. 151–158). New York: Philosophical Library. (Reprinted from: E. Foulkes (Ed.) (1990) *Selected papers: Psychoanalysis and group analysis.* London: Karnac).

Foulkes, S. H. (1975) *Group analytic psychotherapy: Methods and principles.* London: Karnac.

Foulkes, S. H. (1990 [1975]) Problems of the large group. In: E. Foulkes (Ed.) *Selected papers of S.H. Foulkes: Psychoanalysis and group analysis* (pp. 249–270). London: Karnac.

Foulkes, S. H., & Anthony, E. J. (1965) *Group psychotherapy: The psycho-analytic approach* (2nd ed.). Harmondsworth: Penguin.

Freud, S. (1905) Three essays on the theory of sexuality (J. Strachey, trans.). In: J. Strachey (Ed.) *The standard edition of the complete psychological works of Sigmund Freud* (Vol. 7, pp. 135–243). London: Vintage.

Freud, S. (1913) Totem and taboo (J. Strachey, trans.). In J. Strachey (Ed.) *The standard edition of the complete psychological works of Sigmund Freud* (Vol. 18, pp. 1–162). London:Vintage.

Freud, S. (1961 [1923]) The ego and the id. In J. Strachey (Ed.) *The standard edition of the complete psychological works of Sigmund Freud* (Vol. XIX (1923–1925), pp. 1–66). London: Vintage Books.

Freud, S. (2001 [1920]) Beyond the pleasure principle (J. Strachey, trans.). In J. Strachey (Ed.) *The standard edition of the complete psychological works of Sigmund Freud: Volume XVIII* (1920–1922). London: Vintage.

Gibeau, A. M. (1998) Female genital mutilation: When a cultural practice generates clinical and ethical dilemmas. *Journal of Obstetric, Gynecologic, & Neonatal Nursing*, 27(1), pp. 85–91. doi: 10.1111/j.1552-6909.1998.tb02595.x

Goffman, E. (1971) *The presentation of self in everyday life.* Harmondsworth: Penguin.

Hall, S. (1996) Introduction: Who needs identity? In: S. Hall & P. du Gąy (Eds) *Questions of cultural identity* (pp. 1–17). London: Sage.

Harré, R., & Van Langenhove, L. (Eds) (1999) *Positioning theory.* Oxford: Blackwell.

Hopper, E. (2003) *The social unconscious: Selected papers.* London: Jessica Kingsley.

Huffington, C., Armstrong, D., Halton, W., Hoyle, L., & Pooley, J. (Eds) (2004) *Working below the surface: The emotional life of contemporary organizations.* London: Karnac.

Ivey, A. E., Ivey, M. B., & Simek-Morgan, L. (1980) *Counselling and psychotherapy: A multicultural perspective.* Needham Heights: MA: Allyn and Bacon.

Jahoda, G. (1978) Cross-cultural perspectives. In H. Tajfel & C. Fraser (Eds) *Introducing social psychology: An analysis of individual reaction and response* (pp. 68–82). London: Penguin.

Kaës, R. (1979) Introduction à l'analyse transitionelle. In R. Kaës (Ed.) *Crise, rupture et dépassement* (pp. 1–83). Paris: Dunod.

Kaës, R. (1987a) La troisième différence. *Revue de Psychothérapie Psychoanalytique de Groupe*, 9(10), pp. 5–30.

Kaës, R. (1987b) Realité psychique et souffrances dans les institutions. In R. Kaës (Ed.) *L'institution et les institutions* (pp. 53–67). Paris: Dunod.

Kohon, G. (Ed.) (1986) *The British school of psychoanalysis: The independent tradition.* London: Free Association Books.

Kroeber, A. L., & Kluckhohn, C. (1963) *Culture, a critical review of concepts and definitions.* New York: Vintage Books.

Lacan, J. (2006) *Écrits: The first complete edition in English.* New York: Norton.

Laplanche, J., & Pontalis, J.-B. (1973) *The language of psychoanalysis.* London: Hogarth Press.

Le Roy, J. (2000) Group analysis and culture. In: D. Brown & L. Zinkin (Eds.) *The psyche and the social world: Developments in group-analytic theory* (pp. 180–201). London: Jessica Kingsley.

Lecky, P. (1945) *Self-consistency: A theory of personality.* New York: Island Press.

Lewis, G. (2000) *'Race', gender, social welfare: Encounters in a postcolonial society.* Cambridge: Polity Press.

MacDonald, G. (2007) The nature and significance of Scottish ethnic identity (MSc Psychology and Counselling Dissertation), Manchester Metropolitan University, Manchester.

MacDonald, G. (2015) *Culture as a positive resource in therapy.* Unpublished thesis, Doctor in Counselling, The University of Manchester, Manchester.

Masterson, J. F. (1985) *The real self: A developmental, self, and object relations approach.* New York: Brunner/Mazel.

McClintock, A. (1995) *Imperial leather: Race, gender and sexuality in the colonial contest.* London: Routledge.

Miller, J.-A. (1978) Suture: Elements of the logic of the signifier. *Screen*, 18(4), pp. 24–34.

Molino, A. (2004) Kathleen Stewart. In: A. Molino (Ed.) *Culture, subject, psyche: Dialogues in psychoanalysis and anthropology* (pp. 137–155). London: Whurr.

Moodley, R. (2007). (Re)placing multiculturalism in counselling and psychotherapy. *British Journal of Guidance & Counselling*, 35(1), pp. 1–22.

Moodley, R., & Palmer, S. (Eds) (2006) *Race, culture and psychotherapy: Critical perspectives in multicultural practice.* Hove: Routledge.

Mulhearn, F. (2000) *Culture/metaculture.* Abingdon: Routledge.

Obholzer, A., & Roberts, V. Z. (Eds.) (1994) *The unconscious at work.* London: Routledge.

Potter, J., & Wetherell, M. (1987) *Discourse and social psychology: Beyond attitudes and behaviour.* London: Sage.

Roberts, J. P. (1982) Foulkes' concept of the matrix. *Group Analysis*, 15(2), pp. 111–126. doi: 10.1177/053331648201500203

Rouchy, J. C. (1982) Archaic processes and transference in group analysis. *Group Analysis*, 15(3), pp. 235–260.

Rouchy, J. C. (1983) L'eboration des objects incorporés en groupe analyse. *Bulletin de Psychologie*, 363, pp. 71–77.

Rouchy, J. C. (1987) Identité culturelle et groupes d'appartenance. *Revue de Psychothérapie Psychoanalytique de Groupe*, 9, pp. 31–41.

Rouchy, J. C. (1995) Identifications and groups of belonging. *Group Analysis*, 28(2), pp. 129–141.

Saussure, F. D. (1916) Course in general linguistics (W. Bashkin, trans.). In: C. Bally & A. Sechehaye (Eds.) *Course in General Linguistics* (pp. 27–42). Glasgow: Collins Fontana.

Silverman, K. (1983) *The subject of semiotics.* Oxford: Oxford University Press.

Silverman, K. (1996) *The threshold of the visible world.* London: Routledge.

Sontag, S. (1991) *Illness and metaphor & Aids and its metaphors.* London: Penguin.

Stevens, R. (Ed.) (1996) *Understanding the self.* London: Sage.

Stewart, H. (2003) Winnicott, Balint, and the independent tradition. *The American Journal of Psychoanalysis*, 63(3), pp. 207–217.

Stewart, K. (1991) On the politics of cultural theory: A case for 'contaminated' cultural critique. *Social Research*, 58(2), pp. 395–412.

Stewart, K. (1996) *A space on the side of the road: Cultural poetics in an 'other' America*. Princeton, NJ: Princeton University Press.

Stewart, K. (2007) *Ordinary affects*. Durham, NC: Duke University Press.

Taylor, C. (1989) *Sources of the self: The making of modern identity*. Cambridge: Cambridge University Press.

Taylor, S. (2006) Narrative as construction and discursive resource. *Narrative Inquiry*, 16(1), pp. 94–102.

Tiryakian, E. A. (1996) *Three metacultures of modernity: Christian, gnostic, chthonic. Theory, Culture & Society*, 13(1), pp. 99–118. doi: 10.1177/026327696013001005

Tomlinson, J. (1991) *Cultural imperialism: A critical introduction*. London: Continuum.

Urban, G. (2001) *Metaculture: How culture moves through the world*. Minneapolis, MN: University of Minnesota Press.

Wetherell, M. (2001) Themes in discourse research: The case of Diana. In: M. Wetherell, S. Taylor, & S. J. Yates (Eds) *Discourse as data: A guide to analysis* (pp. 14–28). London: Sage.

Wetherell, M., Taylor, S., & Yates, S. J. (2001) Introduction. In M. Wetherell, S. Taylor, & S. J. Yates (Eds) *Discourse as data: A guide to analysis* (pp. 29–48). London: Sage.

Williams, R. (1983) *Keywords: A vocabulary of culture and society* (revised ed.). London: Fontana.

Winnicott, D.W. (1953) Transitional objects and transitional phenomena: A study of the first not-me possession. *The International Journal of Psychoanalysis*, 34, pp. 89–97.

Winnicott, D. W. (1965 [1960]) Ego distortion in terms of true and false self. In: D. W. Winnicott (Ed.) *The maturational process and the facilitating environment* (pp. 140–152). London: Karnac.

Winnicott, D.W. (1965 [1963]) From dependence towards independence in the development of the individual. In: D. W. Winnicott (Ed.) *The maturational process and the facilitating environment* (pp. 83–92). London: Karnac.

Winnicott, D.W. (2005 [1971]) *Playing and reality*. Abingdon: Routledge.

Wolf, M., Gerlach, A., & Merkle, W. (2014) Conflict, trauma, defence mechanisms, and symptom formation. In M. Elzer & A. Gerlach (Eds) *Psychoanalytic psychotherapy: A handbook* (pp. 61–78). London: Karnac.

Žižek, S. (1993) *Tarrying with the negative: Kant, Hegel, and the critique of ideology*. Durham, NC: Duke University Press.

8

CULTURE AS A RESOURCE IN THE CREATION OF MEANING

Part Two

George MacDonald

Overview of research

In this chapter I explore my doctoral research (MacDonald, 2015) into how my participants make use of culture as a positive resource in their lives. In this research I gathered data using semi-structured interviews, and analysed transcripts using a bespoke qualitative methodology. The participants were chosen by purposive sampling to provide useful and relevant data. I avoided recruiting participants who were from traditional stigmatised groups – in terms of race, colour, and religion; although these dimensions were still in evidence. All participants had approached or crossed cultural boundaries, and all were at a sufficiently advanced stage in their lives for patterns to have emerged. The methodology was designed to follow the evolution of a personal culture within the life of an individual and aimed to combine inductive and deductive perspectives. Although I started the study with certain views that I wished to 'road test', I needed flexibility to change or evolve these as the study progressed.

Although the study was situated in the context of therapy, the participants were not current or previous clients, and were not, at the time of the interviews, in any form of therapy. I made this decision for ethical reasons, and because I wished freedom to challenge and explore. This raised questions of validity, and of the isomorphism between research and therapy that I am now further extending to the relationship with everyday life.

The method of data collection aimed to track the life of the participant from birth to the present day. It attempted to map the cultural life of the participant, in their own terms, albeit interpreted through the perception of the researcher, and the process of co-construction that took place in the interview. The analysis followed a three-stage process, each stage of which generated a narrative. The first stage aimed to establish facts. The second stage aimed to identify the cultural resources available to the participant. The third and final stage made use of thematic analysis, to identify and describe the superordinate metacultural themes that were active in the life of the participant. In the discussion section, I attempted to make sense of each individual case and to find commonality between cases.

Research findings

The main findings were that the first role of the cultural world is to provide a place of belonging that an individual has either experienced or is seeking. Beyond this, the cultural world provides a field for growth in which the individual, when they feel secure enough, can search and explore in the manner described by Winnicott and Bowlby. Here, the analogy with Bowlby's model of growth is close. The repetition compulsion is apparent in the expression of cultural life – as a re-enactment of trauma, an attempt to redeem earlier wrongs, or an enjoyable celebration of cultural achievement. The pathway chosen is personal and is strongly influenced by early life experiences.

Belongingness

Personal culture seems to be a symbolic place of safety that can also correspond to a physical or social one. It is reasonable to suspect that this is an evolutionarily adaptive instinct that enhanced the chance of survival in primitive environments. All participants had this from their childhood or sought to create it in later life as a place of safety from physical or psychological threat, where they could seek the companionship of like-minded people. The expression of belongingness could be related to attachment styles and internal working models.

I did not find that a stable, mature sense of cultural belonging could be equated to happiness or contentment. However, I found evidence that it could be a source of strength and resilience (Aldwin, 2007; Aldwin & Gilmer, 2013; Aldwin, Park, & Spiro, 2007; Lazarus, 1985, 1999). My participants all had somewhere to belong – even if it was split, insubstantial or a partial fantasy. There was what Belsey (2002, p. 64) calls 'the longing to belong'. The findings support the idea that culture is a repository for the psychotic anxieties described by Le Roy (2000). One example of this is found in Anderson's (2006) postmodern understanding of nations as 'imagined communities', shaped by history, politics and global migration in the postcolonial era. This can apply to both residents and ex-patriots, whether the nation is a real entity, a personal fantasy or a virtual transnational diaspora (Werbner, 2002).

The malleability of the process is illustrated by the example of Muslim identity in the post 9/11 world (Ewing, 2008). Research has shown that Asian Muslims in Britain, who would previously have declared their nationality in terms of a single or hyphenated country, such as Pakistani-Scottish (Modood, Beishon, & Virdee, 1994), now increasingly declare themselves to be Muslim (Hopkins, 2007; Werbner, 2002). This resonates with the attitude of Freud to his Jewish identity. In 1926, he told an interviewer: 'My language is German. My culture, my attainments are

German. I considered myself German intellectually, until I noticed the growth of anti-Semitic prejudice in Germany and German Austria. Since that time, I prefer to call myself a Jew' (Gay, 1988, p. 448).

Growth

The idea of belongingness seems warm and comfortable, but as Winnicott (2005 [1971], p. 14) points out 'incomplete adaption to need makes objects real, that is to say hated as well as loved'. It seems reasonable that the symbolic place of cultural belonging will be associated with negative as well as positive feelings that will trigger a wish to escape, which may be enacted or acted out in life. Even if there is optimal attunement (Winnicott, 1960), and the feeling toward the place of cultural belonging is broadly positive, the process of growth and separation will still operate, and there will be a normal healthy desire to move outside or beyond. Freud (1917 [1915]) suggested that non-human objects stand in for human objects. I would extend this to cultural resources, and, as previously noted, different attachment styles may apply to these and may be incorporated into working models (Holmes, 2001) as part of a personal culture.

My participants demonstrated a variety of attachment styles in relation to their place of cultural belonging, ranging from secure attachment through anxious insecure attachment to avoidant insecure attachment. Two felt a sense of safety in their home culture but did not feel sustained by it. Both came to see foreign places as objects of desire and made repetitive trips to increasingly remote places. Another felt completely comfortable in her cultural identity but preferred to live abroad, in places that were on or near cultural fault lines. Yet another had mixed cultural roots and could feel at home in none of them. This resulted in the need to find or create new cultural places based on cosmopolitanism and spirituality.

Overall, the word growth has a positive connotation, and I am not sure that the underlying essence of some of the cultural growth that I found was quite so benign. I do not wish to pathologise my participants, but I think there were elements of acting out and avoidant examples of repetition compulsion. However, this demonstrates the search for solutions, which may be an attempt to resolve trauma or right wrongs from the past. The metaphorical revisiting of these situations has therapeutic potential (Grove & Panzer, 1991), and acting out introduces the possibility of interpretation and insight that can transform the acting out into working through (Sandler, Dare, & Holder, 1992). In addition, people undoubtedly derive pleasure, satisfaction and meaning from cultural activity, such as the observance of religious, national or family rituals, travel, or relationship with the culturally different. These provide aesthetic or practical choices that are as valid as any others, and it seemed to me that the most appropriate response is simply to note and very gently interpret the choices made, rather than to judge them.

Case examples

My thesis was based on research data, and I have also collected clinical data and case examples from the 'real world' that support its findings. In this chapter I am going to share one 'real' example based on a published source and two clinical vignettes. These are intended to support the conclusions of the research and indicate the application to clinical work with clients. I believe that the example from the 'real world' enhances the validity of the underlying hermeneutic process, through the availability of full and free access to the source material.

Real-world case example

The processes that I have described are most clearly visible in situations where people have attempted to swim against the cultural current. This is exemplified by the first case example, which I chose because of its recency, relevance, and access to direct testimony from the protagonist. I have documented other (as yet unpublished) case examples that relate to espionage and radicalisation.

Case example 1 – racial dysphoria: Rachel Doležal

Rachel Doležal was a white American civil rights educator and activist who, 'identified as black'. She modified or managed her appearance (through makeup, hair style and dress), and allowed the impression to be given that she was black. The case came to light in June 2015, when she was interviewed on a local news channel in Spokane, Washington. At a certain point the interviewer asked if she was African American. She equivocated and, when pressed, ended the interview and left the studio. A small segment of the interview found its way onto the internet, and an article appeared in a local paper 'outing' her as white.

Thereafter the story went viral. The case produced a flood of overwhelmingly negative reaction. Black groups accused her of cultural appropriation, and of making choices denied to them; and the white community was equally negative, for less obvious reasons. After the initial storm of negative coverage, more balanced comment began to emerge (e.g. Aikenhead, 2017; Ruiz, 2017). Then, in late 2017, Doležal published an autobiography (Doležal, 2017), which put her personal account into the public domain, and provided the source for the material below.

Doležal was born in 1977 to white parents in Troy, Montana; an exclusively white neighbourhood. Her parents were hard working small farmers who lived in a remote mountain area. They were fundamentalist Christians who did not believe in the need for medical support in childbirth. Doležal was the second of two birth children and, as a result, her mother nearly died giving birth to her. She states that her parents blamed her for this, and constantly reminded her of it.

In her home, discipline was strict and work was hard. Her parents subsequently adopted four black children. Up until she left home for college, Doležal was the main carer for these younger adopted siblings. She was shunned at school because of her homemade clothes and restrictions imposed by her parents. From the earliest age, she identified with the outsider, and most especially the black outsider, whom she read about in books.

At college in Mississippi, Doležal was drawn to the minority black community in preference to the white majority. She suspects that she was initially accepted by the black community out of pity, because of her homemade clothes and lack of makeup. She sought out a black mentor, and through this joined a black church. She developed as an artist, and became interested in ethnic black art. And the story continues in this way; of Doležal slipping into a black identity and adopting some of the more radical attitudes of the group she joined. A few people in her life knew of her true ethnic origins; others did not, or did not care.

Doležal makes the point that, as a civil rights activist, she understands the issues around cultural appropriation, yet she does not believe that this is what she was doing. She had little sense of belonging in either her family or home culture and experienced her parents as punitive and uncaring. For a while she established a loving black sub-family, within a hostile white environment. Then, when she went to college, she was welcomed by the black community and found a series of black mentors and father figures. To put it another way, blackness was a resource that came to represent safety and protection, friendship and love. When she had established a place of safety, she chose to seek growth, and it seems understandable that she did this by activism in the civil rights movement. Ultimately, of course, she should have seen the flaw in her scheme and the inevitability of its collapse. However, as I have previously observed (MacDonald, 2007), in cases of deep cultural identification or dis-identification, there is little role for common sense. The processes operate deep in the unconscious, where reality testing is disabled.

Doležal is clear that she constructed her identity in response to life experiences. It could be argued that, at the point the case became public, she was earning a living through her blackness and was motivated by self-interest to maintain this. However, it was not conscious self-interest that moved her into the position in the first place. The difficult and painful experience of being 'outed' has made no difference to the way she intends to live her life.

Clinical case examples

During the time that I was carrying out the study, I conducted a closed, dynamic therapy group in a healthcare setting. Group members had a variety of mental health issues. Most had suffered abuse in their earlier lives, and all were struggling with complex issues. I am going to use two fictionalised case examples from this group.

Case example 2 – cultural hypersensitivity: Charlotte

Charlotte was a 47-year-old female who presented with a medical diagnosis of depression and a history of superficial and unsatisfactory personal relationships. She claimed that she had never had a deep romantic relationship and that every man in her life had used her for sex, and then rejected her. There was no evidence of physical or sexual abuse in her childhood or that any of her sexual relationships had been non-consensual. However, the recent relationships that she described seemed shallow, idealised and lacking any deeper foundation. There was a long history of mental health issues, the most recent episode of which had started approximately three years before, when her employment as an administrator with a professional services firm had been terminated. Since then she had not been unable to hold down a job. Charlotte had mixed ethnic origins, although both of her parents were born in the UK. Her father was half Afro-Caribbean and half white British, and her mother half Irish and half white British. She was born in north-west England where she had lived for the whole of her life. She was the middle child in a family of three, having a younger sister and an older brother. Her parents were both alive and continued to live together although it was hard to avoid the conclusion that their marriage was neither happy nor harmonious. Latterly, communication between the partners had virtually ceased and was limited to written notes left around the home by one partner for the other to find. Her father unfortunately died in the latter stages of the group, and at this time it came to light that Charlotte had a half-sister living in a nearby town.

Charlotte's skin colouration was darker than either of her two siblings. She felt denigrated and scapegoated in the family and had always been closer to her father than her mother. In her view, the two 'less dark' siblings were closer to their mother. Outside the home, people generally regarded her ethnic roots as Southern European or Middle Eastern. She habitually dressed in a manner that, although not revealing, was individualistic and displayed her body shape.

One of the most obvious factors that emerged in the assessment, and was frequently acted out in the group, was her rage. This showed itself in many ways. I first observed it in relation to the pronunciation of her name. This happened in the first minute of the assessment, when I called her Shar-Lot. She immediately went on the offensive, telling me in no uncertain terms that it was Char-Lot and not Shar-Lot. The correction itself did not surprise me, although the aggressive manner of its delivery did. A second way also emerged in the early part of the assessment. This related to sensitivity about her nationality. She made it clear that she was English and proud of it, and that most of the problems in her life resulted from racial prejudice, triggered by her foreign appearance. Some of her statements sounded xenophobic and she even told a female member of the group, who was clinically obese, that she disliked 'fat people' because they were prejudiced.

A third way relates to what I previously called her 'individualistic' manner of dress and emerged in the group when a male group member complimented her on her appearance. This triggered another wave of tempestuous rage over male chauvinism and the part it had played in her life.

At this point I need to say that behind the hurt and anger, I found Charlotte to be sensitive, intelligent and generous. After a stormy introduction to the group she bonded deeply and participated fully. She went on to befriend, outside the group, the woman to whom she had addressed the comment about 'fat people'. The case supported my belief in the small group as a vehicle to address cultural issues (Hearst, 1993) and, I would like to add, deeper issues that express themselves in cultural terms.

On one occasion Charlotte reported meeting up with an old boyfriend. There was an initial euphoria at the renewal of the relationship, quickly followed by disillusion, disappointment and anger. She experienced the reunion as the repetition of an old pattern that she had once again allowed herself to fall for. It seemed to me that she over invested in relationships at an early stage, idealised them and then experienced inevitable rejection, disappointment and feelings of shame that were frequently disguised as anger. This pattern also emerged with a foreign man that she met fleetingly on a short holiday to Italy in the early part of the group. She was so excited by the fantasy of the relationship that, contrary to advice from the group, she returned a week later, only to find that he was married with two children.

Around the mid-point of the group, Charlotte arrived slightly late and in some distress. An apple tree in her parents' garden had been blown down in strong winds. She believed this was because the tree was a hybrid that lacked adequate roots. I think she and the group interpreted this in symbolic terms, although no one spelled out the interpretation. I saw it as a critical point in her integration into the group and perhaps even her recovery. The group ran for just over a year and I did not have the means to follow up on the participants, however I felt optimistic about Charlotte. Toward the end of the group she formed a relationship with a single man, who lived in the same block of flats. This seemed to be more solidly founded on reality, and something that I saw as real progress.

In attachment terms Charlotte displayed a predominant pattern of relating that was ambivalent-anxious (Hazen & Shaver, 1987). I believe this manifested itself in the ways described above and in many other ways that are beyond the scope of this case example. However, the point was that her attachment pattern also expressed itself in her relationship to cultural resources (whether colour, nationality, gender or body shape). She hung onto the sense of belonging that was inherent in her English nationality and raged against any dimension of difference that threatened this sense of belonging or resonated with the various forms of abuse that she had experienced. It seemed that her sense of both personal and cultural belonging had been so undermined that she needed to define its limits by denigrating dimensions of otherness, and by attacking any assumption that was made about her cultural identity, especially those based on aspects of her appearance such as colour or mode of dress. In effect she became hypersensitised to a range of cultural issues and seemed to have lost the ability to mentalize (Bateman, Fonagy, & Allen, 2009) or regulate her emotions in these areas.

This example is complemented by an example of cultural blindness that follows.

Case example 3 – cultural blindness: Hamid

Hamid was a 48-year-old male who presented with a complex combination of issues. He had a medical diagnosis of depression, had suffered abuse and neglect in childhood, and had sustained mild to moderate brain damage in a physical attack.

Hamid was born into a traditional Islamic family in a Middle Eastern country. However, his parents divorced shortly after his birth and both parents remarried in physically separate parts of the country, where they started new families. Hamid remained with his mother but was not accepted by his new stepfather. He was mainly cared for by relatives and suffered neglect. He did not remember much about his mother but continued to miss her.

At the age of five his father came to take him to his home, presumably motivated by stories of the neglect, the request of his ex-wife, or the fact that Hamid was his firstborn son. In his father's home things were no better, and there was some physical and sexual abuse. The father was stern and remote and did not express love toward the boy.

Hamid grew up and found employment. However, he got into bad company and the police caught him drinking alcohol with a friend. Rather than expressing remorse and showing compliance to the authority of the police, which would probably have headed off further action, his friend argued and resisted. This led to prosecution and to Hamid losing his job. Shortly after, he saw an advert encouraging him to immigrate to the UK, which he decided to do.

In the UK Hamid found work and married. However, the couple did not have children, and the marriage ended after a few years. Life seems to have proceeded more or less well up until a point about seven years before when Hamid was the victim of an attack in a northern city. The details of this are unclear, although it seems that it was unprovoked, and perhaps racially motivated. Hamid has no memory of the attack, from a week before until a week after. However, when he regained consciousness his father was with him in the hospital. The father again took him back to his home and provided physical care during the immediate period of recovery. However, Hamid was still not accepted and felt that he did not fit in, so he decided to return to his home in the UK. Here, he was unable to work and remained under medical care for the head injury. Despite police enquiries, no one was ever charged in relation to the assault.

Hamid was a gentle and kind man. He felt a deep sense of the unfairness of his treatment by the world. He believed that he had not received fairness or justice in his family or his home country and had thought that the UK was better. The experience of the assault contradicted this, although he never once mentioned the possibility of racial discrimination. It was as if he had spent his whole life trying to fit into alien environments in which he lacked any sense of belonging and that his very existence depended on denying the possibility of discrimination or blaming the aggressor.

Hamid described a situation in which a female neighbour had complained about him to the local council, because his garden was untidy. The garden was inspected and found to be fine. The neighbour then made veiled threats about what her nephew might do to Hamid. However, Hamid refused to acknowledge that there could be a racial element, and in this case he managed to turn the situation around by kindness and politeness. In another incident, as racial tensions were rising in the UK, he was stopped and searched by the police. But again, he was reluctant to acknowledge the possibility of racial discrimination.

I think the group helped Hamid to acknowledge his own right to exist, the reality of racial discrimination and the possibility of creating a place in which he could belong. He did not talk much in the group about his childhood and early life but, as with Charlotte, I think current and early life issues create interacting patterns in the transitional space of Winnicott's cultural world, and that by engagement with the cultural world we may help to address current issues and heal early traumas (Wilson & Lindy, 2013). Hamid went on to meet a new partner and to make a life for himself in the extended family that he had joined.

Hamid's attachment pattern was much more avoidant, and this applied equally to his use of cultural resources. In his case, I think the therapeutic process led him to greater acceptance of his native culture, and thereby a greater ability to appreciate and survive in the new and different culture in which he had chosen to live.

By now, the reader may be starting to detect similarities between the case examples, and I believe that they illustrate the same, or a very similar, metacultural narrative; with discourses of loss, absence and rejection. This is not the only metacultural narrative, but it is an important one that motivates people to take superficially irrational actions that are potentially damaging to themselves and others. It seems reasonable to suggest that individuals who lack a sense of belonging will seek this out where they can. Doležal found it in blackness, Charlotte in her relational experiences, and Hamid in Islam. From there they moved on to pursue forms of 'growth': Doležal in civil rights, Charlotte through interpersonal relationship, and Hamid in acceptance of his native culture. It is generally recognised that those who lack good objects in their life will seek out idealised versions that are, ultimately, unachievable fantasies (Freud & Burlingham, 1973), while people with good early attachment figures and a secure place in society are less likely to succumb to destructive influences. The small grain of hope is the possibility of earning security in later life (Holmes, 2001), or even of being helped through the underlying issues in some form of therapy.

Conclusion

My main conclusion is that a metacultural view of the world, incorporating ideas of cultural identity, personal culture and culture as a resource, provides a powerful framework that can aid the understanding of individuals and the path they choose in life. It can help to explain more extreme examples of cultural choices and makes it easier to talk about difficult issues such as cultural stereotypes, without being silenced in the name of political correctness. I also believe that it can be a useful tool in therapy; capable of making a powerful contribution in both individual and group therapy. In addition, although I have not covered it here, there is an extremely powerful area of application in the area of deradicalisation. The components of the approach are not new, although the versions of culture as a resource and personal culture that I present are not constructs that I have encountered elsewhere. Above all, I believe that it is necessary to view the cultural world not just as a passive influence, but as a field of expression for more personal and subjective factors.

References

Aikenhead, D. (2017, 25/02/2017) Rachel Dolezal: 'I'm not going to stoop and apologise and grovel' *The Guardian*. Retrieved from www.theguardian.com/us-news/2017/feb/25/rachel-dolezal-not-going-stoop-apologise-grovel

Aldwin, C. M. (2007) *Stress, coping, and development: An integrative perspective* (2nd ed.). New York: Guilford Press.

Aldwin, C. M., & Gilmer, D. F. (2013) *Health, illness, and optimal aging* (2nd ed.). New York: Springer.

Aldwin, C. M., Park, C. L., & Spiro, A. (2007) *Handbook of health psychology and aging*. New York: Guilford Press.

Anderson, B. (2006). *Imagined communities* (new ed.). London: Verso.

Bateman, A., Fonagy, P., & Allen, J. G. (2009) Theory and practice of mentalization-based therapy. In: G. Gabbard (Ed.) *Textbook of psychotherapeutic treatments* (pp. 757–780). Arlington, VA: American Psychiatric Publishing, Inc. US.

Belsey, C. (2002) *Poststructuralism: A very short introduction*. Oxford: Oxford University Press.

Doležal, R. (2017) *In full color: Finding my place in a black and white world*. Dallas, TX: BenBella Books.

Ewing, K. P. (2008) *Being and belonging: Muslims in the United States since 9/11*. New York: Russell Sage Foundation.

Freud, A., & Burlingham, D. T. (1973) Infants without families: Report on the Hampstead nurseries 1939–1945. In: *The writings of Anna Freud (Vol. 3)*. New York: International Universities Press.

Freud, S. (1917 [1915]) Mourning and melancholia. In: J. Strachey (Ed.) *The standard edition of the complete psychological works of Sigmund Freud: Volume XIV (1914–1916)* (Vol. XIV, pp. 239–258). London: Vintage.

Gay, P. (1988) *Freud: A life for our time*. London: Macmillan.

Grove, D. J., & Panzer, B. I. (1991) *Resolving traumatic memories: Metaphors and symbols in psychotherapy*. New York: Irvington Publishers.

Hazen, C., & Shaver, P. (1987) Romantic love conceptualized as an attachment process. *Journal of Personality and Social Psychology*, 52(3), pp. 511–524.

Hearst, L. (1993) Our historical and cultural cargo and its vicissitude in group analysis. *Group Analysis*, 26(4), pp. 389–405.

Holmes, J. (2001) *The search for the secure base: Attachment theory and psychotherapy*. Hove, East Sussex; Philadelphia, PA: Brunner-Routledge.

Hopkins, P. E. (2007) Young Muslim men's experiences of local landscapes after 11 September 2001. In: C. Aitchison, P. E. Hopkins, & M.-P. Kwan (Eds) *Geographies of Muslim identities* (pp. 189–200). Aldershot: Ashgate Publishing.

Lazarus, R. S. (1985) The psychology of stress and coping. *Issues in Mental Health Nursing*, 7(1–4), pp. 399–418.

Lazarus, R. S. (1999) *Stress and emotion: A new synthesis*. New York: Springer.

Le Roy, J. (2000) Group analysis and culture. In D. Brown & L. Zinkin (Eds), *The psyche and the social world: Developments in group-analytic theory* (pp. 180–201). London: Jessica Kingsley.

MacDonald, G. (2007) *The nature and significance of Scottish ethnic identity.* MSc Psychology and Counselling Dissertation, Manchester Metropolitan University, Manchester.

MacDonald, G. (2015) *Culture as a positive resource in therapy.* Unpublished thesis, Doctor in Counselling, The University of Manchester, Manchester.

Modood, T., Beishon, S., & Virdee, S. (1994) *Changing ethnic identities*. London: Policy Studies Institute.

Ruiz, E. M. (2017, 14/04/2017) All Rachel Dolezal did was show that race and identity are complicated. *Observer*. Retrieved from http://observer.com/2017/04/all-rachel-dolezal-did-was-show-that-race-and-identity-are-complicated/

Sandler, J., Dare, C., & Holder, A. (1992) *The patient and the analyst* (revised ed.). London: Karnac.

Werbner, P. (2002). *Imagined diasporas among Manchester Muslims*. Oxford: James Currey.

Wilson, J. P., & Lindy, J. D. (2013) *Trauma, culture, and metaphor: Pathways of transformation and integration* (first ed.). Hove: Routledge.

Winnicott, D. W. (1960) The theory of the parent-infant relationship. In: D. W. Winnicott (Ed.) *The maturational processes and the facilitating environment* (pp. 37–55). London: Hogarth Press.

Winnicott, D.W. (2005 [1971]) *Playing and reality*. Abingdon: Routledge.

PART III

Practice research

9

HOPE IS A ROPE

Living with a difficult present and an uncertain future

John Prysor-Jones

In this chapter hope is presented as a common and universal folk experience, part of the human condition and experienced in every dimension of the human person. The antecedents, characteristics and attributes of hope are discussed arising from research in many disciplines. Drawing on research, counsellors' personal reflections on their counselling experiences identify hope as a liminal experience, simultaneously existing with hopelessness and differentiated experiences of hope present, hope as relational and hope lost. The implications for counsellors' bringing their humanity and using their liminal experiences of hope and hopelessness in practice are identified as a helpful resource for clients living with present difficulties and an uncertain future.

This is an invitation to experience. Following a tragic death in my family as I began doctoral studies, and was unsure of my research focus, it brought to the fore experiences of both hope and hopelessness. It became clear that I needed to research hope to explore it, to find out what it is for me in my life, both personally and professionally. It raised the question how do we human beings cope with adversity and uncertainty in our private, professional or work lives? How do we as counsellors help our clients navigate through difficulties when they experience a loss of personal power and usual ways of coping no longer work? One answer lies in the experience of hope wrestling with hopelessness. In this chapter I consider characteristics and attributes of hope, its liminal nature and implications for the counsellor's approach to their work, drawing on their experiences of hope in counselling relationships. Exposure to and dialogue with their experiences can touch our own and provide a way to experience the inner world of our clients and ourselves, while providing opportunity for deeper reflection and understanding of hope and its potential for human flourishing.

My intention is to encourage your engagement, initially not so much to analyse or interpret, but rather to experience meaning, engage with your own stories and be aware of a deepening ability to make sense of things in relation to hope. Hope is understood here to refer to a common or folk experience found in almost every culture although understood and conceptualised differently. Hope as a well-developed folk concept arises from people's experience; an instinctual desire for a better life and world which, when understood, will have implications for considering hope as a psychological state (Bruininks & Malle, 2005) and its place in therapeutic work. From a biological perspective hope is understood as evolutionary, found in the body and therefore in human nature and a component in human motivation and action (Tiger, 1979, 1999).

Hope has been researched in many disciplines and a vast amount written particularly over the past sixty years. Professional and academic interest and research in hope has been mainly in the fields of medicine, nursing and psychology, and more recently counselling and psychotherapy, and mostly in the USA and Canada. The universality of hope as a common human experience is well recognised (Eliot, 2005). While there has been agreement between most academic disciplines that hope is a significant concept for research, there is less agreement about what hope is and how it is conceptualised even within disciplines. It is important to recognise that hope was a human experience long before it became a psychological construct and the subject of research developing prescriptive approaches.

Hope has been embedded in culture and human life from earliest times and in everyday language and usage, but not always consciously (Averill et al. 1990). The enduring nature of hope is found in the myth of the Indian rope trick. A man throws a rope in the air and it rises high. It does not fall. It appears that the rope has attached itself somewhere, and to prove this the man climbs the rope. The rope does not collapse. *It holds.* This story, with its theme of ascension, has parallels in many religious traditions. For example, it is found in classical India, in Islam, ancient Mexico, the Dutch Indies, in Irish folklore. Versions are even found in the works of Homer and Plato (Eliade, 1965 cited in Desroche, 1979).

Interestingly, the story has never been explained or solved. It suggests that the metaphors of thread and rope engage the active imagination of human beings, and refer to their deepest experiences which cannot be expressed in other symbols or concepts. 'Hope is a rope' (a meditation by Angelus Silesius (1986) a seventeenth-century mystic) is a metaphor for human aspirations, imagination, 'flung in the air'; kept alive, the rope is secured, it holds, and when people grab hold of it, it takes the strain, remains rigid, whether they are climbing toward something or pulling it toward them. It points to a common experience that belongs to us human beings, created, held and shared in these cultural forms.

It is perhaps not surprising that we are more aware of hope when health is threatened. Nursing scholarship, for example, has focused on understanding the nature and role of hope in illness to create knowledge that can inform nursing practice. Hope here has been conceptualised as multi-faceted with six dimensions, affective, cognitive, behavioural, affiliative, temporal and contextual, and established as part of the experience of being human (Dufault & Martoccio, 1985).

Two spheres have been distinguished. The first, a generalised hope that holds a sense of some future beneficial development; an outlook that makes everything worthwhile; a hopeful disposition; a trait, an approach to life (Averill et al., 1990). The second, particularised hope focused on an object concerned with what is most important in a person's life; hope as a state; the present feelings about a situation which may fluctuate over time (Farran et al., 1995; Snyder, 2002).

The utility of hope for caring professions is demonstrated with a proliferation of definitions and theories in the health sciences. This can be threatening to medicalise hope and can presage a reductive view of the human person.

One definition arising from nursing but used widely in multidisciplinary research suggests 'hope can be defined as a process of anticipation that involves the interaction of thinking, acting, feeling and relating, and is directed towards a future fulfilment that is personally meaningful' (Stephenson, 1991: 1459). While broad and flexible it is focused on the individual's hope for themselves and does not allow for a corporate response or hope to be experienced for others. My doctoral research (Prysor-Jones, 2015) demonstrates counsellors experiencing hope for others, as will be demonstrated below.

From the subject of my research, cited above in several contexts, we can draw together some attributes of hope: it is relational, it has a forward-looking dimension; it sustains in the present; it is both a personal experience and a communal one; it involves the search for meaning; it can be experienced cognitively, emotionally, behaviourally and spiritually.

Strangely, hope often comes into awareness when it is absent. Its antecedents can include a response to a threat or a crisis, e.g. loss, life-threatening event, hardship or change, a difficult decision, a challenge. These events can trigger an unsettled state of uncertainty and anxiety. In this way hope is experienced as liminal, not immediately in present awareness, but at its edge, and therefore difficult to access and conceptualise.

Research has established hope as one of four common factors in all forms of therapy contributing to therapeutic change (Lambert, 1992) and experienced relationally (Larsen et al., 2013). It has therefore been realised as an essential component of effective therapy and a focus for research (Larsen & Stege, 2010a 2010b; O'Hara, 2013; Larsen et al., 2014).

Some research has also found that when a client enters counselling, at some level they are already investing a degree of hope in the counselling process (or the counsellor), as a wish to feel differently, though it may fluctuate in strength. The counsellor's task is to work with and nurture that hope (Roche, 1996; Helm, 2004; Rodrigues-Antonucci, 2006).

Having identified hope as a common and universal human experience and some understandings of hope and contributions to research, analysis of the data from my research can serve to illustrate counsellors' fluctuating experiences of hope as part of a contextual meaning-making process, both personally and within the therapeutic relationship. For counsellors, experience is multi-layered as they distinguish between the 'there and then' and 'here and now' of their experience; established experience from experience in the making. Their own words are used as recorded and move in sequence through personal reflections, hope and hopelessness, hope present, hope as relational, hope lost (Prysor-Jones, 2015).

This sense of hope occupying different areas of life (Dufault & Martoccio, 1985) is captured by a counsellor's reflection:

> Speaking entirely for myself, the absence of hope would now have to permeate not just one, but in many areas of my life before I gave up on life. But I wonder, if we don't develop these areas of life or indeed if we lose them, like good health/fitness, being loved by someone, having a family, a career, good friends etc., do those close to suicide have the ability or energy to separate out which area of their life where hope can re-establish itself? Fortunately, I am now able to separate out in life, the areas that give me hope and those that do not. If all areas of my life became hopeless then I know I wouldn't want to stay around.
>
> *Personal communication, used with permission*

Another counsellor speaking out of her own experience as a client describes what it is like "to be in a hopeless place, it's so bleak, so dark. It's frightening. My experience of it was real fear". Reflecting on this experience she realises that

> to have somebody hold the hope, the possibility of not being frightened and of there being something more meaningful, it wasn't spoken, but there was something about … it was holding ….me in the present supporting me in the present, but in doing that it was sort of somehow leading me into a different future.
>
> *Prysor-Jones, 2015: 117*

Within counselling sessions hope is experienced as coexisting with hopelessness and both as powerful and dynamic experiences fluctuating naturally; maintaining it is seen as potentially challenging. Hope and hopelessness are often presented as opposites, in an either/or relationship deeply rooted in everyday language. Research has identified both in therapy as coexisting in a complex dialectic with contradictions where desolation sits with expectations of life and questioning if it is worth living (Flaskas, 2007; O'Hara, 2011, 2013; Prysor-Jones, 2015).

Some counsellors describe having to make a considerable effort when their hope struggles with a client's hopelessness, its effects on the counselling relationship and on themselves, and subsequently how they reflect on this experience. Difficulties can be created when counsellor and client do not share the same hopes (Larsen et al., 2014); there are two aspects to this struggle. First, between counsellor and client: a counsellor reflects, "there would be times when there was this real sense that things could never change, and the struggle between us was immense".

The struggle seems to be sustaining hope with little prospect of change with his hopelessness. The client's personal history is part of the source of this struggle, an abusive childhood. He had grown up in a very hopeless environment or culture. He took that into his experience of life, it became a part of who he is. The counsellor's hope conflicted with the client's life experience.

She gives 'his voice' to that experience:

> That sense that "I must be useless. I must be unworthy if this is the way I've been treated by people … this is what people do to me …. People must have known but nobody came to help", this was a really difficult piece of work. I was thinking it was really tangible … that my hope was tussling with his hopelessness
>
> *Prysor-Jones, 2015: 106*

A counsellor describes another aspect of struggle, that within herself when reflecting on the difficulty she experienced. "I don't think working with this level of hopelessness is easy and I don't think it is easily overcome either. I think that's something that takes a lot of … I say the word 'convincing'." Again, she tries to recreate his experience, "It's something like if 'I'd had that experience I'm not going to believe what you tell me'. You need to do a lot of convincing that actually the world is a hopeful place". Yet she did not give up, it is going to take time. She asks "Was there change? I think there was … but I don't think it was a massive amount of change, but I think he got a glimpse of something different" (Prysor-Jones, 2015: 106).

One implication for counsellors is to strive for a balance or acknowledged distribution of hope and hopelessness, helping clients learn to balance the difficult parts of life with the satisfying and so develop a sense that life is 'good enough' (Bergin & Walsh, 2005: 7).

Counsellors describe positive moments in the counselling relationship when hope is felt to be present as an embodied, visceral and transitory experience in their clients and in themselves. A counsellor describes a quality in her clients:

> I can actually tell you what it is, because I have found this with lots of clients – it's something in their eyes … there's a little spark, even if it only comes now and again, that glint in the eye, the spirit in somebody comes through; it's also hope.

Another counsellor says,

> The presence of hope is almost a physical act, they are looking at me more, giving me more eye contact … the eyes are very significant … it is one signal to me … that their demeanour is slightly more open.

Yet another says, "There is this excitement that something is going to happen or change … I think I see it in their eyes."

Some counsellors describe their own physical and visceral experiences when hope is present. "Hope for me is energy. That's what it feels like. A spark of energy.

It's almost like that essential part of me is excited". And on occasions, "Hope … there's tranquillity about it, a sense of peace. It feels like a life force."

Hope is present as "a feeling of exhilaration, but I need to dampen that down sometimes … for the client's sake".

> It's physiologically, a lightening, it's a sort of … I'm pointing here [she puts her hand on her abdomen], that kind of solid lump loosens and lightens.

> It's a feeling, I can't describe it – I'm going to my midriff [she puts her hand on her stomach] because that's around where it is, it's warm, exciting sometimes, but I damp that down for the client because they've got to get there themselves … it might be frightening for the client.

Another says:

> On a physical level, I'm kind of quite animated, and there is that … I was going to say "joy", playfulness and a good feeling within myself when hope is there. It's more of a … down here [she points to her stomach] feeling. It's almost like a bubble rising up … to the extent you know, I've perhaps got a smile on my face and a "lightness of body."
>
> When hope is present in the room I definitely have a sense of everything being more energized … holding my body up … a bit alert … sitting up more … I have that kind of embodied sense. I feel more connected with the room, more clarity in my thinking … and probably very slight racing of the heart … a little flutter of excitement, my eyes would brighten … it comes from here (she puts her hand on her stomach), so it's an opening actually.

These specific embodied experiences of hope being present in their clients and in themselves they describe as occurring naturally and fluctuating in the flow of counselling. Absence of such explicit experience does not mean that hope is not present or is lost. Hope can still be implicitly present underlying the counselling relationship (Prysor-Jones, 2015).

Counsellors experience hope as relationally dynamic, involving the mutual exchange of feeling and emotion with their clients. They also experience working with a complex, personally sophisticated internal reality that includes awareness of their own hope and allowing a client's experience to have an impact on them; the relationship is with themselves and their clients for whom they hold hope. What is most painful for a client seems to be deepened to a point where it can be shared and explored, displaying a sense of deep connectedness characterised by trust and mutuality.

A counsellor captures working in such a relationship with a client, distressed and traumatised, actively suicidal, who feels hopeless most of the time and does not know of anything that is different in her experience. It suggests chronic experience formed over a long period of time.

> What happens for her is she feels it, she really trusts me, so she believes that I believe for her and that's almost enough. I think she knows that I get it. How much she wants to die and how important that is to her and how desperate that is.
>
> *Prysor-Jones, 2015: 116*

This counsellor knows that the client knows that the counsellor understands her experience. The respectful acceptance includes the possibility she may end her life.

> "When we talk about whether she wants to live or die, I really stay with it's a possibility, yes, this client might choose death in preference. She might choose that and I feel really respectful of that, given her circumstances." What helps the counsellor to hold this possibility is being in touch with a part of herself. "So the place in me which thinks there's no way I could survive that, kind of enables me to hold that equal balance. I'm not sure I could have held on the way that she has, with what she has. Even with my optimistic outlook. I do think I would have given up."
>
> *Prysor-Jones, 2015: 116*

Her internal dialogue manages that possibility of losing hope. "So I don't feel invested in keeping her alive actually." The counsellor is open to her client's experience and her own, but not invested in hope or hopelessness but using her experience meets her client at another level but is not indifferent, as she makes clear:

> From a very personal point of view, I don't want her to kill herself. I really care about her and I'd be deeply upset. But if I really stay with her life and what she has I think actually I'm not in a place to be pulling her one way or the other. This really has to be her choice. So I think it kind of supports me to hold that more equally.
>
> *Prysor-Jones, 2015: 116*

The counsellor feeling at one with her own feelings is able to create a space for the client to be herself, that is, in touch with her own inner reality, which she knows is respected. She is aware of her influence here: "I do believe that what I say really matters." This is a source of hope. Possibly it is true for this counsellor that we can only become aware of possibilities for the future when we experience our own known limits or go beyond them.

The sombre mood of this part of her client's story is lifted a little as the counsellor says, "Just recently, actually, only in the last month for the first time she's started to say 'I know I'm changing.' So now is like the very first time she names some hope for herself". Her client begins to experience hope. "She could see there was movement for her … and therefore the possibility of further movement. She has worked with her for six years." It seems a characteristic of hope here is waiting.

Some counsellors describe losing hope for a client and the accompanying embodied feeling, one of emptiness, another of bleakness, dread and blackness and another of dissatisfaction, and another of failure (Prysor-Jones, 2015). Wosket (1999) suggests that admissions in public of therapists' failures is rare though more common in private. Mearns' (1998) research exploring counsellors' experiences of failure identifies some feelings that show similarity to those of loss of hope, self-doubt, and self-criticism.

Hope has been identified as liminal in these counsellors' experiences as quoted above (Prysor-Jones, 2015). This concept of liminality arising from human experience and behaviour, first identified in anthropology, is now having wider application conceptually in many disciplines, e.g., Social Sciences (Thomassen, 2014) and Education (Land et al., 2016). In capturing human experience, it offers a way of understanding and finding meaning. Liminality's application in therapeutic activity has been narrowly specific and open for further development.

Liminality is understood here as a fluid transitional state of being in which limits are reached: uncertainty, disturbed feelings, doubt, fluctuating behaviour and emotions, moments of powerlessness, moments where the status quo is challenged with potential loss of identity are necessary while navigating the experience, acquiring knowledge, with its potential for growth and experience of inner transformation. Hope, with its deep roots in human life and culture can provide a way to live through this transition.

This suggests an understanding of counselling as reflecting the society in which it takes place. Therefore, relying solely on psychological concepts, language and technical skills can restrict the course of counselling and unintentionally cause neglect of human resources of understanding, for example, intuition, capacity to care and hope; and well-tried effective ways counsellors have experienced as particularly healing (Clarkson, 2003).

Counsellors have been recognised as liminal figures occupying the space between social groups and the wider social world, and their task to help the individual find a place back into that social world (McLeod, 1999). For the client, the event that has brought them to counselling can be the start of this temporal dimension of liminality, on a threshold 'betwixt and between' two sensory states, at the initial stage of a process. Learning to live in this transitional liminal space in which the taken-for-granted order of known experience ceases to exist, replaced by feelings of uncertainty and anxiety, can be challenging.

Trusting meaning and self-understanding has been found to be creative and to lead to changes in behaviour for both client and counsellor, often in unpredictable ways as they moved toward a new point of stability (La Shure, 2005). What the client learns about their hope and hopelessness in such a transitional space can become a resource they take with them as they step over the threshold, back into their social world. On occasions it is possible it places both client and counsellor at the limits of what they know, and requires letting go of the focused attention of what is known (Barron, 2013). How we human beings experience and react to change seems to be at the heart of liminality. For the counsellor, a necessary part of liminal experience is believing that the liminal space provides safe uncertainty (Mason, 1993).

Counsellors bringing their own liminal experiences of hope and hopelessness as liminal specialists (Jennings, 1988) have been found to be a resource for their clients during this time of transition from dislocation to health. The hope counsellors feel for the client they are with and the meaning they give to the relationship is part of what they bring (Dufrane & Leclair, 1984). In this context, hope is an experience of mutual influence (Larsen et al., 2007), both at conscious and unconscious levels (Buechler, 2002). Counsellors cannot give what they have not got themselves (Buechler, 1995; Jevne, 1994); they have to *be* hopeful; it cannot be faked (Prysor-Jones, 2015).

Such hope for and in their clients is associated with better outcomes, and surprisingly more so than clients' own hope (Coppock et al., 2010), though this observation requires further research. Nevertheless, there can be a common assumption that therapists have an infinite amount of hope which is always available (Koenig & Spano, 2007; Cutcliffe, 2004). Levels of therapist hope during therapeutic sessions have been found to fluctuate (Larsen et al., 2013). Yet, sources of hope for a client can be found outside the therapy room in family, friends, spiritual beliefs, symbols, metaphors and in memories of previous experiences of hope (Hollis et al., 2007).

This highlights that counsellors also bring their humanity, which includes personal histories, life experiences, values, philosophy of life, the origins of hope for them, approach to life and belief about its meaning; each of which will shape every aspect of their work and influence the direction of therapy: 'It is who we are, as people … that inspires hope' (Buechler, 2002: 277). There is general agreement that who we are, our 'self' what we bring to the relationship is central to therapeutic practice (Wosket, 1999; Rowan & Jacobs, 2002). As therapists, we have no choice about having an impact, only a choice to recognise it (Buechler, 2002).

In this chapter I have drawn on human experience, which I argue has its own authority (Scott, 1991) and when felt is a means of understanding (Gendlin, [1962] 1997). This, in itself, may help to inform counselling practice, producing 'knowledge in context' (McLeod, 1999: 205). I argue that in opening up to the possibility of hope, counsellors, in particular, can experience hope afresh rather than trying to assimilate it into prior conceptualised understandings of what hope is with its potential and limits. This latter approach is associated with the 'professionalisation' of counselling and its attendant potential to distance the experience of hope. Alternatively, it is emphasised that practitioners draw on their own hope as experienced in different dimensions of their being and areas of their lives: reflecting on how they hold and work with hope in their work and see it as potential in their clients; it is about being 'real' in the relationship (Clarkson, 2003).

This emphasises the challenging circumstances in which counsellors may function and their capacity for personal resilience (Sibbert, 2004). The implication for practice is that counsellors be conversant with both hope and hopelessness in their own experience but focus on the clients' present experiencing, moment by moment. It may also encourage practitioners to reflect on their practice and what they bring of themselves to their work. This can include the time and energy they have invested in self-exploration, developing self-awareness which provides the resilience needed when working with a client's hopelessness. Jevne (1994: 136) neatly captures this approach: '[h]oping is knowing what is provided is not the musical score but an invitation to the concert'.

References

Averill, J.R., Catlin, G., & Chon, K.K. (1990) *Rules of Hope*. New York: Springer-Verlag Inc.

Barron, C. (2013) *Creativity and the Liminal Space*. www.psychologytoday.com/blog/the-creativity-cure/201306/c [Accessed: 25 June 2015].

Bergin, L. & Walsh, S. (2005) 'The role of hope in psychotherapy with older adults'. *Ageing and Mental Health*, 9(1), pp. 7–15.

Bruininks, P. & Malle, B.F. (2005) 'Distinguishing hope from optimism and related affective states'. *Motivation and Emotion*, 29(4), pp. 327–355.

Buechler, S. (1995) 'Hope as inspiration in psychoanalysis'. *Psychoanalytic Dialogues*, 5(1), pp. 63–74.

Buechler, S. (2002) 'Fromm's spirited values and analytic neutrality'. *International Forum of Psychoanalysis*, 11(4), pp. 275–278.

Clarkson, P. (2003) *The Therapeutic Relationship* (2nd Edn). London: Whurr Publishers.

Coppock, T.E., Owen, J.J., Zagarskas, E., & Schmidt, M. (2010) 'The relationship between therapist and client hope with therapy outcomes'. *Psychotherapy Research*, 20(6), pp. 619–626.

Cutcliffe, R. (2004) *The Inspiration of Hope in Bereavement Counselling*. London: Jessica Kingsley Publishers.

Desroche, H. (1979) *The Sociology of Hope*. London: Routledge & Kegan Paul.

Dufault, K. & Martoccio, B.C. (1985) 'Hope: its spheres and dimensions.' *Nursing Clinics of North America*, 20(2), pp. 379–391.

Dufrane, K. & Leclair, S.W. (1984) 'Using hope in the counselling process'. *Counselling & Values*, 29(1), pp. 32–41.

Eliade, M. (1965) *The Two and the One* (trans. J.M. Cohen). Chicago, IL: Chicago University Press.

Eliot, J. (Ed.) (2005) *Interdisciplinary Perspectives on Hope*. New York: Nova Science Inc.

Farran, C.J., Herth, K.A., & Popovich, J.M. (1995) *Hope and Hopelessness: Critical Clinical Constructs*. Thousand Oaks, CA: Sage Publications.

Flaskas, C. (2007) 'Holding hope and hopelessness: therapeutic engagements with the balance of hope'. *Journal of Family Therapy*, 29, pp. 186–202.

Gendlin, E.T. ([1962], 1997) *Experiencing and the Creation of Meaning: A Philosophical and Psychological Approach to the Subjective*. Evanston, IL: North Western University Press.

Helm, F.L. (2004) 'Hope is curative'. *Psychoanalytical Psychology*, 21(4), pp. 554–566.

Hollis, V., Massey, K., & Jevne, R. (2007) 'An introduction to the intentional use of hope'. *Journal of Allied Health*, 36(1), pp. 52–56.

Jennings, S. (1988) 'The loneliness of the long distance therapist'. *British Journal of Psychotherapy*, 4(3), pp. 297–301.

Jevne, R. (1994) *The Voice of Hope: Heard Across the Heart of Life*. San Diego, CA: Lura Media.

Koenig, T. & Spano, R. (2007) 'The cultivation of social workers' hope in personal life and professional practice'. *Journal of Religion & Spirituality in Social Work*, 26(3), pp. 45–61.

Lambert, M.J. (1992) 'Implications of psychotherapy outcome research for psychotherapy integration'. In: J.C. Norcross & M.R. Goldfried (Eds.) *Handbook of Psychotherapy Integration* (pp. 94–129). New York: Basic Books.

Land, R., Meyer, J.H.F., & Flanagan, M.T. (Eds) (2016) *Threshold Concepts in Practice.* Rotterdam: Sense Publishers.

Larsen, D., Edey, W., & LeMay, L. (2007) 'Understanding the role of hope in counselling: exploring the intentional uses of hope'. *Counselling Psychology Quarterly*, 20(4), pp. 401–416.

Larsen, D. & Stege, R. (2010a) 'Hope-focused practices during early psychotherapy sessions: Part I: implicit approaches'. *Journal of Psychotherapy Integration*, 20(3), pp. 271–292.

Larsen, D. & Stege, R. (2010b) 'Hope-focused practices during early psychotherapy sessions: Part II: explicit approaches'. *Journal of Psychotherapy Integration*, 20(3), pp. 293–311.

Larsen, D., Stege, R., & Flesaker, K. (2013) '"It's important for me not to let go of hope": psychologists' in-session experiences of hope'. *Reflective Practice: International and Multidisciplinary Perspectives*, 14(4), pp. 472–486.

Larsen, D., Stege, R., Edey, W., & Ewasiw, J. (2014) 'Working with unrealistic or unshared hope in the counselling session'. *British Journal of Guidance & Counselling*, 42(3), pp. 271–283.

La Shure, C. (2005) *What Is Liminality?* www.liminality.org/whatisliminality/ [Accessed 27 May 2015].

Mason, B. (1993) 'Towards positions of safe uncertainty.' *Human Systems: The Journal of Systemic Consultation and Management*, 4, pp. 189–200.

McLeod, J. (1999) 'Counselling as a social process'. *Counselling*, August, pp. 217–222.

Mearns, D. (1998) 'The counsellor's experience of failure'. In: D. Mearns & W. Dryden (Eds) *Experiences of Counselling in Action* (pp. 80–96). London: Sage.

O'Hara, D.J. (2011) 'Psychotherapy and the dialectics of hope and despair'. *Counselling Psychology Quarterly*, 24(4), pp. 323–329.

O'Hara, D.J. (2013) *Hope in Counselling & Psychotherapy*. London: Sage.

Prysor-Jones, J.G. (2015) *Hope Springs Internal: Counsellors' Experiences of Hope in the Counselling Relationship*. Unpublished Doctoral thesis. University of Manchester, UK.

Roche, K. (1996) Counselling in Loss and Grief: A Critical Evaluation – Holding Hope. Unpublished paper.

Rodrigues-Antonucci, S. (2006) 'Essential and elusive: the role of hope in counselling'. *Crossing Boundaries: An Interdisciplinary Journal*, 1(1), pp. 68–79.

Rowan, J. & Jacobs, M. (2002) *The Therapist's Use of Self.* Buckingham: Open University Press.

Scott, J.W. (1991) 'The evidence of experience', *Critical Inquiry*, 17(4), summer.

Sibbert, C. (2004) Liminality: Living and Practising at the Threshold. Paper at 3rd global conference: *Making Sense of Health, Illness and Disease*, St. Catherine's College, Oxford, July 2004.

Silesius, A. (1986) *Angelus Silesius: The Cherubinic Wanderer* (trans. M. Shrady). Mahwah, NJ: Paulist Press.

Snyder, C.R. (2002) 'Hope theory: rainbows in the mind'. Psychological Inquiry, 13(4), pp. 249–275.

Stephenson, C. (1991) 'The concept of hope revisited for nursing'. *Journal of Advanced Nursing*, 16, pp. 1456–1461.

Thomassen, B. (2014) *Liminality and the Modern: Living Through the In-Between.* Farnham: Ashgate Publishing Limited.

Tiger, L. (1979) *Optimism: The Biology of Hope*. New York: Simon & Schuster.

Tiger, L. (1999) 'Hope springs internal'. *Social Research*, 66(2), pp. 611–623.

Wosket, V. (1999) *The Therapeutic Use of Self: Counselling Practice, Research and Supervision.* London: Routledge.

10

A CHOCOLATE SANTA

Imaging the liminal moment with reverie in research

Lynn McVey

Introduction

This chapter explores a form of experiencing known as 'reverie' in the psychoanalytic literature. Reverie has been defined as the therapist's receptive, containing state of mind, which she or he can use to help clients transform unprocessed mental contents into useful elements from which they can learn (Bion, 1962). It has also been described as a kind of associative, metaphorical daydreaming that uses the therapist's stream of consciousness to convey otherwise inaccessible information about the therapeutic relationship, through fleeting mental impressions, images, memories, fantasies or bodily sensations (Ogden, 1999a).

One feature of psychotherapeutic reverie that is emphasised in all accounts is its profoundly liminal nature. Ephemeral and almost too subtle to notice, it teeters on the boundary between conscious and non-conscious states and between therapist and client, so much so, indeed, that the boundary may become porous, permitting non-conscious material to emerge (only just perceptibly) into consciousness and making aspects of the client's experiencing available, empathically, to the therapist, who contains them and helps the client to process them. When attended to, then, the mental impressions generated by reverie can offer rich intersubjective and empathic data – liminal images of the other as it were – that can elucidate and deepen the therapeutic relationship and detoxify the client's emotions.

Although much writing about reverie focuses on its therapeutic uses, here I extend the horizon of inquiry beyond therapy to research. I aim to (re-)create an image of a liminal reverie moment that a research participant and I – a counsellor and researcher – shared in a qualitative interview, during a small-scale exploratory study into therapy clients' experiences of emotionally evocative language (McVey, 2013).[1] The meanings we created from this experience and how these impacted on the research will be explored, before implications for counselling and psychotherapy research are reviewed more generally.

What is reverie?

I begin by reviewing the phenomenon in more detail from the perspective of psychoanalytic authors, as well as those from other therapeutic modalities. The term 'reverie' was first applied fully to psychotherapeutic practice by the British psychoanalyst Wilfred Bion (1962), who traced its origins to the mother–infant relationship. Bion suggested that infants are unable initially to make sense of the mass of perceptions and emotions – which he called 'beta-elements' (p. 6) – that assail them, and can only react involuntarily to them by attempting to project them mentally into caregivers, both to rid themselves of discomfort and as a primitive form of communication. In a healthy relationship, the receptive caregiver takes in or *contains* the projected beta-elements – even those that express negative feelings such as fury or pain – and makes sense of them for the baby, returning them to him as processed thoughts, which Bion called 'alpha-elements' (ibid.). The child is comforted and, through many repeated interactions of this kind, begins to learn what his own feelings mean.

Reverie is the open, empathic state of mind that makes such containment possible; a state that enables the caregiver to share her own mature capacity for understanding with her child, feeling her way into his emotional experiencing and translating that experiencing into meaningful thought. For instance, when her baby screams, she takes in his distress with empathy and love and draws on the resultant alpha-elements (split-second mental images, feelings, sensations and so on) to interpret his cries more or less accurately and respond accordingly, perhaps by feeding and cuddling him. In Bion's (1963) words, the relieved infant then 'sucks its bad property, now translated into goodness, back again' (p. 31). In so doing he learns how to translate painful, raw sensation into adaptive responses, shaped and infused with reverie-inspired alpha-elements. Bion suggested that the process continues throughout life and in therapy, albeit in a more sophisticated form, when therapists use their reverie to transform clients' projected beta-elements into tolerable alpha-elements from which they can learn.

Bion (1962) noted that reverie could take almost any form. A number of contemporary reverie authors have elaborated on those forms, including the relational psychoanalyst Thomas Ogden, who describes his own reverie minutely, experienced in ruminations, daydreams, mental images, memories and bodily sensations. Through the mechanisms of projection and empathic sharing described above, Ogden claims that these states of reverie express not only his own, but also his clients' emotional experiencing; their subjectivities overlap, as it were, creating a mutual subjectivity known as the analytic third (Ogden, 1994). For Ogden (1999a), no matter how trivial or irrelevant reverie seems, it relates intersubjectively to the analytic third and forms a kind of metaphorical commentary on what is occurring unconsciously between analyst and analysand. When the former fine-tunes his/her attention and becomes aware of reveries, they can provide an (only just) conscious expression of otherwise inaccessible relational mentation, which is then available to be worked on and transformed.

Take, for example, the following case of a reverie Ogden (1999b) experienced in a session with a patient, Ms. S. During much of their long-term work together, Ms. S. had existed in a deadening state of psychological detachment. Now, however, she was awakening from that state and starting to think she might be ready to end the analysis. In the session concerned she recounted a dream that centred on new feelings of attachment and aliveness. As she talked, Ogden's mind wandered fleetingly. He mused about the forthcoming trip home of his grown-up son (who lived in another part of the country), whom he would meet at the airport. His momentary daydream had a visual quality – it contained an image of the airport where he often met his son, with its stark fluorescent lighting – and an emotional resonance, which he describes as a feeling of sourness and disguised fearfulness.

Ogden acknowledges that reveries like this can feel like distractions from analytic work, but he views them, conversely, as valuable clinical facts; mechanisms by which analysts talk to themselves, in the 'language' of their own subjective memories and sensations, about what is occurring unconsciously between them and their patients. So, at this point in the session, rather than dismissing his reverie or regarding it as an interruption to his work with Ms. S., Ogden sought meaning in it. He recognised in the airport image a 'visceral memory of feelings of sadness, emptiness and fear' (Ogden, 1999b, p. 985) from an occasion years before when he had waited for a flight to visit his dying father at that same airport, under those same lights. He had been filled with sadness not only about his father, but also about his (then teenage) son growing up and leaving home; something that felt like another death to him at that time, although in fact, he realised now, it heralded new life. Ogden linked the reverie with his experience in the session with Ms. S., who was also 'growing up' and getting ready to 'leave home' as she began to contemplate the end of their work together. Having processed the reverie, Ogden spoke from the feeling of it to the analysand, suggesting to her that perhaps she was afraid that her development as a person might mean not only the end of the analysis, but that they would be separated utterly, as if by death. The suggestion connected with something deep within Ms. S. and they ended the session united in silence and quiet feelings of love and sadness.

I have quoted this clinical vignette quite extensively because it illustrates powerfully what it can be like to experience and make clinical use of reverie. When Ogden writes about the remembered fluorescent airport lights, for instance, he manages to convey the liminal nature of such experiencing, which can be indistinct and fleeting while at the same time evoking utterly specific sensations and memories. Reveries (like dreams) seem peculiarly well-suited to expressing the subtle simultaneity and ambivalence of many-layered human *being* in this way, owing to their dream-like, condensed nature. What is more, when *I* read Ogden's account, I see what he describes in my *own* mind's eye, translating his description into my own idiom, with different but, for me, equally potent, associations. I thereby understand emotionally (and not only intellectually) what it is to have a reverie; learning by experience, as Bion (1962) puts it, through the evocative mechanism of empathic imagination, triggered by language. Readers, too, may wish to ponder on their own sensing at this point, and what it might tell them about the meaning they make of Ogden's words and my recounting of them, and, potentially, of their experiencing when with clients and others, and how this affects them and their work.

Toward a broader definition of therapeutic reverie

Bion and Ogden use the term 'reverie' to refer to an ephemeral, liminal inner experience within a specifically psychoanalytic context. Yet it can be argued that this same experience features in the clinical accounts of therapists from non-psychoanalytic backgrounds, using different terminology (McVey, 2018). Carl Rogers (1980), for instance, founder of the person-centred modality, wrote about 'seeing' a mental image of a client as a pleading little boy in a session and using that image to understand his client more fully. His account resembles phenomenologically (if not theoretically) the clinical vignettes of Ogden and other psychoanalytic reverie writers, and his image could be regarded as an 'alpha-element' (Bion, 1962, p. 6); a product of reverie.

Another humanistic case for attending to inner experiencing (whether we call it 'reverie' or not) is made by Gendlin (2003, 1996) when he writes about focusing on the bodily felt sense. The felt sense is an 'internal aura that encompasses everything you feel and know about the given subject at the given time' (Gendlin, 2003, p. 33), just as reverie expresses what therapists feel and know about their relationships with clients in a particular moment. Further, Gendlin suggests that focusing on the felt sense can reveal insights into our own and others' needs and concerns. Such focusing is a profoundly liminal process, which involves 'attending directly in that "edge", that "zone" between conscious and unconscious' (Gendlin, 1986, p. 105); a zone with which reverie practitioners such as Ogden (1999a) are intimately familiar, as they track fleeting inner experiencing to access relational information. For Gendlin, manifestations associated with reverie, such as feelings, memories or mental images, while not synonymous with the felt sense, can act as 'avenues' (Gendlin, 1996, p. 170) to it, and he advocates working with as many avenues as possible to deepen our understanding of others and ourselves.

Extending the horizon of therapeutic reverie to research

Perhaps we should not be surprised that non-psychoanalytic accounts of reverie-type experiencing exist – like those mentioned above – given Bion's (1962) insistence on its universal, extra-therapeutic origins in the caregiver–child relationship. Looked at this way, reverie, or at least aspects of it, can be viewed as a ubiquitous human relational, sense-making phenomenon. And if this is so, why should it not occur and be used in other empathic relationships that seek to make meaning, including research relationships, especially research in counselling and psychotherapy, which sets such store by relational process?

There is growing evidence for the utility of reverie in research (Holmes, 2019), particularly qualitative research which incorporates researcher reflexivity; reflexive feminist writers have, after all, included 'transgressive data' (St Pierre, 1997, p. 180) like dreams and other products of 'alpha function' (Bion, 1962, p. 2) in their research for decades. Other examples, specifically related to therapeutic research, include Nolan's (2008) account of qualitative research interviews with clinical supervisors. In one interview he perceived a kind of energy field or aura around a participant, allowing him to enter deeply into the latter's own description of 'seeing into' clients at a transpersonal level. And in a study about adolescent depression, Holmes (2019) used his reverie about being excluded from a rather aloof participant's warm relationship with her therapist 'where they joked about regimented research meetings, such as the one we were in the midst of' (p. 84) to enrich his empathic understanding of the participant's feelings of exclusion on learning about her therapist's pregnancy. He observes: 'So we see how a reverie-guided intervention brought what would otherwise have been a flat, somewhat depersonalised interview to life, and led on to interesting material about the therapist's pregnancy and its unconscious resonance for the interviewee' (Holmes, 2019, p. 85).

I and co-authors have written about similar reverie-infused experiences in research also (McVey, Lees & Nolan, 2015, 2016), focusing on examples where images from my own past – in one case of a department store café and in another of childhood bedtimes – helped me gain deeper insight into participants' experiencing. We concluded that reverie can provide a route to empathy and reflexivity in qualitative research, offering 'researchers insight into the relational processes taking place during data collection and analysis' (McVey *et al.*, 2015, p. 148).

An example: the chocolate Santa

We turn now to an example from a small-scale qualitative study in which I interviewed therapy clients about their experiences of emotionally evocative language (McVey, 2013), which, I suggest, offers further evidence of the way that reverie can enrich research. The example centres on my shared experience of reverie with a participant in the study, and how that experience impacted on the research. The participant, referred to here by the pseudonym Bella, was a client in her twenties (I did not interview my own clients, but only clients working with other therapists). She gave informed consent to participate in the research and to me using the example here. The following extract from our conversation includes some transcription symbols used in conversation analysis to convey non- and paraverbal features such as pauses ('5.0', for example, relates to a pause of five seconds), overlaps in speech, and intonation (see Appendix for a key to the symbols). The interview was video-recorded to help me study non-verbal elements like these, and in the extracts below body language and gesture are recorded in double brackets. Such features are often omitted from reports of both research and psychotherapeutic conversations but they are included here to provide a fuller sense of what it was like to be there. They are resources readers can use to situate themselves mentally in the interview room alongside Bella and me, where you can study us and your own inner responses to us, whatever these may be.

The following extract from my research conversation with Bella occurred about 20 minutes into our meeting, which lasted for around an hour. Just before, Bella had been talking about her experience of feeling alone as a teenager, which she linked with feeling hollow:

Bella: (5.0) Just a bit *hollow* really (2.0) yeah, like a [hollowness]
Lynn: [Mm] is it anywhere (2.0) *in* you? ((Moves both hands in front of torso)).
Bella: (6.0) No, I don't, [I don't] ((rests head on right hand))
Lynn: [Mm]
Bella: think I can feel it sort of *physically* but (1.0) the image that just sort of flashed up then was, erm (3.0) thinking of hollowness: you know like those chocolate Santas or things [like that?].

As the extract begins, Bella paused for five seconds. During the pause she seemed to be trying to 'get into' the experience of aloneness so that she could represent it to me in some way, and she did so powerfully, identifying a feeling of hollowness. Perhaps she was trying, unconsciously, to minimise the painful finality of the word 'hollow' by prefacing it with the phrase 'just a bit', but in fact the contrast between her words intensified their impact on me. This sense of contrast was a strong feature of our interaction, as we will see. I asked if Bella could feel the hollowness in her body, moving my hands in front of my torso to indicate where such a feeling might be located. After another long contemplative pause of six seconds, during which she rested her head on her hands thoughtfully, Bella explained she could not identify a physical feeling but instead an image of a chocolate Santa 'just sort of flashed up'. The ephemeral yet specific nature of Bella's mental image echoes the form taken by reverie in the descriptions we have reviewed above: this time, however, the reverie was experienced by a research participant and not a therapist.

I responded to it in the moment with a reverie of my own, which, like Bella's, 'just flashed up' suddenly and vividly. It was over in a moment and yet left a strong impression on me. My mind was filled in that instant with a gaudy mental image of the crinkly red, black and silver foil covering of a chocolate Santa. I had a sense of Christmas shopping trips from the past, full of frenetic bustle, hemmed in by shoppers, fairy lights, and shelves full of brightly coloured goods. Something about this image also evoked a faint childhood memory of chocolate Santas hanging on the family Christmas tree, with its sharp, ferny scent. Although in the moment I felt a fleeting sense of gladness about the reverie because it was so attractive and familiar, I also felt some discomfort, because it seemed irrelevant or even contradictory to Bella's experience, given that my reverie was full (of people, colour, things), whereas Bella had been exploring aloneness and hollowness. As our conversation continued, I became more and more aware of the contrast between my full reverie and Bella's sense of hollowness and the effect this was having on me, but I did not express it immediately, instead encouraging Bella to go on:

Lynn: [Ye::ah]
Bella: where it might seem like a *s::olid object* but then (2.0) you sort of break it open and inside (.) it's just, it's completely hollow (2.0). That just sort of sprang to mind then with that word.
Lynn: (4.0) That's really, erm (2.0) that sort of brings things to mind for me as well, that chocolate Santa ((I have a warm facial expression. Bella laughs)). It's like a kind of, there's a pathos ((pinches wrist with right hand)) in that, 'cos it's something that, it's quite a cheery, erm (2.0) sort of outwardly (2.0) well, a cheerful, sort of sweet thing [and]
Bella: [M::m].
Lynn: and, and I'm thinking but quite (1.0) there's that feeling of hollowness though, the sad- ((looks down and holds head in hand)) (.) I feel *sad* thinking [about that].

My drawn-out, rising 'ye::ah' at the beginning of this extract and warm facial expression throughout the exchange expressed my engagement with Bella's image, to which she seemed to respond, in turn, by laughing and murmuring 'mm' under my words. She went on to develop the metaphorical implications of her chocolate Santa reverie, which seemed 'like a *s::olid object* but … inside … it's completely hollow', her words flowing, with shorter pauses than before. Using verbal and paraverbal expressions to underline the contrast between the apparent solidity of the Santa and its hollowness, she emphasised the word 'solid' by elongating its initial vowel sound, before saying that, in fact, the Santa was 'completely hollow'. I was moved by that phrase 'completely hollow', which emerged from the brutal act of breaking open the poor Santa. Mirroring Bella, I continued to emphasise contrast, setting the words 'cheery' and 'sweet' alongside the halting, fragmentary 'sad-', where I appear about to say 'sadness' but was broken off, like the Santa. I named what the contrast brought up for me: pathos and sadness, pinching my wrist to mirror the sharp pain that I sensed alongside these feelings. Bella responded:

Bella: [Ye::ah] (2.0) And I suppose when you, when you break it open, you sort of (1.0) realise that it's actually (.) I mean the, the chocolate is actually quite *thin* ((brings together thumb and forefinger of left hand)) and it's quite *fragile* (2.0)
Lynn: Yeah
Bella: So it seems like a *sturdy* object but it's actually quite *fragile*.
Lynn: Yeah. It doesn't (1.0) its outward appearance doesn't really (2.0) tell you that much about what it's really like ((nodding)).
Bella: Mm (3.0) I think that sums up me actually (.) at that sort of age.

The elongated, falling 'ye::ah' which prefaced Bella's talk here sounded resigned (and contrasted – again – with the rising intonation on the 'ye::ah' I had uttered a few moments before). She brought her thumb and forefinger together to show just how thin the chocolate was and named it 'fragile'. This is an important word whose significance Bella marked by using it twice with tonal emphasis, and by contrasting the word with its antonym 'sturdy'. That word 'sturdy' brought to my mind rosy-cheeked toddlers, robust yet vulnerable: a link with infancy that my reverie also hinted at, with its suggestion of the chocolate Santas hanging on my childhood Christmas tree. This link had a specific emotional effect on me in the interview, evoking a sense of protectiveness and the compassionate sadness that I named 'pathos'.

Bella and I were not only *feeling* emotion evoked by reverie and language at this point in the interview: we were also *using* the emotion to make sense of these feelings and of the experiences under discussion: we were sharing our alpha function in reverie, in Bion's (1962) terms. Another way of looking at the process, this time inspired by hermeneutics, the study of interpretation, is to regard it as the development of mutual or common understanding through dialogue, which the hermeneuticist Gadamer (1960/2004) calls a 'fusion of horizons' (p. 306) or perspectives, in which what is expressed 'is not only mine … but common' (p. 390). Bella and I were developing common meaning of this kind during our research conversation, as we worked together on the chocolate Santa metaphor to understand more fully her remembered feeling of hollowness. Taking up Bella's theme of the fragility and ambiguity in hollowness, I went on to remark that 'its outward appearance doesn't really tell you that much about what it's really like'. Bella paused for three seconds to take in (contain) this statement and the meaning it conveyed, and then linked it to herself as a teenager. She spoke in a wondering tone, as if this were a discovery and a surprise. It seemed the attention we were paying to our reveries was giving us a deeper, shared understanding – a fusion of horizons, as it were – of her past experience of contrast when, like a chocolate Santa, Bella's solid-looking exterior concealed inner fragility.

Implications for researchers

My reverie with Bella offered me a lived, visceral perspective on my subject of study: emotionally evocative language. In particular, it showed me ways that metaphor and analogy evoke emotion, like the analogy of the chocolate Santa that arose in Bella through a metaphorical mental image. For Ogden (2001, 1999a) reverie is an intrinsically metaphorical process, transforming unconscious experience into verbal symbols that show what that experience is *like*. Gendlin (1986), too, acknowledges the evocative power of metaphor, pointing to its sense-making function which involves past and present experiences interacting or *crossing* each other (just as my reverie included a crossing of Christmases past and present, and a crossing of Bella's and my own feelings too). Crossing paves the way for implicit understanding of a situation, and can offer deep, embodied insight (Gendlin, 2009), similar perhaps to the insight Bella and I gained into her teenage experience of hollowness through her use of metaphor.

The chocolate Santa reverie ensured that my understanding of Bella's metaphorical language was not only cognitive but also emotional. I *felt* the pain of pathos as I spoke and that pain was sharp and real *because* of reverie. Conjured by Bella's words, my reverie put me in a place that was guaranteed to evoke a kind of frenetic fullness in me, furnished as it was by the particular memories and emotions I have described above, and as a result the 'drop' into Bella's contrasting hollowness was all the more powerful. I do not suggest that these evocative effects were intentional, however; a case of the researcher's (or therapist's) mind cleverly fabricating a response to achieve certain research/therapeutic ends. Rather, like Ogden (1994), I believe reverie to be an intersubjective 'fact' (p. 61); a manifestation of how we are bound to interact with a specific other in a specific moment of time, given each person's unique ways of being and our histories up to that point. Attending to reverie can allow us to access those intersubjective facts *as they are unfolding*, which, I suggest, gives it powerful potential as a research tool, because it can sharpen our immediate awareness of transient phenomena that we might not otherwise notice, or that we might forget quickly. And when these phenomena are available to us, we can make sense of them in ways that deepen our understanding of the topic we are studying, as Bella and I did when we unpacked the implications of the chocolate Santa.

And yet, if we accept that reverie can help researchers access their unfolding responses to participants and the topic under investigation, as I believe this example shows, do not such responses belong solely to the researcher, rather than the participant? Could a focus on reverie, therefore, detract from research into others' experience, leading instead to solipsism? I asked myself this question frequently during this research, which related to participants' (not my own) experiences of emotionally evocative language, and I ask it too when I use reverie in my work with my own clients, who consult me to explore their experience and not to provide me with an opportunity to examine mine. Concerns of this kind cause some writers to advise caution in the use of reverie: Meissner (2000), for example, notes that 'the greater the focus of attention on the other, the less on the self, and *vice versa*' (p. 361) and counsels against overbalance in either direction. And Ogden (1999a) himself is clear that viewing reverie as an inherently intersubjective phenomenon does not mean that we are free to assume our every thought or feeling mirrors the other's experience, and still less that we are entitled to impose those assumptions on others. To the contrary, he points out that: 'the experience of reverie is rarely, if ever, "translatable" in a one-to-one fashion into an understanding of what is going on in the analytic relationship' (Ogden, 1999a, p. 160). Instead, he urges therapists to use reverie in a cautious, disciplined way that respects clients' otherness as well as recognising potential connections with them.

In my encounter with Bella I aimed to work in a similar way, giving her space to disagree with my comments and move in new directions if she wished. For example, when, in response to my question 'Is it anywhere in you?' Bella could not locate the feeling of hollowness in her body, I did not pursue the matter (which relates to my own interest in focusing on the bodily felt sense), but instead followed her into more intersubjective territory where the image of the chocolate Santa was located. Such tentativeness is essential if we are to work with reverie in research in a way that respects participants and their alterity, making it more likely that the understandings we reach are *inter-* rather than wholly *intra*subjective, while not dismissing the extraordinarily rich data-source afforded by reverie. Worked with in this manner, that source can provide an empathic way to share meanings, rather than impose our meaning on others, and can help us to achieve a real 'fusion of horizons' (Gadamer, 1960/2004, p. 306).

Conclusion

A major task in research about lived experience, as in therapy, is to understand others (and ourselves) as fully as we can. Buber (1965) claims that such understanding requires an act of intuitive imagination that has much in common with reverie. He calls this act 'imagining the real' (p. 80): 'Not a looking at the other, but a bold swinging – demanding the most intensive stirring of one's being – into the life of the other' (p. 81).

In this chapter I have considered the role that reverie can play in imaging/imagining the 'real' that exists in the liminal space between two people, but is otherwise invisible. In so doing, I have sought to extend the horizon of reverie from clinical practice to research, and then to consider how two people's horizons can fuse in deep, mutual understanding. I end by asking you, reader, to think about how you have used your own capacity for reverie and imagination as you have encountered my words, here …

> Ask yourself, now, what went on for you as you read about the chocolate Santa?
>
> Did you see it in your mind's eye or associate it with memories or places from your own life?
>
> What, if any, bodily felt sense (Gendlin, 2003) did it evoke in you?
>
> Can you use this embodied knowledge to develop your understanding of how you are in relation to reverie and liminal experiences in therapy and research?

I encourage you to welcome these inner goings-on and to wonder about them, because it is only by experiencing the ongoing reverie stream yourself first-hand and holding such experience in awareness long enough to examine and question it, that you can appreciate the specific forms it takes for you, and, consequently, its relevance to your own research and practice.

Acknowledgements: I thank 'Bella' for her generosity in participating in the research outlined in this chapter and agreeing to use of the extract from her interview.

Appendix: transcription symbols

(.)	Pause of less than 1 second
(1.0)	Minimum countable pause (1 second)
((sniff))	Non-speech sounds and body language
Lo::ng	Colons denote a drawn-out sound
word↑	Rising intonation
word↓	Falling intonation
italics	italics for emphasis
Over[lap]	Square brackets denote start and finish of overlapping talk

Source: Turnbull (2003)

Note

1 Findings from this work informed research methodology in a subsequent PhD investigation (McVey, 2017).

References

Bion, W.R. 1962. *Learning from experience*. London: Maresfield Library.

Bion, W.R. 1963. *Elements of psycho-analysis*. London: Maresfield Reprints.

Buber, M. 1965. *The knowledge of man*. New York: Harper Torchbooks.

Gadamer, H.G. 1960/2004. *Truth and method*. 2nd, revised ed. London: Continuum.

Gendlin, E.T. 1986. *Let your body interpret your dreams*. Wilmette, IL: Chiron Publications.

Gendlin, E.T. 1996. *Focusing-oriented psychotherapy: A manual of the experiential method*. New York: The Guilford Press.

Gendlin, E.T. 2003. *Focusing: How to gain direct access to your body's knowledge* (Revised ed.). London: Rider.

Gendlin, E.T. 2009. What first and third person processes really are. *Journal of Consciousness Studies*, 16(10–12), pp. 332–362.

Holmes, J. 2019. *A practical psychoanalytic guide to reflexive research: The reverie research method*. London: Routledge.

McVey, L. 2013. *Deep roots, fuzzy clues and new personal meaning: An interpretive phenomenological analysis of therapy clients' experiences of emotionally-evocative language*. Unpublished Master's dissertation. University of Leeds, Leeds, UK.

McVey, L. 2017. *'Pied beauty': Exploring psychological therapists' inner experiencing in reverie*. Unpublished PhD thesis. University of Leeds. Available at: http://etheses.whiterose.ac.uk/19588/

McVey, L. 2018. Sharing a living room: Empathy, reverie and connection. *Self and Society*, 46(2), pp. 51–57. Available at: http://eprints.whiterose.ac.uk/133019/

McVey, L., Lees, J. & Nolan, G. 2015. Practitioner-based research and qualitative interviewing: Using therapeutic skills to enrich research in counselling and psychotherapy. *Counselling and Psychotherapy Research*, 15(2), pp. 147–154. Available from: http://onlinelibrary.wiley.com/doi/10.1002/capr.12014/full

McVey, L., Lees, J. & Nolan, G. 2016. Reflective-verbal language and reverie in a qualitative interview. *Counselling and Psychotherapy Research*, 16(2), pp. 132–140. Available from: http://onlinelibrary.wiley.com/doi/10.1002/capr.12059/full

Meissner, W.W. 2000. On analytic listening. *Psychoanalytic Quarterly*, 69(2), pp. 317–367. Available from: http://dx.doi.org/10.1002/j.2167–4086.2000.tb00565.x

Nolan, G.J.C. 2008. *Mirrors and echoes: Meaning-moments in counselling supervision*. Unpublished Doctoral thesis, University of Manchester, UK.

Ogden, T.H. 1994. *Subjects of analysis*. London: Karnac Books.

Ogden, T.H. 1999a. *Reverie and interpretation: Sensing something human*. London: Karnac.

Ogden, T.H. 1999b. 'The music of what happens' in poetry and psychoanalysis. *International Journal of Psycho-Analysis*, 80, pp. 979–994.

Ogden, T.H. 2001. *Conversations at the frontier of dreaming*. London: Karnac.

Rogers, C.R. 1980. *A way of being*. Boston, MA: Houghton Mifflin.

St Pierre, E.A. 1997. Methodology in the fold and the irruption of transgressive data. *International Journal of Qualitative Studies in Education*, 10(2), pp. 175–189. Available from: http://dx.doi.org/10.1080/095183997237278

Turnbull, W. 2003. *Language in action: Psychological models of conversation*. Hove: Psychology Press.

11

MOMENTS OF DEEP ENCOUNTER IN LISTENING RELATIONSHIPS

Resisting limiting the interpretive frame to enhance beneficial encounter

James N. Tebbutt

Introduction

Moments of deep encounter can be understood to be beneficial and often profound experiences within listening relationships. These can occur when, with safety and trust established between the parties, the talker gains a new 'penny-dropping' insight into themselves or their concerns, accompanied also by a sense of something beyond or greater than the parties themselves (albeit that this 'sense of something beyond or greater' might be understood in a great variety of ways).

I began to identify such moments and their beneficial effect as the 'listener', or as the 'talker', in various counselling and pastoral relationships while undertaking training some twenty years ago. I undertook initial training to become a psychotherapist as well as training to become a Methodist minister, and occasionally experienced these moments of deep encounter in both counselling and ministerial contexts. (This was so notwithstanding that, when listening in 'secular' counselling contexts, I tried to maintain – so far as it is ever possible – a 'neutrality' of perspective, and my faith background was not disclosed to clients.) This involvement in both fields enabled me to bring wider insights and perspectives, and curiosity as to whether others also experienced such moments.

As I began to explore the literature of both fields, it became apparent that moments of deep encounter were not frequently or universally experienced or acknowledged, but instances nonetheless appeared to be spread across several therapeutic and pastoral approaches (I use 'therapeutic' to cover psychotherapy and counselling, and 'pastoral' to cover various approaches within pastoral care and counselling in largely Christian contexts). While generally lasting for only a short episode (although reflecting and working through it might take longer), such moments generally appeared to be beneficial, and indeed sometimes had profound and lasting effects. This then raised a question as to whether such moments might be encouraged or facilitated to increase their likelihood or frequency, thereby enhancing therapeutic and pastoral practice. Curiosity also grew as to why some approaches seemed to exhibit or acknowledge these moments more than others, including some (but not all) secular approaches, compared to many pastoral approaches. In addition, I began to note the diverse and potentially competing understandings and explanations of such moments that different approaches appeared to offer or imply.

My investigation became focused in my PhD research (Tebbutt, 2014). This explored questions about identifying, analysing, and classifying moments of deep encounter; about what might lead to or facilitate their occurrence; about how they might be understood or interpreted; and about whether and how competing accounts and interpretations might be related to each other.

Ultimately, my research invited the conclusion that an open-minded approach to such experiences and their possible interpretation might be therapeutically more beneficial than any tendency to apply a rigid interpretive or theoretical framework. In the context of this book, my subject therefore invites and affirms practitioners of various approaches to remain open and willing (if required) to extend their theoretical and practice horizons, so as to allow moments of deep encounter to occur and unfold, and for possible understandings to emerge, in ways that might be helpful for those to whom they are listening. It also invites an openness and dialogue between different potential understandings, in the moment itself or in its aftermath, and, more generally, between different interpretive frameworks.

In this chapter, I will describe and distinguish moments of deep encounter in more detail, before briefly summarising some of my research. I will then offer two key and related implications from the research findings, which invite, first, respect and dialogue between different interpretive frameworks and, second, open-minded attentiveness in the occurrence and unfolding of moments of deep encounter themselves.

Identifying and distinguishing moments of deep encounter

Unwittingly, I first offered a description of moments of deep encounter in a report of a long-term training placement when I was a student counsellor at Cruse Bereavement Care, Birmingham in 1999–2000 (and thus in a secular context with a primarily person-centred approach). I reported that the therapeutic encounters with various clients were central to my placement experience, including, at the deepest level, particular moments that appeared to focus or release the positive transforming effects that could occur when the therapeutic relationship and process were working well. These were:

> those occasions when the heart of the encounter was revealed. The client would be in touch with their feelings when, through their own process or because of my intervention, they went deeper another notch or two. There could then be the clearest sense of mutual connection, of being present to each other, whilst also being vividly present to the client's particular insight,

> memory, issue or emotion. In such indescribable but palpable moments of encounter, there was almost a mystical quality …
>
> *Tebbutt, 2000, pp. 37–38*

As I continued to notice and reflect upon such moments as a listener or talker in a variety of counselling and ministerial settings, I revisited this earlier description, now with greater attention and appreciation. The placement description, in effect, represented an original piece of data, albeit unwittingly authored by myself. As indicated, my growing intent was then to seek out other relevant data, i.e., other accounts and insights concerning similar moments.

Within the literature, it became apparent that various types of moments could be discerned, each one of course unique, but sometimes with similar elements or characteristics, enabling a degree of categorisation. In particular, iterative analysis of various moments confirmed that one, two or three aspects might be present, with 'moments of deep encounter' themselves seeming to possess all three. I set out the three aspects in Box 11.1, but, in doing so, I stress that I am not thereby implying (or limiting) each aspect to any particular understanding or interpretation. Indeed, in studying the different aspects, I endeavoured to remain open and attentive to the variety of meanings and understandings implied or given for them by the different participants involved in the various moments, or by the authors describing and discussing them.

To illustrate a moment of deep encounter with its three constituting aspects, I set out below an excerpt from Robert Hobson (1985), describing a session with a client.

> We sat in silence. It was a very different sort of silence from the tense closed-upness of the first few weeks. Neither of us seemed either to fight against,

BOX 11.1 CONSTITUENT ELEMENTS OR ASPECTS WITHIN A MOMENT OF DEEP ENCOUNTER

1. An '*intrapersonal*' or intra-psychic aspect within each of the parties (both parties will have their own inner processes, but the main focus will be on those occurring within the talker), and, for the talker (although sometimes also the listener), a new and sometimes profound insight;
2. an '*interpersonal*' or relational aspect that operates between the parties (including involving a level of safety and trust); and
3. a '*transpersonal*' aspect that conveys a sense of something beyond or greater than the parties, which one or both parties will experience or allude to as being an additional aspect of the experience.

> or to withdraw into it; we sat in it each alone and yet together. Eventually Sam spoke with a new seriousness and decisiveness and I sensed a note of confidence and trust in me, and in himself. 'I had a dream the other night,' he said. He had told me before about a few dreams, in a casual way, but now he spoke with a strange intensity, akin to awe. 'I was by a dark pool. It was filthy and there were all sorts of horrible monsters in it. I was scared but I dived in and at the bottom was a great big oyster and in it a terrific pearl. I got it and swam up again.' I felt myself caught up in mystery, in a sense of otherness. At the time, my few words seemed very lame, but I was right to reply in the present tense. 'That's good. Brave, too. You've got it, though, and pearls are pretty valuable.' We said nothing more about the dream, then, but this interview was followed by another important step. Sam began to express his feelings and thoughts, his hopes and fears, and I was able to use my book knowledge in formulating his problems.
>
> *Hobson, 1985, p. 5*

The passage illustrates the presence of each aspect: an intrapersonal (the client, Sam, relaying and reflecting on his internal process); an interpersonal (including the description of being 'alone and yet together'); and a transpersonal aspect (suggested by the references to 'awe', 'mystery' and 'sense of otherness'). (See Tebbutt, 2014, pp. 71–78, for a full analysis, including according to the thematic coding referred to below.)

Again, not all three aspects were present in every type of moment, so that the presence, absence, or combination of these different elements, suggested the classification set out in Figure 11.1, involving various subsets, and applying some descriptive terms that I devised or adopted.

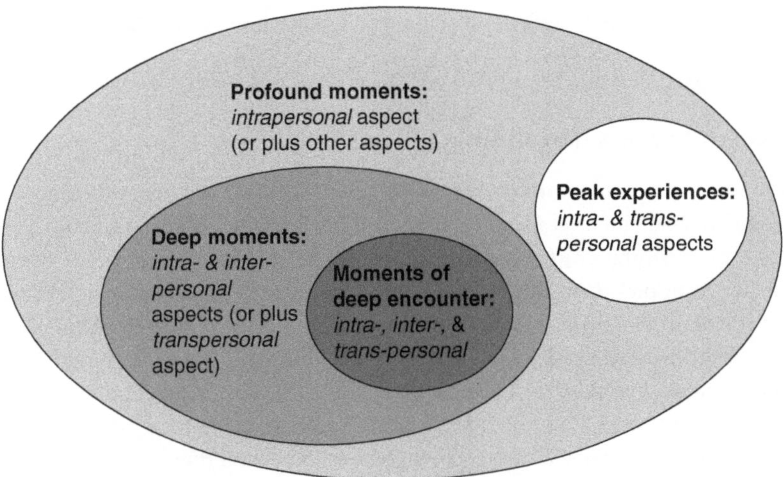

FIGURE 11.1 The permutations of different aspects involved in various experiences

While I focused on 'moments of deep encounter' with their three aspects, to a degree I also considered the wider group of 'deep moments', where sometimes there was no evident transpersonal aspect, or where, at other times, the possible presence of a 'transpersonal' aspect was unclear and could be argued either way (which is why I used the term 'deep moments' to cover two or three aspect possibilities, rather than only for two aspects). This larger group provided some confirmatory or distinguishing insights compared with the smaller group of moments of deep encounter.

Once more, the different aspects could be understood or emphasised in various ways; especially the 'transpersonal'. Thus, some understood the transpersonal aspect in spiritual terms (which additionally might include, or reject, the possibility of a 'divine', however understood); while others argued that the 'transpersonal' aspect could be explained in intra- or interpersonal terms alone. (See Tebbutt, 2014, pp. 27–31, for indicative references, and a discussion about using 'transpersonal' as a suitable or least-worst term for describing this aspect, including to allow for various interpretive possibilities).

Differences in understanding and emphasis, including regarding any transpersonal aspect, often reflected that different and sometimes competing theoretical perspectives were present in and underlying any consideration of deep moments. (For example, the passage cited from Hobson above naturally reflected some of the concerns and foci of his particular therapeutic approach: his 'Conversational Model', subsequently developed into the 'Interpersonal Psychodynamic' approach, with its relational and psychodynamic emphases.) Consequently, any consideration of these differences mean that moments of deep encounter can act as a lens to illuminate any underlying theoretical frameworks, and the related questions about how those frameworks and their different understandings of deep moments might, or might not, be brought into dialogue, or even related to each other. This suggested that the study of moments of deep encounter offered a wider relevance and interest beyond simply their beneficial effect, even if that alone was sufficient to justify their study.

Research process and findings

Some initial research identified various moments of deep encounter within some relevant fields of literature, and raised some pertinent questions (Tebbutt, 2008). From this, a natural course might have been to undertake face-to-face research with (for example) therapists and/or clients, in order to gain further insights and understanding. However, I judged that mapping and analysing the data already available in the various accounts and insights within the literature might, at that point, be more immediately effective at moving forward understanding. As far as I could discern, only Rowan (2005, pp. 162–173) had previously attempted any form of overall summary of this type of phenomenon, and then only in a relatively brief summary and without detailed analysis. Additionally, my decision, to assimilate and analyse the data and analyses already available, resonated with a subsequent call by McLeod (2011, pp. 286–287) for researchers within counselling and psychotherapy to undertake this type of study, rather than always seeking to generate new data. Accordingly, in my doctoral research I devised and undertook a *meta-study*.

Meta-studies are often quantitative types of research, but they can also take a qualitative form if they compare and analyse qualitative insights from other reported studies or accounts, as in my research. With my subject, while there were some relevant published analyses and studies, most of my data came from the largely uncollated and not yet analysed deep-moment accounts and insights that I found in a wide range of relevant literature. Drawing on the methodological insights of Paterson et al. (2001) and others, I then devised a meta-study in three stages. (See Tebbutt, 2014, pp. 34–58, for a detailed methodology, and navigation of the competing principles and objectives of various research paradigms, including valuing the concerns of constructivism-interpretivism, but also affirming the principles of critical realism.)

The first stage involved data identification and its *thematic analysis*, undertaken by discerning, developing and applying six clusters of interconnected thematic codes. These emerged from iterative analysis of potential data in a wide range of Psychodynamic, Humanistic, Eclectic or Integrative, Transpersonal, Spiritual, and Pastoral approaches (my initial research having suggested that these approaches might be the most data-rich for deep-moment indicators and insights). Stage two, a *meta-analysis*, involved comparing and contrasting the commonalities and differences revealed by the thematic findings in a critical dialogue, including to reveal the nature, limits and merits of different interpretive positions. The third stage, a *meta-synthesis*, mapped the meta-analytic findings for each thematic code into a provisional explanatory framework, including to explain and relate different understandings of moments of deep encounter, so as to provide a first extensive overview of the subject (Tebbutt, 2014).

In the broadest terms, findings for the six interconnected clusters of thematic codes revealed:

1. a significant number of *indicators* of moments of deep encounter, which if not large in overall numbers, appeared to be increasing in occurrence or reporting, with greater prevalence in some rather than other approaches;
2. the presence of inter-, intra- and transpersonal *aspects*, albeit with different understandings and emphases;
3. some identifiable causal or *facilitative factors* that appear to encourage the occurrence of deep moments;
4. the presence of some potentially pertinent psychological, professional/ethical, and/or transpersonal *boundary issues*;
5. the influence on the occurrence and/or interpretation of deep moments of the diverse *theoretical frameworks* and perspectives of different authors and approaches; and,
6. various *interpretations* of moments of deep encounter that coalesce into three competing but sometimes complementary groups.

I hope in later publications to present and discuss these thematic findings in more detail, together with those for the meta-analysis and meta-synthesis. However, for the purposes of this chapter, I want to consider further the issues of interpretation and facilitation (although, in doing so, I will allude also to some of the other interconnected findings), but again without here being able to offer a full presentation or discussion of, for example, the particular interpretations of the various authors studied.

In considering interpretation before facilitation, I am arguably taking these issues in the wrong order, but I do so in order to draw attention to, and to try to subvert, what I suggest is our innate tendency to apply or impose previous understandings to a repeat or new phenomenon, and thus to risk inhibiting, undermining, or misunderstanding a new unfolding experience. By first introducing the principal types of deep-moment interpretation revealed by the research, it may become more apparent how such interpretations might be introduced, not only to interpret deep moments after the event, but inadvertently or deliberately to influence or interfere with the occurrence and unfolding of such moments in the first place.

Issues of interpretation

Many different explanations of moments of deep encounter were offered or could be inferred from an approach's theoretical perspectives. However, while every author's interpretive position might include particular nuances or emphases, I found that broadly they could be grouped into three principal categories, involving Earlier Life, Relational, or Spiritual interpretations. Some authors then offer a combination of two or three of these understandings to allow multiple factors and aspects to be in view, or, on occasion, suggest a bespoke understanding of a particular moment according to whatever contextual issues or circumstances may have been in play in that particular moment. The distinct or combined interpretive positions could then be plotted as in Figure 11.2 (Tebbutt, 2014, p. 235, and see p. 261 for a mapping onto this of the different interpretations of various authors or approaches).

Those authors who, explicitly or implicitly, primarily promoted one type of understanding against others, whether Earlier Life, Relational, or Spiritual, were essentially offering interpretations that were competing with others, and often they did so by reflecting and drawing on their preferred underlying theoretical frames.

For example, given the Psychodynamic approach's emphasis that previous life experience affects the present, the Psychodynamic tradition naturally leant towards a range of possible Earlier Life explanations for moments of deep encounter (including explicitly or implicitly interpreting them as various projective/transferential, regressive, transitional, or intersubjective phenomena). Some within the Psychodynamic tradition might also allow for (present) relational factors and/or spiritual possibilities to play a part (see Tebbutt (2014, pp. 112–115, 118–123) for references, for example, to Bion and Jung). However, those who share Freud's (1913, 1927) interpretation, that the 'spiritual' and any reference to a 'divine' are signs of projection or regression, would be likely to dismiss any possibility of a Spiritual type

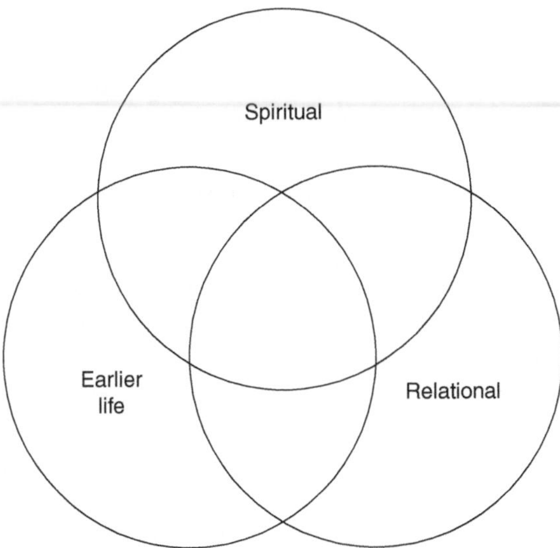

FIGURE 11.2 Overlapping categories of interpretation

interpretation of both the transpersonal aspect, and the moment of deep encounter as a whole. In contrast, other traditions and approaches might resist dismissing and instead readily look to the possibility of a Spiritual interpretation (for example, Lines 2006), West (2000); and see summary references for Spiritual interpretations in various traditions at Tebbutt (2014, pp. 191–192, 234 and 261)).

Even within the same tradition, competing interpretations can arise. For example, from the Person-centred approach within the Humanistic tradition, Dave Mearns, in Mearns and Thorne (2000), rejects spiritual possibilities in favour of existential and relational explanations, interpreting what others might identify as a transpersonal aspect in interpersonal terms, and offering a predominantly Relational interpretation of the 'moments of relational depth' that he describes (Mearns & Cooper, 2005; see Tebbutt (2014, p. 28) for precise references), and which I construe, given the indications of three aspects being present, as moments of deep encounter. In contrast from within the same approach, Brian Thorne offers a spiritual understanding of the transpersonal aspect of the 'magical', 'mystical' and 'intense and transformational', etc., moments that he describes (which again I construe as constituting moments of deep encounter), in Thorne's case applying a Christian understanding of the transpersonal, so that, overall, he offers a combination of a Spiritual and a Relational interpretation (Thorne, 1991/2000, 1998, 2002; Mearns & Thorne, 2000; see Tebbutt (2014, pp. 69–70) for precise references).

That there can be competing understandings from even within the same approach raises questions about which interpretations might be better or worse, or more or less 'correct', and about how best to assess and choose between different possible explanations. This may be less of a challenge for those who, through choice or instinct, prefer an eclectic or integrative approach. However, for those who prefer a single or predominant approach, inevitably they will be guided, or risk sometimes being limited, in their interpretive choices by the precepts and horizons of their preferred tradition. At worst, tribal loyalty to favoured theoretical frameworks and the attendant promotion of particular versions of 'truth', may restrict openness to the possible meaning (or even occurrence) of individual deep moments, and also risk missing the potential explanatory insights that other theoretical perspectives may have to offer for understanding an individual moment. Obviously, I am expressing this in fairly strong terms to make a point, but a logical outworking from the reality of competing interpretations (and their underlying theories) might sometimes lead to a limiting or inaccurate interpretation of particular moments (or even to their occurring, which I discuss later in connection with the issue of facilitation).

While the issue of weighing, championing, or reconciling different competing theoretical and practical approaches goes much wider than the issue of deep-moment interpretation, this discussion of deep-moment interpretation illustrates and illuminates a general conundrum for theory and practice in the fields of psychotherapy and counselling, and of pastoral care and counselling, as a whole, about how to weigh and relate competing theoretical voices. This raises various epistemological and hermeneutical issues (as acknowledged in my methodology: Tebbutt, 201, pp. 34–58), but my objective here is not to engage with them, but to draw attention to the practical implication that my research invited.

Given the rich insights that the research revealed as residing in the diverse approaches studied, raising a wide number of possible 'truths' rather than outrightly condemning the attitudes of some or exclusively supporting the claims of other approaches, my research invited and endorsed the implication that it is better to be open rather than closed to different interpretative possibilities; in other words, to treat each moment on its merits, investigating and considering the different factors that might on each occasion be in play, to help the understanding of the meaning of that particular moment. This encouraging of open theoretical horizons is not to suggest that all positions or interpretations might be equally valid or cogent at all times: I am not arguing for a constant equalising or relativising of every theoretical position (which would also dilute and potentially undermine every position at all times); rather, my research endorsed the virtue of being willing with every deep moment to keep in view, consider and choose from the various interpretive possibilities that might be available, in order to determine each time what might be the most applicable, and therefore the most helpful, understanding for that particular moment. In turn, this might help to release the full therapeutic and healing potential of each moment of deep encounter.

The research, therefore, invited a keeping open, and if necessary a willingness to extend, one's existing theoretical and interpretive horizons, in order not to be limited or bound to particular pre-conceived interpretations, but rather to allow for whatever possibilities might emerge or apply, through careful attention to all pertinent interpretive possibilities. In open-mindedly paying attention to the particular features of any deep moment, this might sometimes mean, for example, allowing for transpersonal or even spiritual possibilities, even when they might not routinely be encountered or countenanced. Conversely, it might sometimes mean discerning and taking into account possible issues of projection or regression, either alongside, or instead of, any spiritual possibilities that might be present, depending again on the particular features present in each moment of deep encounter. Overall, a more perceptive, accurate and collaborative (between the parties to the encounter, and more widely with different voices in the relevant fields) discernment of a deep moment's meaning may result, according, once more, to the particular features present.

As will be apparent, this invitation to keep open and, if necessary, extend theoretical horizons leads on from the 'micro' level (i.e. a consideration of the interpretive possibilities for a particular deep moment) to the 'macro' level (i.e. a consideration of the cogency and interrelation of the different interpretive principles and theories offered by different authors and approaches), and back again, with each level potentially informing the other about the interpretive insights being considered. Put another way, moments of deep encounter can again function as a lens to illuminate the wider issue of how different approaches and competing paradigms might relate to one another, so that the invitation to open-mindedness extends into a wider invitation for competing approaches and different theoretical frameworks to remain in dialogue, respectfully listening to and learning from each other's particular insights and concerns, and extending if necessary their own theoretical horizons. This would, of course, mirror something of the therapeutic or pastoral process itself, and in turn would feed back into practice.

At other times, a discussion at the 'macro' level might lead into consideration of the virtues, challenges, possibilities and impossibilities of reconciling different frameworks; and thus into a discussion of eclectic, integrative and pluralistic issues in psychotherapy and counselling (Norcross & Grencavage, 1990; Hollanders, 2000; Clarkson, 2000; Cooper & McLeod, 2007); a discussion of correlative and other dialogical methods of theological reflection in practical theology and pastoral care (e.g. Graham et al., 2005, pp. 154–161; Swinton & Mowat, 2006, pp. 77–82); or a consideration, for example, of the pertinence of hermeneutics (e.g. Messer et al. (1988), Polkinghorne (2000), or Gadamer (2004), whose concept of a 'fusion of horizons' resonates with the invitation to keep open and extend theoretical and interpretative horizons when considering moments of deep encounter).

However, in this chapter, I want to return to the 'micro' of individual encounters, because I want to argue that embodying an attentive open-mindedness is of benefit not only when considering the meaning and interpretation of particular moments of deep encounter, but it can also help facilitate their occurrence in the first place.

Issues of facilitation

My research suggested that few authors consider that moments of deep encounter can be engineered or caused to happen, but that many authors claim or imply that such moments can be facilitated. My research then identified and collated the various insights (whether expressed or implied) as to which attitudes and qualities might allow or even make moments of deep encounter more likely to occur. These involved first some general qualities and emphases, and second some specific factors (see Tebbutt (2014, pp. 211–223, 256–259), including for relevant authors).

Unsurprisingly, it appeared that the general *relational qualities* that are commonly upheld as being necessary for cultivating a supportive, listening environment (including respectful, trustworthy listening, etc.) were, in effect, a pre-condition for moments of deep encounter to occur. In connection with these, a willingness to encourage rather than discourage the *present interpersonal*, and to allow for rather than discourage any *transpersonal* elements or aspects, was important; as also was a willingness to respect professional/ethical, personal/psychological and transpersonal *boundaries* (but sometimes with their temporary lowering: see later).

In addition to the above general qualities and emphases, *seven specific factors* could be identified as occurring, individually or in combinations, across a range of approaches, to suggest that these were common factors that might facilitate moments of deep encounter. Three were more generic relational attitudes or qualities that were frequently cited (and described in terms that often resonated with characteristics of the Person-centred approach, but the concepts and even terms involved were replicated in many other approaches). These were:

1 *accepting* and *recognising* the individual;
2 a profound *empathic connectedness*, and being 'in tune' with the individual; and
3 a quality of *presence*, being a term and concept that appeared to have a wide currency, albeit with different nuances for different authors.

Two additional factors were cited that involved staying with difficult feelings or material, and then risking going an extra step in order to go further into the feelings, material or the listening relationship, and thus sometimes into the unknown, being:

4 *risking staying with* and *going deeper*; and
5 *waiting* in the not-knowing, silence, and/or aloneness.

Finally, two specific factors were cited by authors with particular theoretical frameworks, although these factors were still relatively common and referred to by authors practising in a surprisingly wide range of approaches (for factor (6), Psychodynamic, Humanistic, and Eclectic/Integrative approaches; and, for factor (7), the same range, plus various approaches that could be described as having a Spiritual or Pastoral framework):

6 a *mothering, holding environment*, including sometimes the facilitating of regression;
7 a maintaining or even cultivating of *spiritual* awareness, and, in some cases also, of a spiritual discipline.

A necessary emphasis on the present interpersonal (supported by some of the specific relational factors also identified), and a willingness not to discourage (rather than necessarily to encourage) transpersonal possibilities, probably helps to explain the patterns of occurrence revealed for moments of deep encounter across various approaches (summarised in more detail in Tebbutt (2014, pp. 201–211), in order to illustrate the relevance of the principles involved).

Most indicators were identified in the Humanistic approaches or in various Eclectic and Integrative approaches, perhaps unsurprisingly given their usual emphasis on the listening relationship and the present interpersonal, and a willingness (at least in some cases) not to discourage transpersonal possibilities. Where there was antipathy to transpersonal possibilities, moments of deep encounter were less evident (for example, the earlier Carl Rogers preferred humanistic to spiritual understandings, and his earlier reporting of deep moments involved intra- and inter- but not transpersonal aspects, so as to constitute 'deep moments' rather than 'moments of deep encounter' (Tebbutt, 2014, pp. 24–25). However, when authors appear more open to transpersonal possibilities, moments of deep encounter exhibiting all three aspects become more evident (see Rogers' later more spiritually sympathetic account of 'presence', which I argue constituted a 'moment of deep encounter' (Rogers, 1990, pp. 137–138; Tebbutt, 2014, p. 25).

In contrast, fewer moments of deep encounter were reported in the Psychodynamic approaches, perhaps unsurprisingly given that tradition's historic emphasis on the past interpersonal (including its focus on transference), rather than on the present interpersonal (albeit the shift by many towards more relational approaches has led to a greater incidence of reported deep moments within the Psychodynamic tradition). Additionally, the Freudian reductionist approach to transpersonal issues may have meant not only interpreting any transpersonal aspect in earlier life terms, but perhaps also discouragement of its emergence (reflecting perhaps the risk that pre-understanding and prior interpretation may prevent new experience and understanding emerging; although this may apply in similar or different ways in every approach).

Similarly, the Transpersonal and Pastoral approaches' common emphasis on intrapersonal and transpersonal, rather than on interpersonal aspects, may explain why, somewhat surprising as it may at first appear, these approaches also exhibit relatively few indicators of moments of deep encounter. In contrast, the generally greater emphasis on the present interpersonal within what I have described as 'Spiritual' approaches, probably explains the greater incidence of moments of deep encounter reported amonst them (see Lines (2006), West (2000, 2003, 2004, 2011) and Tebbutt (2014, pp. 186–192) for precise references and further examples). In short, promotion of the transpersonal alone does not lead to more moments of deep encounter; rather, an emphasis on the present interpersonal is required, plus a willingness (at the least) not to discourage any transpersonal aspects.

Beyond these general emphases that also help to explain the patterns of occurrence, the cultivating and embodying of the specific factors referred to above may then help to explain when moments of deep encounter do occur, and, if applied, may potentially help to facilitate their occurrence in future. Again, not all seven factors were present on every occasion, but alone or in combinations they featured sufficiently regularly to be identified as potentially significant factors.

Factors (1) to (3): *acceptance*, *deep empathy*, *presence*; are more generic and not, I suggest, especially contentious. They are distinct factors, but since they are indicated across several approaches, they may potentially be attractive to a wide range of practitioners, who may therefore be willing to deploy them in order to help facilitate or cultivate moments of deep encounter. In contrast, notwithstanding some incidences across various approaches, factors (6) and (7), involving fostering a *holding environment* (and sometimes encouraging regression), and maintaining *spiritual awareness* (and even discipline), may be more – or less – attractive, and more or less willingly promoted as a means of facilitating moments of deep encounter, according, inevitably, to the preferred frameworks and approaches of individual practitioners.

Here, I want to highlight factors (4) and (5): *risking staying with* and *going deeper*, and *waiting* in the not-knowing, silence, and/or aloneness. These may sometimes be less familiar or less acknowledged features of a listening process, but they especially illustrate the wider point I am making: that if practitioners wish to allow for or even to facilitate the possibility of deep moments occurring, they need to be open to the unfolding of moments of deep encounter, and accordingly they need to avoid pre-judging or limiting the nature, meaning or possible interpretation of the experience, before and during its occurrence, as much as, as was emphasised earlier, afterwards.

My earlier excerpt from Hobson (1985) illustrates the two factors being highlighted, with Sam first staying with his difficult material, and then risking interpersonal disclosure, but only after both parties had neither fought nor withdrawn into the silence, while 'alone and yet together'. Thorne similarly illustrates both a risking of trust (e.g. Thorne, 1991/2000, p. 81), and the waiting sometimes required, and in particular that:

> Often such magic moments seem to have resulted from the acceptance of powerlessness, which is not a sign of resignation but of a positive stance that unites counsellor and client and leads to a waiting without hope but also without despair.
>
> *Thorne, 1998, p. 46*

This risking of staying with and going deeper sometimes appears also to involve a temporary lowering of boundaries (albeit generally in a balanced and appropriate way), either of professional/ethical boundaries (involving adjustments to the usual therapeutic frame), personal/psychological boundaries (involving an experience of close connection between the parties, which sometimes goes so far as to be described as 'merging'), and/or of what might be described as transpersonal boundaries (leading to 'spiritual' experience) (see the summary at Tebbutt (2014, pp. 214–223)).

This risking of depth and sometimes lowered boundaries, and the waiting in a state of silent, powerless, not-knowing, can be alien and uncomfortable for both parties. For the listening practitioner, it may necessitate a suspending, bracketing, or letting go of pre-existing ideas and understandings, including regarding the transpersonal (whether negatively, or positively, understood) (see Tebbutt (2014, pp. 41–44) for some of the principles and challenges involved). Again, it will mean not pre-judging or limiting the possible aspects and meaning of a deep moment as it unfolds. It will mean heeding Mearns and Cooper's (2005, pp. 114–118) call for a letting go of aims, anticipations and techniques; and Bion's advocacy (using Keats' poetic phrase) of a 'negative capability', without 'memory or desire' (Bion, 1970; Sullivan, 2010, pp. 214–218).

Yet if, along with embodying the other facilitative emphases and factors, depth can be risked, and the sometimes silent, unknowing waiting endured, a moment of deep encounter may be allowed or encouraged to occur. It is worth emphasising again, such moments can bring a healing, 'liminal' experience, of encountering and going deeper into an appreciation and understanding of oneself, the other person, and the 'Other' (the 'Other' in terms of whatever may be conceived or existing beyond or greater than the two parties themselves, whether understood in interpersonal, transpersonal, and/or spiritual terms). This can deepen each party's experience of being and extend their horizons of understanding.

Thus, whereas previously I cautioned against privileging or excluding certain interpretations following a moment of deep encounter without first open-mindedly attending to its particular features, here I am emphasising the same principle, but invoking it also for before and during a moment's occurrence. Hence, in its facilitation and unfolding, the 'macro' issue of competing theoretical frameworks must not prevent or inhibit the moment's course or even occurrence, thus enabling each moment to be freely experienced and reflected upon, and for its healing potential to be released; and maybe occasionally also to inform thinking at a macro level.

Conclusion

I have sought to explain how moments of deep encounter can represent a beneficial focusing of therapeutic or pastoral qualities, which potentially can enable both parties to grow in understanding and being. In referring to my research, I have distinguished moments of deep encounter by their three aspects; summarised why and how I undertook my research; and indicated the type of findings produced. In this chapter I have focused first on issues of interpretation, introducing Earlier Life, Relational and/or Spiritual understandings and referring to their underlying frameworks; and second, on issues of facilitation, identifying emphases, qualities and factors that also help to explain the occurrence patterns of moments of deep encounter.

With both interpretation and facilitation, I have invited an open-minded attentiveness. With facilitation, this extends to inviting practitioners to risk waiting, holding their nerve, and resisting introducing a particular understanding, so as to allow moments of deep encounter to emerge and proceed unfettered. Afterwards, this creative holding of the tension needs to continue, so as not hastily or prejudicially to collapse the tension by foreclosing on any preferred understandings, but rather to attend open-mindedly to the particular features of each moment, so as to reflect, identify and allow appropriate meaning to emerge, and thus to help release the beneficial and healing effects of both the experience and the understanding.

The micro can inform the macro and vice versa, for I have suggested that moments of deep encounter offer a lens for illuminating wider issues of theory and practice, including by bringing the insights of competing interpretations and approaches into a creative dialogue, in which maintaining and not collapsing the inherent tensions may again be beneficial. If so, just as moments of deep encounter can extend their participants' horizons of being and understanding, a wider open-minded and attentive consideration of moments of deep encounter may, in turn, help to extend some wider horizons of understanding regarding theory and practice.

References

Bion, W.R. (1970) *Attention and Interpretation: A Scientific Approach to Insight in Psycho-analysis and Groups*. London: Tavistock.

Clarkson, P. (2000) 'Eclectic, Integrative and Integrating Psychotherapy or Beyond Schoolism'. In: Palmer, S. & Woolfe, R. (eds) *Integrative and Eclectic Counselling and Psychotherapy*. London/Thousand Oaks/New Delhi/Singapore: Sage (pp. 305–314).

Cooper, M. & McLeod, J. (2007) 'A pluralistic framework for counselling and psychotherapy: Implications for research'. *Counselling and Psychotherapy Research*, 7(3), pp. 135–143.

Freud, S. (1913) 'Totem and Taboo'. In: Dickson, A. (ed.) *The Origins of Religion: The Penguin Freud Library Volume 13* (1985/1990). London: Penguin (pp. 43–224).

Freud, S. (1927) 'The Future of an Illusion'. In: Dickson, A. (ed.) *Civilization, Society and Religion: The Penguin Freud Library Volume 12* (1985/1991). London: Penguin (pp. 179–242).

Gadamer, H.-G. (2004) *Truth and Method*. 2nd revised edn. New York/London: Continuum.

Graham, E., Walton, H. & Ward, F. (2005) *Theological Reflection: Methods*. London: SCM.

Hobson, R.F. (1985) *Forms of Feeling: The Heart of Psychotherapy*. London: Tavistock.

Hollanders, H. (2000) 'Eclecticism/Integration: Some Key Issues and Research'. In: Palmer, S. & Woolfe, R. (eds) *Integrative and Eclectic Counselling and Psychotherapy*. London/Thousand Oaks/New Delhi/Singapore: Sage (pp. 31–55).

Lines, D. (2006) *Spirituality in Counselling and Psychotherapy*. London/Thousand Oaks/New Delhi: Sage.

McLeod, J. (2011) *Qualitative Research in Counselling and Psychotherapy*. 2nd edn. London/Thousand Oaks/New Delhi/Singapore: Sage.

Mearns, D. & Cooper, M. (2005) *Working at Relational Depth in Counselling and Psychotherapy*. London/Thousand Oaks/New Delhi: Sage.

Mearns, D. & Thorne, B. (2000) *Person-Centred Therapy Today: New Frontiers in Theory and Practice*. London/Thousand Oaks/New Delhi: Sage.

Messer, S.B., Sass, L.A., & Woolfolk, R.L. (eds) (1988) *Hermeneutics and Psychological Theory: Interpretive Perspectives on Personality, Psychotherapy, and Psychology*. New Brunswick/London: Rutgers University Press.

Norcross, J.C. & Grencavage, L.M. (1990) 'Eclecticism and Integration in Counselling and Psychotherapy: Major Themes and Obstacles'. In: Dryden, W. & Norcross, J.C. (eds) *Eclecticism and Integration in Counselling and Psychotherapy*. Loughton: Gale Centre Publications (pp. 1–33).

Paterson, B.L., Thorne, S.E., Canam, C., & Jillings, C. (2001) *Meta-Study of Qualitative Health Research: A Practical Guide to Meta-Analysis and Meta-Synthesis*. Thousand Oaks/London/New Delhi: Sage.

Polkinghorne, D.E. (2000) 'Psychological inquiry and the pragmatic and hermeneutic traditions.' *Theory & Psychology*, 10(4), pp. 453–479.

Rogers, C.R. (1990) 'A Client-centred/Person-centred Approach to Therapy'. In: Kirschenbaum, H. & Henderson, V.L. (eds) *The Carl Rogers Reader*. London: Constable (pp. 135–152).

Rowan, J. (2005) *The Transpersonal: Spirituality in Psychotherapy and Counselling*. 2nd ed. London/New York: Routledge.

Sullivan, B.S. (2010) *The Mystery of Analytical Work: Weavings from Jung and Bion*. Hove/New York: Routledge.

Swinton, J. & Mowat, H. (2006) *Practical Theology and Qualitative Research*. London: SCM.

Tebbutt, J.N. (2000) *Placement Report of a placement at Cruse Bereavement Care, Birmingham on 22 days between October 1999 and March 2000*. Report submitted to The University of Birmingham as part of an M.Phil. (B) in Contextual Theology.

Tebbutt, J.N. (2008) *A Preliminary Study of Moments of Deep Encounter in Therapeutic Relationships*. M.Phil. thesis, Department of Theology, School of Historical Studies, The University of Birmingham.

Tebbutt, J.N. (2014) *A Comparative and Theoretical Study of Moments of Deep Encounter in Therapeutic and Pastoral Relationships*. Ph.D. thesis, School of Environment, Education, and Development, The University of Manchester, accessible at: www.escholar.manchester.ac.uk/uk-ac-man-scw:240817.

Thorne, B. (1991/2000) *Person-Centred Counselling: Therapeutic & Spiritual Dimensions*. London: Whurr Publishers.

Thorne, B. (1998) *Person-Centred Counselling and Christian Spirituality: The Secular and the Holy*. London: Whurr Publishers.

Thorne, B. (2002) *The Mystical Power of Person-Centred Therapy: Hope Beyond Despair*. London/Philadelphia: Whurr Publishers.

West, W. (2000) *Psychotherapy and Spirituality: Crossing the Line between Therapy and Religion*. London/Thousand Oaks/New Delhi: Sage.

West, W. (2003) 'Humanistic Integrative Spiritual Psychotherapy with a Sufi Convert'. In Richards, P.S. & Bergin, A.E. (eds) *Casebook for a Spiritual Strategy in Counselling and Psychotherapy*. Washington, DC: American Psychological Association (pp. 201–212).

West, W. (2004) *Spiritual Issues in Therapy: Relating Experience to Practice*. Basingstoke/New York: Palgrave MacMillan.

West, W. (2011) 'Introduction', 'Spirituality and Therapy: The Tensions and Possibilities', 'When Counselling becomes Healing', 'Research in Spirituality and Healing', and 'Practice around Therapy, Spirituality and Healing'. In West, W. (ed.) *Exploring Therapy, Spirituality and Healing*. Basingstoke/New York: Palgrave Macmillan (pp. 1–10, pp. 13–27, pp. 131–141, pp. 189–202, & pp. 214–223).

PART IV
Clinical practice

12

THERE IS NO HORIZON, THIS SIDE OR THAT SIDE, OF OUR OWN SHADOW

Risking the relational (l)edge in clinical supervision

Greg Nolan

Introduction

This chapter considers Carl Jung's ideas, originating from *Liber Novus: The Red Book*, his notions of the relational 'third' and 'fourth' (Jung, 1952/70), his search for personal and spiritual meaning (Jung, 2009, 1952/54 & 1956/58), and how this thinking propelled him toward investigating the nature of phenomenological meaning and human existence. Jung showed the mind's capacity for function at its broadest reaches when making some meaningful sense at the edges of perception, of how consciousness links with unconscious thought at the roots of awareness, its outer fringes and beyond. How these phenomena may emerge is explored with a case example of an encounter in clinical supervision. Potential for love of an other (or others) and its polar equivalent for destructive hate are discussed, particularly where existential and spiritual angst may pivot on 'the hinge of our own shadow' (Ulanov, 2007b, p. 595). These ideas are shown as illustration of risk and opportunity when indwelling on this (l)edge with the other; how relational intimacy and insight, particularly with our own shadow, enables a firmer, more secure, base when straddling our liminal horizons; these extremes sensed as transcending the everyday toward an 'infinity' (Levinas, 1961/69) of positive and/or negative potential.

Origins and ideas

Liber Novus: The Red Book (Jung, 2009), as illustrated synthesis of Jung's Black Book journals, contains his wonderings while in a transformational struggle with nightmare dreams, sense of self, identity, personal belief and professional meanings when in the middle stage of life. Begun following his break with Sigmund Freud in 1912–13, which Jung saw as being inevitable, following publication of *Transformations and Symbols of the Libido* (Jung, 1912),[1] which text separated his ideas from those of his father-figure and mentor: 'I knew in advance that it would cost me my friendship with Freud' (Jung, 1961/63, p. 191). Their personal and professional links had been increasingly faltering, evidenced in their exchange of letters during 1912–13 (Freud & Jung, 1974).

Significantly for Jung, he had felt that the church rituals performed by his father as Presbyterian minister 'seemed automatic and devoid of any authentic religious experience' (Boechat, 2017, p. 13); he had also, at school, encountered the fundamentalist Catholicism of Jesuit teachers. Together, these challenged Jung's faith in organised religion and led to the search for meanings in his dreams (see Jung, 1961/63, pp. 26 and 50), expressed visually through his paintings in *The Red Book*, illustrating his journeying to find personal spiritual meaning. Having rejected Christian certainties, Jung needed to find a replacement that was his own: 'these images portray his need to seek personal, original values so that he could express the transcendental' (Boechat, 2017, p. 15).

Paul Bishop (2014) discusses the links with German classicism in *The Red Book*, of which Jung had a large library dating from medieval times; his classical education gave him access to original Greek and Latin texts, a curiosity in archaeology and an awareness of recent discoveries of ancient civilisations. Sonu Shamdasani's (2012) illustrated biography celebrates Jung's love of books and thirst for knowledge; it encounters Jung's collection of 16th-century handwritten illuminated manuscripts, the beauty and hidden wisdom in the texts and later iconic images, which together foreshadowed the distillation of thoughts and ideas from his formative Black Book diaries, and gathered into *The Red Book*. Of significant influence were the works of Friedrich Nietzsche and Johann Wolfgang von Goethe. Drawing comparisons with Goethe as a polymath, Paul Bishop (2014) notes that,

> Jung, the scientist, the psychologist, the phenomenologist ... turns to painting, to architecture, and sculpture ... to poetry, and to the visual and literary exercise of *The Red Book*, in order to carry out his investigations into the depths of the psyche and into the inner sources of the self.
>
> *Bishop, 2014, p. 15*

Its collation in the early 20th century emerged at a time of social and economic disturbance and of a battle for political power that, in its seeking, fed national populations with propagandised perceptions of challenge and threat from the different 'other' in justifying the waging of war. A milieu/*Zeitgeist* of ideas posed alternatives to those of the established order, offering philosophical underpinning to new political ideologies. Europe and its colonies, led by those promoting and defending their privileged power, floundered in the face of these changes, whole populations falling into conflict. Similar social, political and economic challenges of recent decades, exacerbated by war, associated population displacement and an increased nationalist focus in domestic and global politics, present evident parallels in a polarisation of political ideologies and belief systems. These together generate associated anxieties toward an uncertain future continually fed by media hype, hysteria and the manipulation of news. This is a necessary perspective for practitioners to be mindful of in alerting clients to their wider context, and away from binary oppositions that can both corrupt and distort, where 'truth' is an ungraspable fog.

These parallel contexts reflect certain features of Nietzsche's (1969, 1974) *eternal return*, or *the eternal recurrence of the same* (see also Gadamer, 1993/96; Heidegger, 1961/84). A prescient idea, given that we are currently within what seems a cyclical re-run of history, with populist movements driving 'others-who-are-not-me' posturing, feeding enactments serving to undermine and disempower (or ultimately destroy) the 'other'. Psychiatrist Eva Cybulska (2013) sees the *eternal return* as a Jungian mandala, representing 'the self-healing tendency of the mind to rescue itself from a state of overwhelming dread and disintegration' (p. 7). In offering a route beyond this cycle, Nietzsche emphasised the source of one's potential for empowerment in reaching for their *Übermensch*, the 'overman' within us that offers some element of control over life events. The person might thereby gain self-judgement and insights, avoiding being subject to others' propaganda or rhetoric, be it political and/or faith-bound. In an unfortunate perversion of its intention, the idea of the *Übermensch* was later adopted and misused in Nazi propaganda as a means to justify the idea of a superior race. Cybulska, (2012) clarifies that,

> [t]he *Übermensch* is not a Nazi. Nietzsche's anti-semitic sister Elisabeth invited Hitler to her brother's shrine in Weimar in 1934 and essentially made an offering of his philosophy. … (Hitler) adopted the *Übermensch* as a symbol of a master-race.
>
> *Cybulska, 2012, p. 10*

Developing reflection on *the eternal return*, Kathleen O'Dwyer (2011, p. 255) defines a 'more concrete form', quoting from Nietzsche's *Thus Spoke Zarathustra*, 'Did you ever say Yes, to one joy? … then you said Yes to all woe as well. All things are chained and entwined together, all things are in love' (Nietzsche, 1969, pp. 331–332). In embracing a re-run of one's life, O'Dwyer sees that this affirmation challenges the individual's capacity to see the interconnectedness of *all* our actions and experiences; who and what one is at any moment is influenced and created by all of one's past. To live life in such a way to want it over again helps us select what is important and significant in life. But O'Dwyer argues that 'eternal recurrence' fails to provide a definitive answer in the measuring of our lives, questioning Nietzsche's call for 'acceptance of all the experiences', including involuntary ones, particularly when instances are

> outside of one's control or volition, it is difficult to reconcile acceptance and understanding with the reality of loss, and injury that may be unwittingly visited on the individual. It may be rationally argued that acceptance, of self and of reality, is the key to happiness and integrity; however, we are also

> emotional beings, and sometimes our emotional response is in conflict with such rationalism.
>
> *O'Dwyer, 2011, p. 257*

She emphasises that our emotions, as well as rational thought, are equally valid sources in assessing 'personal truth and knowledge' in our lives, that we are, or could be, our own life-authors, and that moments experienced as an interconnected process of emotional significance can be 'glimpses of joy and beauty' that impact on all of life. The light and shade being necessary balances when, as author, taking ownership of the whole and thereby an autonomy that allows self-empowerment. These elements of Nietzsche's *eternal return* and the 'overman' inspired Jung's formulation of the concept of 'individuation', a transformational process toward owning self-responsibility for the second half of life.

Jung also saw that 'scholarliness alone is not enough; there is a knowledge of the heart that gives deeper insight' (Jung, 2009, p. 233). Jung explored his troubled psyche through dream images and symbols in a process that he would later call 'active imagination'. Through his Soul, his feminine psyche or 'anima' (Jung, 1961/63, pp. 210–211), he engages with archetypal figures from myth and legend and those from later religions and faiths in 'a constant process of confrontation, the ethical position of the conscious ego that subsequently takes a stand when faced with the content of the unconscious, which is personified by the various characters in the book' (Boechat, 2017, p. 19).

In *The Red Book*, Jung engages centrally through a wise 'guru' figure Philemon, who psychologically 'represented superior insight' (Jung, 1961/63, p. 208), and another archetypal figure, Abraxas, 'the God … [who] is the uniting of the Christian God with Satan' (Jung, 2009, p. 370, Appendix C). Abraxas is paradoxical in that he 'produces truth and lying, good and evil, light and darkness, in the same word and in the same act' (Jung, 2009, *Scrutinies* p. 350, cited in Maillard, 2014, p. 89); he represents the broad span of good and evil in human behaviour, being 'a renovating deity different to the Judaeo-Christian … in the form of the Gnostic God Abraxas' (Boechat, 2017, p. 15).

In *The Red Book*, Jung is 'turning theory back into a language of evocation' (Shamdasani, 2011, my verbatim notes). Through words and images Jung (2009) illustrates his journey toward self-awareness, plumbing his psychical archaeology, his phylogeny, articulated in pre-verbal symbol and archetype, imaged in the first instance as the thought-origin, then in language that speaks as a search for soul in a libidinous drive to transcend beyond the everyday and construct a sense of self-in-the-universe. It is the source from which he both derived and developed his subsequent work and publications of ideas on individuation, the collective unconscious and synchronicity.

Jung (1952/54, 1956/58), in *Answer to Job*, furthers the elements explored in the Black Book journals. He presents his questioning thoughts on the nature of God's omnipotence as presented in the Old and New Testaments. He discusses the likely impact of religious belief on the emerging human psyche, particularly the oppositions between the Early Judaeo-Christian position that viewed God as monotheistic, and the later Church of the Middle ages that took a dualistic position. In his *CW11* Prefatory Note to 'Answer to Job', Jung (1956/58) observes:

> Clement of Rome taught that God rules the world with a right and a left hand, the right being Christ, the left being Satan. Clement's view is clearly *monotheistic*, as it unites the opposites in one God ... Later Christianity, however, is dualistic, inasmuch as it separates off one half of the opposites, personified in Satan ... If Christianity claims to be a monotheism, it becomes unavoidable to assume the opposites as being contained within God.
>
> *Jung, 1956/58, pp. 357–358*

In Jung's (1952/54, 1956/58) discussion, one view of God's power is presented as absolute, worshipped and revered as at the very height of mortal human aspiration; it is also argued to be contrary, confused and at times irrationally vindictive and jealous, seen in a mirror-image of the darkest aspects of human nature. Displaying overly righteous actions of evil and intent toward human mortals, Jung sees God as defending against the threats, as He perceives them, toward His infinite sovereign right to power over temporal human thoughts and actions. Intriguingly, there is an apparent emerging perspective on God here as a troubled personality. Evident in Jung's discussion are traits that might be seen in 'narcissism', indicative aspects of personality where there is an apparent splitting off between 'good' and 'evil' in oneself, projecting one's own darker and denied aspects of self on to 'other'(s).

Stephen Gross (2013) on 'narcissism', suggests that Martin Buber's notion of 'I-Thou' and 'I-It' may be applied, not just in a one-to-one intersubjective relationship, but 'to the individual in relation to a collective other and also to the relation between collectives themselves' (Gross, 2013, p. 46). He adds that this has profound social and political implications, seeing 'the issues posed by the hostility towards immigrants and asylum seekers, especially those perceived as embodying excessive "otherness"' (ibid.) as leading to a relational 'I-It'. He further cites Zimbardo's (2007) extension of Buber's 'I-Thou' and 'I-It' into a form of negative relating, that of 'It–It', an alienating perspective acting as a negative and 'dehumanising agent'. 'The misperception of certain others as subhuman, bad humans, inhuman, dispensable, or "animals" is facilitated by means of labels, stereotypes, slogans and propaganda images' (Zimbardo, 2007 cited in Gross, 2013, p. 47). The 'others' become a projected 'It' that can then be denied any possibility of being relational 'others'. Having been dehumanised, this enables the ego of 'I' to be defended against the reality of their violence toward another human being (see also Nolan, 2016).[2]

Stiffell and Holtom (2016) discuss 'the seductive face of narcissism', observing 'the narcissist's conviction that he is the most loathsome and utterly unlovable self (that) must be hidden beneath tiers of reaction formations such as grandiosity and omnipotence, projections and denials' (Stiffell & Holtom, p. 39).

Jung (1952/54 & 1956/58) suggests that the origins of religious beliefs lie within the natures of human behaviour, and that in splitting off 'good' and 'evil' as separate entities, within any faith or any person, it can serve to both absolve responsibility and offload the blame onto others, the social consequences of which recycle in an *eternal recurrence of the same.* Jung's idea of 'individuation' (inspired by the debate in Nietzsche's *Thus Spoke Zarathustra* on the notion of the *Übermensch*, the 'Overman') is a position aspired toward by letting go of dependency on a greater power, and the need for the person to find their own soul in order to fulfil life's potential. Originating from Jung's own personal, professional and spiritual journey, 'individuation' in *The Red Book* and subsequent texts in the *Collected Works*, is seen as a developmental process where the person begins to psychologically assume responsibility for their actions and their consequences. It offers a way forward beyond the avoidance of one's 'shadow' and toward an integration of conflicting aspects of self. Only then may the person begin to accommodate the vagaries of rights and wrongs, both meted out on them (including those 'outside of one's control or volition'), by their own actions on others, and thereby the chance of making sufficient meanings of (and within) a temporal, time-limited life.

Implications for therapeutic practice

How might these ideas on Jung's 'individuation' support therapeutic interventions in the helping professions? This discussion will consider an instance of practice from an encounter in clinical supervision; this process informed by relational psychoanalytic and Jungian thinking on the 'third' and the 'fourth', and conducted within a reflective and intersubjective relationship, where open reflections on interpersonal phenomena are shown as helping to unravel meanings and further insight.

The 'third' and the 'fourth'

Psychoanalyst and supervising analyst, Ann Ulanov (2007a, 2007b), discusses Jungian notions of the 'third', a co-created relational language from which narrative emerges when engaging with the other. The third offers opportunity for a dialogue where 'either/or' polar positions might give way into 'open-ended constructions of meaning' (Ulanov, 2007b, p. 585). Ulanov (2007a, 2007b) considers the 'third' as enabling a co-created relational language from which narrative emerges when engaging with the other. It offers opportunity for a dialogue where 'either/or' polar positions might give way into 'open-ended constructions of meaning' (Ulanov, 2007b, p. 585); she cites Benjamin et al. (2004) in highlighting the relational third as being 'the mutative agent' in therapeutic treatment.

Developing this notion, she sees the third as originating from within a Jungian 'fourth' (Jung, 1938/58, 1944/68, 1952/70), the latter seen as an area that lies beyond rational, verbal and symbolic meaning, and links to the whole of our lived-in reality. The fourth remains shadowy, containing areas otherwise rejected and protecting those elements that we might 'leave out of our conscious identity' (ibid.). The fourth defines the third in that it acts as a bridge to a broader reality that is 'beyond psyche' and each individual's worldview; it is 'only known by living it, for we are part of the larger reality it discloses' (Ulanov, 2007b, p. 585); the 'shadow' of the fourth enables the third into a 'mysterious something' that is healing, enabling a 'creative aliveness that undoes deadness' (ibid.).

Ulanov juxtaposes this Jungian stance with Winnicott's (1971/91) 'transitional space', where the mother/infant relationship parallels the as-if therapist/client relationship. The subjective other is able to 'survive our destructiveness' (ibid.), the relational space offering both a mirror of regard and an objective otherness that can recognise and contemplate a separate self, an openness to intersubjective relationship. She cites Thomas Ogden's (1999) idea of an 'unconscious permeability' that exists between analyst and analysand, where in reverie the analyst monitors their countertransference as a rhythmic interplay 'of connection, breakdown and repair'.

> It functions to create new insights in us and in the analysand and between us. But more is here. I suggest that we cannot see this third except in the shadow of the fourth, something Jung explored decades ago that has postmodern implications for clinical work and for understanding reality.
>
> *Ulanov, 2007b, p. 589*

Creative discovery in the therapeutic relationship, particularly where Bion (1962) and Ogden's (1999) notions of 'reverie' may inform transference and countertransference interactions, can generate a complexity of feelings from within the third, from where a 'transformational' moment may emerge from the midst of 'an "avalanche" of empathic engagement' (Cambray, 2006, p. 11). This moment contains a feeling of significant mutual understanding, a resonance of temporal realities – a place where the 'historicity' (Gadamer, 1975/89) of each is interlinked in a 'fusion of horizons'; 'whilst separated by different horizons of understanding … mutual understanding comes through overlapping consensus, merging of horizons rather than through the abandonment by one of the interlocutors of his or her initial horizon' (Moran, 2000, p. 252).

As *noetic horizons* (Churchill, 1998, p. 86), they facilitate ever-extending limits of awareness from accumulating perceptions, each moment adding to and experientially modifying the widening mutually perceived view. They are anticipatory, guiding intentionality toward a particular direction, 'thus connecting a present perception with the future unfolding profiles' (ibid.). In helping articulate a bridge between the 'third' and the 'fourth', *noetic horizons* can help disentangle the informational inter-psychic relationship; it offers a cyclical unification through to the 'one' (Jung, 1953/68, 1961/63), a place of pre-existing 'synthesis of the four in a unity' (Jung, 1961/63, para. 619, cited in Ulanov, 2007b, p. 592). Ulanov represents the 'fourth' as a place of transcendence within both the analyst and analysand, each sharing the potentiality of experiencing the 'one'.

Jung's focused 'third' may be seen as a source of timeless moments within the 'analytic third' (Ogden, 1994, 2004); acting as 'gateway' to the 'fourth', it allows the possibility of momentary 'synthesis' with the world, a sense of unifying completeness and that 'every kind of thing will be well' (Julian of Norwich, 1670/

1978, p. 229; see also Jantzen (2000) for further discussion on Julian); 'the One' or 'the Good' of Neoplatonist philosopher Plotinus (d. AD270) is 'the ultimate cause of everything … [that] cannot be grasped by thought or given any positive determination' (Emilsson, 2000, p. 683), yet emerges from, 'a culmination of a series of experiences going from that of the material world to those of self-knowledge in soul, and in intellect' (O'Meara, 1993, p. 108). And Wilfred Bion's (1970/83) similarly elaborated formulation of 'O',

> the ultimate reality, absolute truth, the godhead, the infinite, the thing-in-itself. O does not fall in the domain of knowledge or learning save incidentally; it can be 'become', but it cannot be 'known'. It is darkness and formlessness … (until) it has evolved to a point where it can be known, through knowledge gained by experience, and formulated in terms derived from sensuous experience; its existence is conjectured phenomenologically.
>
> *Bion 1970/83, p. 26*

Perspectives are offered in the Hindu spiritual treatises, *The Upanishads*, as,

> Atman, the Spirit of Vision, is never born and never dies. Before him there was nothing, and he is ONE for evermore. Never-born and eternal, beyond times gone or to come, he does not die when the body dies.
>
> *Mascaró, 1965, 'Katha Upanishad', p. 59*

A sense of peace and at-Oneness, however briefly perceived and felt in therapy and its supervision, can serve to sustain transformational shifts in ease with self, thereby facilitating psychical confidence toward potentiality and change. However, Ulanov includes a necessary caveat in the experiencing of such 'grounded' and 'embodied wisdom': this sense of 'wholeness to match the inclusiveness of reality as a whole … [it] burdens us with the good as well as the bad' (Ulanov, 2007b, p. 594), requiring that the practitioner assumes responsibility to fully live the human condition. In so doing, and in openness to these 'good' and 'bad' sides of self, '[t]he fourth can get us through whatever lurks in the shadows; the door is unlocked because there we are undeveloped, without the arm of our consciousness' (ibid., p. 596).

Ulanov (1996) takes care to highlight the 'incredible risks of relating in a deeply open and perceptive way' (Ulanov, 1996, p. 6), and that they are 'fraught with dangers … to allow oneself to be oneself' (Milner, 1979, p. 43, cited in Ulanov, 1996, p. 6). It necessitates that the therapist knows the worst about themselves, and thereby avoids 'the hinge of our own shadow that trips the trap door through which we fall' (Ulanov, 2007b, p. 595).

Our sense of Reality, the 'one' or God, or nothingness, or whatever each of us may call this origin point, 'is engineering us, each in our different ways, to mirror its conversation with us', our meeting with the other extends relation by 'mirroring this transcendent presence' (ibid., p. 603) with joy and light as well as its abyssal shadow of darkness and destruction.

A mutual encounter in clinical supervision

Maddy (an agreed pseudonym) is an experienced practitioner who has worked for several years with clients who bring issues of significant childhood sexual abuse. We have over time developed a necessarily trusting professional intimacy when engaging with clinical frame material. In this additional supervision session that she had specifically requested, Maddy wished to reflect on the previous week, a session during which we had mutually experienced her turbulent reaction, driven from within the client's presenting narrative, that had 'hooked' into her own psychological 'story' in a disturbing way. We had been considering her client's reluctance and apparent balking at any implied further unfolding of her childhood abuse narrative when, in recalling the clinical frame, there had been a sharp shift, within an extended moment, where Maddy had flipped into a momentary 'dissociation', manifested in her curled-up-into-the-chair frightened child self and driven from her client's transference projection scraping against her hitherto shielded core, the 'shell' containing her remembered inner-child.

Within the supervisory frame, it was a moment that had also hooked into several layers of my countertransference-felt reactions: in the initial microsecond there was my instinct to reach out and protectively hold her, but which I knew would inappropriately intrude and deny her access to indwelling with the phenomenon – there was also a barely concealed anger and unexpressed murderous hatred. Alongside in the countertransference was a momentary dark shadowy pull to erotically abuse; unremembered at this time, and unfolded later in my own clinical supervision, it was a not unexpected countertransference reaction in the supervision of therapy with a client's vulnerabilities of need and, having been groomed, then subjected to sexual abuse. Dialogue in supervision engages with the therapist's psyche, inevitably generating reactions in response to client projections, then echoed in the parallel process of the supervisory frame.

> Psychotherapy with patients sexually abused as children necessarily involves taking on perverse aspects in the transference and countertransference, and if these manifestations can be held and understood alongside the therapist's personal experiences, then it is possible further to expand awareness of the erotic transference as a way of creating a possibility for healing, creativity and increased spontaneity.
>
> *Gardner, 1999, p. 149*

I subsequently shared this realisation with Maddy, which she acknowledged as also having been part of her own experiencing toward her client, helping recognise the 'countertransference enchantment' (Schaverien, 2007, p. 61) with her client's fears.

> The therapist travels with the patient into the recesses of the conscious mind and permits the dark material from the psyche to permeate a layer of her being … the role of the supervisor is an important one in confronting the

> shared imaginal world of the patient and therapist and breaking the spell of the countertransference enchantment.
>
> *Schaverien, 2007, pp. 60–61*

These later observations informed Maddy's insight into the client's transference, and her (until then unconscious) fear of the erotic being re-enacted in the vulnerability of the therapy frame – a clear example of the necessity for both the therapist and supervisor to recognise, know and own their shadow, to 'know the worst about themselves' in order to openly own, separate and understand from where such feelings and fantasies are so generated.

All these elements in the supervision were experienced by me within a fraction-of-a-second micro moment … that then swiftly shifted, resting in a sense of my own remembered child self, one similarly but differently distraught who had also needed to have been 'seen', and loved … I dwelt within this as-if self, while quietly reminding Maddy of the day, the time and where we were in the consulting room. Moments later, as she returned to the here-and-now, I disclosed my own as-if child felt within that moment, and who had also sensed her fearful aloneness.

In this additional supervision session Maddy asked how I had experienced the extended moment where she was curled up in the chair, which to her had felt as an embarrassing and unprofessional 'dissociative enactment' (Stern, 2010, 2019), and was questioning her own competence. I expanded upon my felt sense, where I had recognised and empathised with her distress from a similarly but different bereft place, and that from my initial as-if parental instinct to 'rescue', I had allowed my inner-child reaction to share the space within which we both had then dwelt. She owned that this intimate connection between us had been a surprise for her, this perspective not having been experienced or expressed before in her personal therapy – at this point our mutual gaze became a moment of 'recognition' in 'knowing' the acknowledged agape love between us.

> Both the uncertainty of our knowledge and the necessity of struggling toward mutual accommodation of difference are contained in this conception of dialogue. It is the constantly renewed commitment to restoring the thirdness of intersubjectivity that allows us to get beyond a struggle of your meaning versus my meaning, to a sense of working together to transcend complementarity in favor of mutual recognition.
>
> *Benjamin, 1999, pp. 207–208*

This follow-up session was an opportunity for a 'space to play' (Winnicott, 1971/91), a place within which to explore the parallels of her uncertainties with those of her client, of the ambivalence of wanting to 'know' yet 'not know' of her client's dissociated child's experiencing of significant and sadistic abuse, which had triggered elements of her own hitherto similarly avoided childhood events (having chosen so in her own therapy, on having perceived a 'good enough' place, for now, within which to be); 'knowing' yet not wishing to unnecessarily re-visit, and thereby re-encounter, particularly unpleasant and nasty memories that, while recognised and known, were better left in the past and with no apparent power. Maddy realised, in the parallel process of the moment we had observed, that the client was indicating similarly, and that there was, at this stage, no need to unnecessarily, and damagingly, pursue what each of them can mutually and pre-consciously recognise and acknowledge. In so doing, she was seeing, for now, that this was enough. Also observed in the parallel process and recognised by Maddy was the sensed power of the adult-as-survivor, the vengeful parent's latent threat of hate and murderous anger in protection of their own inner-child, and how the fear of its enactment had been stirred by the clinical frame material.

These reflections on supervision illustrate how insights into the processes of therapeutic and supervisory engagement can be heightened through engagement with the interpersonal, intersubjective relationship. It happens when both parties sit in mutual recognition within the immediacy of an open encounter; engaging in the 'dialogical-interpersonal' (Hycner, 1991, p. 74) and perceiving the client's internal world by being openly curious in exploring phenomena sensed from the 'dialectical-intrapsychic' field (ibid.). Close intimacy and relational transparency in supervision serve to inform the relational 'third' through 'the shadow of the fourth' (Ulanov, 2007b), releasing insights from within the (hitherto hidden) embodied memory of the reified therapeutic frame.

In the parallel processes, we had indwelt with Harold Searles' notion of a 'therapeutic symbiosis',

> which is in part of delusional-transference origin but in part based upon the actual state of the relatedness between us, a relatedness which involves symbiosis participated in by both of us, and in which we function in terms of the power to create one another.
>
> *Searles, 1972, p. 9*

This aspect of intersubjective experiencing, linked to early developmental processes in the infant–mother, infant–caregiver or client–therapist dyads (Aron, 2006; BCPSG, 1998, 2002, 2010; Tronick, 1998), is helpful for exploring options in sense-making within the immediacy of the relational experiencing moment; initially this is at a non-verbal level, with therapist and supervisor interventions that are intuitively instinctive: 'these moments open up the way to the elaboration of a more complex and coherent way of being together, with associated change in how relational possibilities are represented in each participant's relational knowing' (BCPSG, 1998, p. 288).

In the mutual recognition of the 'third', we were each as if 'alone' in the presence of the other, who is also alone, but together able to momentarily peer into the void, into the awe-full abyss of the 'fourth', to recognise, resonate with, and witness 'the larger reality it discloses' (Ulanov, 2007b, p. 585).

Experiencing a transformational event in a therapeutic or supervisory relationship gives witness to its ideation; subsequent dialogue acknowledges this 'witness' – which may also be non-verbal in a meeting of the eyes that says, 'I know that you know that I know that what we just experienced is significant' – concretising the phenomenon into ideated meaning and a transformational shift. We had together dwelt in our own shadows, visiting

> a boundless expanse full of uncertainty, with apparently no outside, no above and below, no here and there, no mine and thine, no good or bad. It is the world of water, where all life floats in suspension; where the realm of the sympathetic system, the soul of everything living, begins; where I am indivisibly this *and* that; where I experience the other in myself and the other-than-myself experiences me.
>
> *Jung, 1954/59/68, pp. 21–22*

At the clinical session following our supervision presented above, Maddy's client announced her preparedness to move beyond her 'for now' place; it was as if she had been present at our supervision sessions and, having witnessed the discussion, allowed herself permission to risk the next stage of her journey. This had also enabled Maddy to acknowledge a further shift in her own therapy process, to move beyond, recognising this as an unsolicited but welcome 'gift' from her client. We had, together in our mutual relational trust, taken the risk of stretching the elasticity of the supervisory frame as 'container' of the therapeutic frame, thereby facilitating unexpected insights.[3]

Significant shifts in awareness such as these can arise when recognising, and then dwelling within, parallel process phenomena (Doehrman, 1976; Jacobs, 1996; Ogden, 2005), or Searles' (1955) 'reflective process', that emerge in the relational supervisory frame. Ogden (2005) sees the therapist and supervisor 'dreaming a patient into existence' through contemplation, in so doing creating a narrative manifested in words, voice, body language and gestures, fleshed out in the projective identifications and 'the unconscious re-creation in the supervisory setting of the supervisee's experience of the intersubjective process' (Ogden, 2005, p. 1267). Disentangling this inherent complexity can be aided by holding in mind the extended relational matrix, in so doing the therapist has the freedom to be 'alive to all that is happening in the analytic and the supervisory relationship, as well as in the dynamic interplay between the two'; 'aliveness' manifested in the 'single set' of relationships (ibid., p. 1269).

In conclusion

Jung's ideas from *The Red Book* and his other texts on his search for existential and spiritual meaning, his utilising of ancient myths and archetypes from human phylogeny in seeking answers that might make, for him, a different and more meaningful sense of life, presaged the notion of 'individuation'. Its origins in Nietzsche's *Übermensch*, explored in making contemporary links with Jung's struggle and the notion of *eternal return*, suggest ways of gaining empowerment and some control over the endless recycling of events. Juxtaposed with Ann Ulanov's scholarly analysis of

Jung's 'third' and 'fourth', the supervision sessions presented above illustrate how the therapist-as-supervisee may usefully intuit information that had been hitherto reveal-ingly concealed[4] within the weft and weave of the recalled therapeutic relationship. While, in her terms, struggling against becoming 'enchanted' in the client's world, Maddy and I had explored our embodied countertransference reactions within a co-created and intersubjective supervisory space, where conscious awareness of parallel processes had served to extend our horizons of experiencing (Gadamer, 1975/89),[5] allowing us to dwell within and contemplate the void beyond, the (l)edge.

All aspects of what it means to be human – the good, the bad and the unsavoury – can become readily enacted within the therapeutic space and then reified in clinical supervision. When in intimate presence and dialogue with an 'other', each is focusing attention toward an enhanced level of awareness, both of self and the mutuality of the other person (Levinas's [1961/69] 'ethical' presence) and, by proxy, of the rest of humanity and the rest of the universe, 'that the stuff of matter is the stuff of psyche and vice versa' (Ulanov, 2007a, p. 172).

> Interpersonally, we experience this connectedness as the interdependence of all peoples, that in our tiny subjectivity dwells as well an ecumenical spirit thrown open to all cultures, languages, laws. Imaginally we are citizens of the world, where everyone on the city street, the rural path, the far away nation is our neighbour because they, too, are subjects of this subject within us, this power far outside us.
>
> *ibid., p. 181*

This perspective on supervision offers a lens into the relationship,[6] a focus that can integrate across joy, beauty and the sometimes shadowy 'abyss' of being human, each of which may emerge in seeking meaning from the clinical frame. An openly trusting and ethically contained relational intimacy allows open exploration across a continuum of love, hate and 'psychic nullity', inter-psychically risking soul-to-soul, touching the edge of 'infinity' (Levinas, 1961/69) in the 'one' (Jung, 1953/68, 1961/63). The mutually witnessed experience, resonating within an interconnected web of relational being, becomes an ideated and embedded memory, a 'mutative agent' (Ulanov, 2007b, p. 585), releasing shifts toward sufficient therapeutic meaning, and insightful for each in the supervisory triad.

Questions for practitioners

As supervisor: Have there been occasions where I held back from saying something that I had thought, felt, or seen in my 'mind's eye', and later wished I had said to my supervisee?

a) What held me back?
b) What was the risk in saying this?
c) What might they or I gain if I said it?

As supervisee: Have there been occasions where I held back from saying something that I had thought, felt, or seen in my 'mind's eye', and later wished that I had said to my supervisor?

a) What held me back?
b) What was the risk in saying this?
c) What might they or I gain if I said it?

Notes

1 *Transformations and Symbols of the Libido* (Jung, 1912) was extensively revised by Jung in 1952, published in English as *Symbols of Transformation*, *CW*5 (Jung, 1952/70).
2 Nolan (2016) offers a contextual discussion on suicidal killing, 'internalised as retaliation in defence against annihilation of both self and avowed worldview' (p. 310), linking Emmanuel Levinas's (1961/69) notion of the *ethical relation* with Judith Butler's (2004) *Precarious Life*, the latter's essay in which she holds a lens to sense-making of terrorism and the events of 9/11 in New York.
3 Renn (2013, pp. 142–143), discusses sexuality in the consulting room and the need for ethical guidelines, the maintenance of a safe and boundaried therapeutic frame and that therapists necessarily 'do no harm'. He notes Feltham (2007) on the potential to 'slide into a defensive mind-set of "Take no risks"' (Renn, 2013, pp. 142–143). In maintaining an ethical frame by rigid adherence to prescriptive protocols, the therapist 'may foreclose the space to develop a humane, intersubjective relationship', leaving the patient with a sense of having been abused by a too rigidly correct therapist. 'Take no risks' may breach the 'do no harm' injunction – 'in effect, the treatment becomes iatrogenic, that is, actively harmful' (ibid.).
4 Martin Heidegger (1927/62) explores the nature of the person as an existential 'Being', describing their ontological presence as *Dasein*, their 'Being-in-the-world'. His later work (1953/2000, 1975/82) recognises that a person's Being is their meaning-making, their ontology; the individual self, in their *Dasein*, perceives the world 'as it is', and in the first instance, cannot perceive it otherwise. It is dependent on a Being's self-awareness of being, confirmed and constructed in and through social relationship, where 'Being revealingly conceals itself in beings' (Caputo, 1982, pp. 151–152), self-awareness emerging from relationship with others.
5 See Nolan (2007, 2015) on research with clinical supervisors, where qualitative data analyses of interviews demonstrate instances of parallel processes and phenomenal experiencing; McVey, Lees and Nolan (2015) and McVey (2017) offer examples from research with practising therapists.
6 An astronomical term, 'gravitational lensing', might be seen as a metaphor for this form of heightened perception, a phenomenon where light, in a focused line-of-sight view, is seen as being bent around the edge of a significantly large object, such as a galaxy (Hubblesite, 2019; Sauer, 2010), its gravity 'bending' space-time so as to bring forward distant objects that are behind the source of gravity, unseen and otherwise too distant to be perceived.

References

Aron, L. (2006) Analytic impasse and the third: Clinical implications of intersubjectivity theory. *International Journal of Psychoanalysis*, **87**, pp. 349–368.

BCPSG (Boston Change Process Study Group) (1998) Implicit relational knowing: Its role in development and psychoanalytic treatment. *Infant Mental Health Journal*, **19**(3), pp. 282–289.

——. (2002) Explicating the explicit: The local level and the microprocess of change in the analytic situation. *International Journal of Psychoanalysis*, **83**, pp. 1051–1062.

——. (2010) *Change in Psychotherapy: A Unifying Paradigm*. New York: Norton.

Benjamin, J. (1999) Recognition and Destruction: An outline of intersubjectivity. In: S. Mitchell (Ed.) *Relational Psychoanalysis. Vol 1: The Emergence of a Tradition*, pp. 181–209. Hillsdale, NJ: The Analytic Press.

Benjamin, J. et al. (2004) The Third in psychoanalysis. *Psychoanalytic Quarterly*, LXXIII, 1.

Bion, W. (1962) A Theory of Thinking. In: *Second Thoughts*. London: Karnac, 1967.

——. (1970/83) *Attention and Interpretation*. Lanham, MD: Rowman and Littlefield.

Bishop, P. (2014) Jung and the Quest for Beauty. In: T. Kirsch & G. Hogensen (Eds) *The Red Book: Reflections on C.G. Jung's Liber Novus* (pp. 11–35). London: Routledge.

Boechat, W. (2017) *The Red Book of C. G. Jung: A Journey into Unknown Depths*. London: Karnac.

Butler, J. (2004) Precarious Life. In J. Butler (Ed.) *Precarious Life: The Powers of Mourning and Violence* (pp. 128–151). New York: Verso.

Cambray, J. (2006) Towards the feeling of emergence. *Journal of Analytical Psychology*, **51**(1), pp. 1–20.

Caputo, J.D. (1982) *Heidegger and Aquinas: An Essay on Overcoming Metaphysics*. New York: Fordham University Press.

Churchill, S.D. (1998) The Intentionality of Diagnostic Seeing: A phenomenological investigation of clinical impression formation. In: R. Valle (Ed.) *Phenomenological Inquiry in Psychology* (pp. 175–207). New York: Plenum.

Cybulska, E. (2012) Nietzsche's Übermensch: A hero of our time? *Philosophy Now*, **93**, pp. 10–12. Retrieved 4 January 2019 from https://philosophynow.org/issues/93/Nietzsches_Ubermensch_A_Hero_of_Our_Time

——. (2013) Nietzsche's eternal return: Unriddling the vision, a psychodynamic approach. *Indo-Pacific Journal of Phenomenology*, **13**(1), pp. 1–13. Retrieved 4 January 2019 from https://doi.org/10.2989/IPJP.2013.13.1.2.1168

Doehrman, J.G. (1976) Parallel process in supervision and psychotherapy. *Bulletin of the Menninger Clinic*, **40**(1), pp. 9–104.

Emilsson, E.K. (2000) Plotinus (AD 204/5–70). In: *Concise Routledge Encyclopedia of Philosophy*. London: Routledge.

Feltham, C. (2007) Ethical agonizing. *Therapy Today*, **18**(7), pp. 4–6.

Freud, S. & Jung, C.G. (1974) *The Freud/Jung Letters* (ed. W. McGuire, trans. R. Manheim & R.F.C. Hull). Princeton, NJ: Princeton University Press.

Gadamer, H.-G. (1975/89) *Truth and Method* (2nd edn, trans. Rev. J. Weinsheimer & D.G. Marshall). London: Sheed & Ward.

——. (1993/96) *The Enigma of Health* (trans. J. Gaiger & N. Walker). Cambridge: Polity Press.

Gardner, F. (1999) A Sense of All Conditions. In: D. Mann (Ed.) *Erotic Transference and Countertransference: Clinical practice in psychotherapy* (pp. 140–149). London: Routledge.

Gross, S. (2013) The I-Thou Relationship. In: C. Driver, S. Crawford, & J. Stewart (Eds), *Being and Relating in Psychotherapy: Ontology and therapeutic practice* (pp. 36–48). Basingstoke: Palgrave Macmillan.

Heidegger, M. (1927/62) *Being and Time* (trans. J. Macquarrie & E. Robinson). New York: Harper & Row.

——. (1953/2000) *Introduction to Metaphysics* (trans. G. Fried & R. Polt). New Haven, CT: Yale Nota Bene.

——. (1961/84) *Nietzsche. Vol. 2: The Eternal Return* (trans. D.F. Krell). New York: Harper & Row.

——. (1975/82) *The Basic Problems of Phenomenology* (trans. A. Hofstadter). Bloomington & Indianapolis: Indiana University Press.

Hubblesite (2019) NASA's Hubble Helps Astronomers Uncover the Brightest Quasar in the Early Universe. 9 January 2019. Retrieved from http://hubblesite.org/news_release/news/2019-03/18-gravitational-lensing, Retrieved 10 February 2019.

Hycner, R.H. (1991) *Between Person and Person: Toward a dialogical therapy*. Highland, NY: Centre for Gestalt Development.

Jacobs, M. (1996) Parallel process: confirmation and critique. *Psychodynamic Counselling*, **2**(1), pp. 55–66.

Jantzen, G.M. (2000) *Julian of Norwich: Mystic and theologian* (2nd edn). London: SPCK.

Julian of Norwich. (1670/1978) *Showings* (trans. E. Colledge & J. Walsh). Mahwah, NJ: Paulist Press.

Jung, C.G. (1938/58) *A Psychological Approach to the Dogma of the Trinity, Complete Works, Vol. 11* (trans. R.F.C. Hull) (pp. 148–200). London: Routledge & Kegan Paul.

——. (1944/68) *Psychology and Alchemy, Complete Works, Vol. 12* (2nd edn, trans. R.F.C Hull). London: Routledge & Kegan Paul.

——. (1952/54) *Answer to Job*. London: Routledge & Kegan Paul.

——. (1952/70) *Symbols of Transformation, Complete Works, Vol. 5* (2nd edn, trans. R.F.C. Hull). London: Routledge & Kegan Paul.

——. (1953/68) *Psychology and Alchemy, Complete Works, Vol. 12* (trans. R.F.C. Hull). London: Routledge & Kegan Paul.

——. (1954/59/68) Archetypes of the Collective Unconscious. In: *Archetypes and the Collective Unconscious, Complete Works, Vol. 9, Part I*, (2nd edn, trans. R.F.C. Hull). London: Routledge & Kegan Paul.

——. (1956/58) Prefatory Note, Answer to Job. In: *Psychology and Religion: West and East, Complete Works, Vol. 11* (trans. R.F.C. Hull) (pp. 355–470). London: Routledge & Kegan Paul.

——. (1961/63) *Memories, Dreams, Reflections*. London: Collins Fontana.

——. (2009) *The Red Book. Liber Novus* (trans. M. Kyburz, J. Peck, & S. Shamdasani). New York: W.W. Norton.

Levinas, E. (1961/69) *Totality and Infinity* (trans. A. Lingis). Pittsburgh, PN: Duquesne University Press.

Maillard, C. (2014) Jung's Seven Sermons to the Dead (1916). In: T. Kirsch & G. Hogensen (Eds) *The Red Book: Reflections on C.G. Jung's Liber Novus* (pp. 81–93). London: Routledge.

Mascaró, J. (1965) *The Upanishads*. London: Penguin Classics.

McVey, L. (2017) *Pied beauty: Exploring psychological therapists' inner experiencing in reverie*. Unpublished PhD thesis. University of Leeds, UK. Retrieved 18 September 2018 from http://etheses.whiterose.ac.uk/19588/

McVey, L., Lees, J., & Nolan, G. (2015) Practitioner-based research and qualitative interviewing: Using therapeutic skills to enrich research in counselling and psychotherapy. *Counselling and Psychotherapy Research*, **15**(2), pp. 147–154.

Moran, D. (2000) *Introduction to Phenomenology*. London: Routledge.

Nietzsche, F. (1969) *Thus Spoke Zarathustra* (trans. R.J. Hollingdale). London: Penguin Books Ltd.

——. (1974) *The Gay Science* (trans. W. Kaufmann). New York: Vintage.

Nolan, G. (2007) *Mirrors and Echoes: Meaning-Moments in Counselling Supervision*. Unpublished DCouns thesis, University of Manchester, UK.

——. (2015) Perspectives at the Edge of Experiencing in Clinical Supervision. In: G. Nolan & W. West (Eds) *Therapy, Culture and Spirituality: Developing Therapeutic Practice* (pp. 138–158). Basingstoke: Palgrave Macmillan.

——. (2016) A precarious ecstasy: Beyond temporality in self and other. *British Journal of Guidance & Counselling*, **44**(3), pp. 306–315.

O'Dwyer, K. (2011) Nietzsche's challenge: Eternal recurrence. *Journal of Humanistic Psychology*, **51**(2), pp. 250–259.

Ogden, T. (1999) *Reverie and Interpretation*. London: Karnac.

——. (2005) On psychoanalytic supervision. *International Journal of Psycho-Analysis*, **86**(5), pp. 1265–1280.

O'Meara, D.J. (1993) *Plotinus: An Introduction to the Enneads*. Oxford: Clarendon Press.

Renn, P. (2013) Moments of meeting: The relational challenges of sexuality in the consulting room. *British Journal of Psychotherapy*, **29**(2), pp. 135–153.

Sauer, T. (2010) A brief history of gravitational lensing. In: *Einstein Online*, **04**, p. 1005.

Schaverien, J. (2007) Framing Enchantment: Countertransference in analytical art psychotherapy supervision. In: J. Schaverien & C. Case (Eds) *Supervision of Art Psychotherapy* (pp. 45–63). Hove: Routledge.

Searles, H.F. (1955) The Informational Value of the Supervisor's Emotional Experiences. In: H.F. Searles *Collected Papers on Schizophrenia and Related Subjects* (1965, pp. 157–176). London: Hogarth Press/Institute of Psychoanalysis.

——. (1972) The function of the patient's realistic perceptions of the analyst in delusional transference. *British Journal of Medical Psychology*, **45**: 1–18.

Shamdasani, S. (2011) 'After *Liber Novus*'. Paper presented at the Joint Conference of the Society of Analytical Psychology/Journal of Analytical Psychology, *The Red Book Two Years On: What Have We Learned?* London, 11–12 November 2011.

——. (2012) *C.G. Jung: A Biography in Books*. New York: W.W. Norton & Co.

Stern, D.B. (2010) *Partners in Thought: Working with unformulated experience, dissociation, and enactment*. New York: Routledge.

——. (2019) *The Infinity of the Unsaid*. Abingdon: Routledge.

Stiffell, G., & Holtom, R. (2016) Beware the song of the siren: Reflections on the seductive face of narcissism. *British Journal of Psychotherapy*, **32**(1), pp. 37–52.

Tronick, E.Z. (1998) Dyadically expanded states of consciousness and the process of therapeutic change. *Infant Mental Health Journal*, **19**(3), pp. 290–299.

Ulanov, A.B. (1996) *The Transcendent in Intrapsychic Work*. Wilmette, IL: Chiron Publications.

——. (2007a) *The Unshuttered Heart: Opening to aliveness and deadness in the self*. Nashville, TN: Abingdon Press.

——. (2007b) The third in the shadow of the fourth. *Journal of Analytical Psychology*, **52**, pp. 585–605.

Winnicott, D.W. (1971/91) *Playing and Reality*. London: Routledge.

Zimbardo, P. (2007) *The Lucifer Effect: How good people turn evil*. London: Rider/Ebury Press.

13

A DIALOGUE WITH THREE VOICES

Creating a therapeutic triad between therapist, asylum seeker and interpreter

Lynn Learman

> In the waiting room and when we went to the counselling room, … believe me I looked at my counsellor carefully. Can I trust her? … When you stay in one room, even if we talk the same language if you don't feel comfortable in your heart …. It's faces … sometimes, when you see a person you feel comfortable at the beginning …. In her face I felt 100% she understand me. Better than anyone else.
>
> *Nadia (client)*

This is a description of a first encounter between a client, a therapist and an interpreter. This is, of course, the ideal scenario, the point at which the interpreter melts seamlessly into the therapy and the contact between therapist and client is complete. Yet if you try to define the emotional engagement that can happen in the therapy room, it becomes elusive. At its heart it's a simple yet profound emotional alliance, a connection felt and shared between people. Boundaries create safety and structure in a therapeutic relationship but through liminality we can explore the experiences that overlap, the human and emotional connections that lie between those boundaries. My passion for working with interpreters has come from my experience of working with asylum seekers who have been traumatised. Often clients will say 'I trust you' or 'it feels safe in here' because 'I can see it in your eyes and in your face' even though we have no common language.

Across the country there is increased demand for non-European linguists and challenges in how to incorporate the work of interpreters in counselling, psychotherapy and psychology. I have seen the addition of a good interpreter bring powerful change in my clients. I have also had some bad experiences. This chapter is based on 15 years of experience and findings from my doctoral thesis at Manchester University (Learman 2015). It uses verbatim quotes from therapists, interpreters and clients to explore how I and my colleagues have been able, at times, to create an emotional connection with people who have experienced trauma, torture and betrayal without sharing a common language. These are clients at the margins, who are some of the most in need and require the best we can provide but often receive some of the worst services available. Ideally bilingual and appropriate bicultural therapists should provide these services. However, in reality, this is an impossible task. I manage an asylum seeker and refugee therapy service called Spinning World, part of PSS, a large third sector social care organisation based in Liverpool where 43 different languages have been used in therapy in the last nine years. So 'a properly resourced, supervised and utilised Interpreter service is the most quickly achievable means of raising the standard of mental health services for this population' (Summerfield, 2001, p. 162).

Communication

When practitioners first contemplate working with an interpreter they usually focus on linguistic difference. Yet Mehrabian (2009) claimed that only 7% of communication rests in the words we use. How we communicate and what precisely we communicate become even more important when you consider that human beings believe non-verbal signals more than verbal ones when faced with conflicting messages (Stiff et al., 1990). This means that when working in a therapeutic triad, non-verbal communication becomes paramount.

> Sometimes I get lost in what the clients saying, even though I don't understand, I'm picking up their body language and emotions .... it just depends how emotional the dialogue is.
>
> *Isara (therapist)*

Non-verbal communication

The universal face

MRI scans have resulted in advances in neurobiology and neuro-anatomy adding to our knowledge about the links between the brain and the universality of some human responses (Trimble, 2012). 'Crying has now been recognised as a universal emotional response, especially to sadness, feelings of loss and the death of a loved one' (Trimble, 2012, p. 19). It is also possible to identify emotional expressions such as happiness, anger and surprise regardless of the culture of the person displaying the emotion (Ekman, 2007).

Involuntary expressions occur in the human face in as fast as 1/25 of a second (Haggard and Isaacs, 1966). This means that people can read your feelings far more accurately than you may think. So if a practitioner feels ill at ease, whatever they do, the client will know. Clients I interviewed said that because of the vocal delay, they relied on their observations and gut feelings to decide if they trusted the therapist and/or interpreter. When it worked, the auditory and visual stimulus including facial expressions and the tone and pace of the therapist's voice, mirrored by the interpreter reflecting the client's emotion, added to the therapeutic atmosphere in the room.

> It's especially her voice; believe me it's very, very soft. And anyone's just depressed, when you listen, it feel like you are going to heaven.
>
> *Nadia (client)*

> 'Cos some people get very emotional and look in your face, and if you are not reflecting their emotion, if you were smiling or something like that, they won't be confident or would not trust you.
>
> *Majid (interpreter)*

The culturally specific

'Just as emotional expression may be a universal "language" different "accents" or "dialects" may vary in subtle ways across cultures' (Elfenbein and Ambady, 2003, p. 21). A client's affect and demeanour are usually important indications of their wellbeing (Cushing, 2003). This will combine the content and the form in which the client speaks, their facial expressions and bodily movements. In the UK, mental health care is generally provided by staff from an indigenous population, drawing from their own cultural reference points (Raval, 2003). Yet some non-verbal communications have different and sometimes opposite meanings in different cultures (Knapp and Hall, 2006, p. 10) so there is the danger that practitioners may misunderstand these communications (Cushing, 2003). Samovar and Porter (2004) identify possible barriers in inter-cultural communication as seeking similarities; uncertainty reduction; withdrawal; stereotyping; prejudice; racism; and ethnocentrism (pp. 284–300). It is vital that therapists identify and understand their own cultural patterns of meaning before they try to interpret someone else's.

> I suggest that nearly all communication is to some degree cross-cultural in the sense that no two people have exactly the same background and, consequently precisely the same expectations about the interaction between them. Expectations, however, are more strikingly different when backgrounds diverge more drastically.
>
> *Tannen, 1980, p. 327*

In my study, all the practitioners warned against making assumptions based on body language.

> I've felt as though I haven't connected with the client to the extent I've wanted to when I've had the interpreter with me, but I've completely misread the situation and when it's come to an end, I've had this huge rush of

> affection from the client … I don't know if it's because I didn't hear the tone or I didn't read the body language because the person has been so reserved because of their culture.
>
> *Donna (therapist)*

A therapist related an instance in which she thought the client was angry when they were actually relating a funny story:

> Afterwards I processed that and I thought I was concentrating too much on the tone and I'd obviously missed something, completely missed it … we'd got enough relationship built up … and we were able to laugh about it together.
>
> *Victoria (therapist)*

Therapists gave many examples of interpreting non-verbal clues wrongly, warning that in their experience it was a mixture of the universal, the culturally specific and the personal, further complicated because of the delay between auditory and visual stimuli when using an interpreter.

Silence

Silence can be seen as another liminality, a space between spoken language and body language. Although counselling and psychotherapy are often characterised as 'talking therapies', silences and non-verbal communication form a significant part of all therapeutic interactions and connections can occur in subtle and nuanced ways. Clinicians working in the field of psycho-traumatology write about how silence communicates more than words: 'The fragility of language and the limitations of what can be tolerated in our conceptual thinking tend to render the words to describe these horrific memories void and redundant' (Hassan, 2009, p. 11). Therapists working with interpreters have to explore both their own and their clients' cultural patterning of meanings in order to explore what is not being said, to explore the implicit (Krause, 2002).

The interpreters I interviewed saw non-verbal communication as part of their professional responsibility but said the use of silence was unique to therapeutic interpreting.

> [T]he silences, which we may quite like because it gives you time to think … you don't tend to get those silences (in other interpreting contexts). It's more a case of getting information quickly.
>
> *Kim (interpreter)*

Three clients I interviewed identified silence as space and time to express emotion that is beyond words. They said that when they came for therapy they were unable to function or speak and displayed great distress. They were allowed to process this distress in a therapeutic safe space which resulted in an emotional catharsis. In 'Speech and Silence' (Ross, 2001), an account of the public hearings of the South African truth and reconciliation commission, women who had experienced brutal treatment of rape and violence during apartheid did not speak openly about their experience. Yet it was acknowledged in their testimonies: 'Women's silence can be recognised as language, and we need carefully to probe the cadences of silences, the gaps between fragile words, in order to hear what it is that women say' (Ross 2001, p. 273).

Language

As many asylum seekers speak multiple languages there is a danger of services using easily accessible languages rather than the best language for the client (Edwards, 1995). Getting the right language may be the first step to facilitating an effective therapeutic relationship. Languages are not neutral mediums but have the potential to impact in positive or negative ways on the client, particularly in the context of discrimination and racism. It is necessary to beware of bringing a client's oppressor into the room symbolically in the form of an easily available language. My experience is to ask at the referral stage which language the client wishes to use in therapy.

Interpretation

> Interpretation is a very much more complex process than a word-for-word translation….it calls for the deciphering of two linguistic codes, each with its own geographical, cultural, historical and linguistic traditions.
>
> *Farooq and Fear, 2003, p. 105*

The interpreters I interviewed talked about the challenges of working in a therapeutic culture, where conveying emotion and working with silences were new experiences. The style of facilitation and use of open questions used by therapists also caused problems. Some words and concepts are unique to a specific language, making direct translations impossible and the need to encode very different meanings, the '"in-between" of languages' (Burck, 2004, p. 334).

> The language (used in therapy) is sometimes quite vague … and it's not always easy to translate … talking about things like being in a safe place. If you translate that, it means a safe place, literally … it doesn't mean your state of mind at all.
>
> *Kim (interpreter)*

So it is vital to use an interpreter who is not only linguistically competent but also understands mental health and the subtleties of what you are trying to convey.

The therapeutic value of speaking in a mother tongue

The therapeutic impact of speaking in a mother tongue is slowly emerging (Costa and Dewaele, 2012; Pavlenko, 2012; Harris, 2006). Intense emotions developed in early years will have been encoded in the native language, (Harris, 2006). When clients have a basic understanding of English there is a temptation to work as a dyad. Yet this can limit the depth of the intervention, 'certain experiences can best, and possibly only be, elicited in a first language. This is why it is so important to work with an interpreter' (Burck, 2004, p. 334).

Sometimes the therapy session is the only opportunity that a client has to talk in their own language. It has the potential to connect them to a resilience and attachment that they may have had before the trauma. Working in their mother tongue is also a respect and an affirmation of a culture and life they have left behind. A connection to severed roots they may never find again.

What makes a good therapeutic team?

Research by the United States Army identified gifted, innate communicators. They found that there were cognitive, behavioural, and affective/motivational components that enable specific individuals to adapt effectively in inter-cultural environments (Abbe, Gulick and Herman 2007). If non-verbal communication is a mixture of the universal, the culturally specific and the personal, natural communicators, both therapists and interpreters, are comfortable with an out-of-conscious level of information exchange (Hall, 1959).

For a long time, therapists have agreed that 'Who provides the treatment is a much more important determinant of success than what treatment is provided' (Miller, Hubble and Duncan, 2008, p. 15). I believe that the qualities of a good therapeutic interpreter should match those of a good therapist. The British Association for Counselling and Psychotherapy (BACP) Ethical Framework for the Counselling Professions (2018b, pp. 10–11) identifies these qualities: 'candour, care, courage, diligence, empathy, fairness, humility, identity, integrity, resilience, respect, sincerity and wisdom'.

As well as the obvious linguistic skills, the interpreter has to work collaboratively, be emotionally literate, sensitive, mature and self-aware. Above all the interpreter has to positively choose to do this work. The interpreters I interviewed were all extremely experienced before they started working in this field, yet they all made it clear that working in a therapeutic setting was different to any other context they had ever worked in.

> [W]hen I came here I realised that it is different, what was expected, in the way of the environment, the situation, in the way of the topic, too many differences. So I realised, this is another world of interpreting than the way we usually do.
>
> *Majid (interpreter)*

The interpreters were concerned about the levels of distress they saw and the possibility of vicarious trauma. They discussed how they had struggled to stay professional when working at a deep emotional level. The spontaneity of therapy meant that the interpreter was tested personally and professionally. There was an acknowledgement that as well as capturing, processing and delivering the right words, tone and pace, they had to maintain a dignified and professional demeanour:

> [S]ometimes it's hard to keep control of emotions, you know, 'cos you don't want to show shock, particularly shock.
>
> *Kim (interpreter)*

> You have to show that you can get emotional too, to show your humanity, but mainly you have to control, to not affect the situation.
>
> *Majid (interpreter)*

Procurement

Because of the importance of the three-way alliance, the therapists in my research went so far as to ascribe success or failure of the therapy to the temperament of their interpreter as co-worker.

Miller et al. (2005), makes the crucial point that individual interpreters may have the appropriate language skills but might not be temperamentally suited to this work. This has implications for some practitioners working within the NHS who could be faced with a random interpreter and no opportunity to brief the interpreter before the client arrives. This might explain why some NHS practitioners do not believe working therapeutically with an interpreter is possible: 'some counsellors reported feeling that the counselling was "inferior" and that the work felt "compromised"' (Century, Leavey and Payne, 2007, p. 30). The interpreter was perceived as 'a cumbersome conduit in dealing with highly sensitive issues' (Century, Leavey and Payne, 2007, p. 30). This is in direct contrast to my personal experience, echoed by my research in the third sector, where there is often more control over procurement.

> It feels like we are one person for a bit … really engaged.
>
> *Rita (therapist)*

> I've had the situation with a client and interpreter where the warmth and the affection in the room between the three of us is quite clear, you know, it's worked. It's been wonderful.
>
> *Donna (therapist)*

> I felt like they are my sisters. We don't have the same blood, we don't, but we are sisters. S (the interpreter) too. Part of my life, I can't forget her like that.
>
> *Nadia (client)*

With two staff present at each session there are clear cost implications when working with an interpreter. However, without this facility, service users can remain in the mental health system for years. Black and mixed race men are three or more times more likely than the general population to be admitted to a psychiatric unit (Gajwani et al., 2016; Quality Care Commission, 2010). It has been argued that the higher prevalence of BAME (Black, Asian and Minority Ethnic) patients in in-patient facilities is precisely because people cannot access appropriate early help. Therefore, putting additional resources into services that use interpreters in primary care is, I believe, a long-term 'Invest to Save' model.

Teamwork

All the practitioners I interviewed agreed that the therapist and interpreter must work together with a shared aim and mutual respect for each other's roles. This required the two practitioners to view each other as professionals with different but inter-dependent skills. The therapists admitted that when they started, they had felt that their practice was under scrutiny. The interpreters stressed that they trusted the therapist and were too busy doing their own job to judge:

> I think three people in a room, this affects the therapist more than the interpreter.
>
> *Martin (interpreter)*

The interpreters wanted to be considered as part of a team and asked for help with the emotionally demanding aspects of the work. The best practice guidelines from the BACP (2018) and the British Psychological Society (BPS; 2017) advocate a debrief after every session:

> I think that's another very positive thing for us that counsellors will offer that debrief … all professionals should do that but it's very rare … I was offered it once when I worked with Macmillan staff at the hospital and someone was dying but it tends to be exceptional rather than routine …. I know that if there's something I have been stressing about or that there is an issue, we can take a few minutes to sort it out.
>
> *Kim (interpreter)*

Dynamics

There is a need for a fluid, organic approach to the dynamics in the therapy room as these may change and re-configure a number of times during the course of the therapy. The therapists I interviewed admitted that because they could not understand what the interpreter was saying to the client they had to relinquish some control and trust in the interpreter and the therapeutic process. If the therapist has previously worked within their own community, they may find themselves culturally outnumbered for the first time.

> All these different nuances (race, culture, language, identity) make a difference in how the relationship evolves. So it's always different. And you have to work with that.
>
> *Isara (therapist)*

The dynamics will change and develop as the relationship develops. Sometimes alliances are two-way, particularly linguistically and culturally, but gradually the three people begin to develop a unique culture of their own within the room. They begin to speak the same body language as they attune to each other and develop a shared narrative. I believe that there is a danger of making cultural dynamics sound complicated and the practicalities of this are simpler than the analysis. If you imagine describing a conversation between any three people, it could be seen as having linguistic, cultural, and emotional alliances as well as socio-economic and power issues. I would suggest that professional therapists deal with these dynamics in any therapeutic relationship. In my study the therapists saw facilitating dynamics as part of their usual therapeutic role:

> I don't see it as any different to any other therapeutic relationship and sometimes it works and sometimes it doesn't.
>
> Isara (therapist)

Added value

I believe that the presence of a third party can, on occasion, enhance the therapeutic relationship and be a positive element to bearing witness within the therapeutic alliance. Bot and Wadensjö (2004) state that their patients 'liked the fact that two people heard their stories' (p. 375).

> [B]ecause my experience was so emotional .... I was crying .... The interpreter and the counsellor, they are crying ... people ... sharing their experience like your experience ... It was very, very amazing for me, strange for me ... That was very, very special.
>
> *Mariam (client)*

The presence of the interpreter can provide extra support for the client. Not only are two people bearing witness to the trauma narrative, but one person comes from within the client's own community while the other represents an external and different society, providing a double validation for the client.

> I often feel that the other person is enabling that relationship. I really like it when interpreters use the same tone of voice as me and it feels like we're one person for a little bit, or when they look like they're really trying to find the

> right word or they're really engaged. They search around and maybe sometimes they apologise but .... I think that's really good, it's like two people are saying to the client, 'you are worth this, we're giving our time, we're being there for you.' We are working together. It's giving even more respect to a client than one sometimes.
>
> *Rita (therapist)*

When an interpreter becomes part of the therapeutic alliance, the presence of an extra skilled professional may support both the therapist and the client when listening to distressing trauma narratives.

> Having someone there is company in the situation. You're not alone (with the trauma) ... just to feel that understanding, that's something you can't get when it's just you and the client.
>
> *Rita (therapist)*

Another world of working

This is specialised work that might not suit all practitioners. Even the gifted communicators I interviewed felt out of their comfort zone when they began. The adjectives used to describe how the therapists and interpreters felt before they started this work included: *nervous, de-skilled, scary, daunted, unnerving, anxious, challenging, terrified.*

The adjectives chosen to describe how they feel now, reflect their changed perspective and their personal and professional commitment to working in a therapeutic triad: *fantastic, confident, positive, comfortable, fascinating, intense, glad, grateful.*

The therapists I interviewed recounted stories of when triads had not worked, which they attributed to the particular interpreter not understanding the subtlety of the therapeutic alliance. The therapists felt that the interpreter needed to respect and value the client, to understand the differing roles between them, and have an understanding of what the therapy was trying to achieve and the subtle nuances of the therapeutic alliance.

The interpreters identified that what may be obvious to a mental health practitioner might not be clear to a professional interpreter. Whether the interpreter is born in this country or elsewhere, they emphasised that it is necessary for the professional to meet a new interpreter before any sessions are completed, to fully brief them. They asked that the therapist explain what interventions will be used and what is expected from them. All the practitioners agreed that it was the therapist's responsibility to induct the interpreter into the work. When this did not happen there was more likelihood of problems later.

They all agreed that the issue of mental health as a concept was often difficult to explain:

> The clients think it is an extension of their medical treatment and when the counsellor asks 'what happened to you?' you can read their faces, they are

> thinking: 'What the hell am I doing here, I came for treatment, and then you remind me about the trauma'.
>
> *Majid (interpreter)*

> I was scared and everything was in my head. I just ask myself why did this woman want to know all my life? ... maybe she will kill me ... who is that woman and what does she want? She say 'I want you to feel well'. Why was she being so kind? The counsellor tell me something very interesting. She say talk with someone, this will divide your problem!
>
> *Mariam (client)*

Interpreters and clients talked about the unique culture created by therapy itself:

> Usually (therapy) it's such an unfamiliar concept ... but I think it is for a lot of English people, isn't it? ... there again most clients get used to the idea quite quickly and understand through the relationships.
>
> *Kim (interpreter)*

My findings showed that of the three cohorts, the interpreters had adapted their professional practice the most. They had to become brokers between at least two cultures and understand issues of mental health. They had to mitigate between belief systems and understand psychological therapies. They had experience of other mental health settings but said that they all expected the therapist to give advice and were confused at the start of the work. Above all, they cited facing distressing and disturbing material, bearing witness week after week as unique to therapeutic triads.

The therapists had to change their way of working too. They had to work as part of a team instead of independently, were observed throughout, worked with clients from diverse cultures and backgrounds and may have been culturally outnumbered for the first time in their professional or even personal lives, dealt with barriers to communication including auditory and visual delay, and had to understand the issues of the professional interpreter. One of the therapists, who had been a practitioner for over 15 years before she started working with an interpreter (Isara) said, 'it's opened up my world'.

In my research, the triadic experience was easiest for the client. They accessed interpreters wherever they went and so expected to have an interpreter when they came for therapy. Undoubtedly the clients had complex needs. They had PTSD and were deeply traumatised. They were faced with emotional, cultural and linguistic challenges but the issue of working in a triad rather than a dyad was very low on their list of concerns.

Conclusion

In my professional opinion, linguistic competency is not enough to employ an interpreter in a therapeutic setting. The baseline should be innate communicators who are skilled interpreters. Mearns and Cooper (2005) identify specific 'moments of encounter' and a particular 'quality of relationship' in effective therapeutic interventions. This can only happen when there is nuanced and subtle communication. When there is synchronicity, a joining of hearts and minds with bodies mirroring and reflecting each other:

> even though the interpreter might seem sort of in the background .... I can feel that they are feeling, and the client can feel that, so even though you're not actually saying it, you can pick that up in the room.
>
> *Isara (therapist)*

> Many of the therapists we spoke to said that their most in-depth moments of relating occurred in silence: a second of eye contact, a touch on the shoulder, a laugh shared between themselves and their clients.
>
> *Mearns and Cooper, 2005, p. xii*

As practitioners we are privileged to be part of these encounters. They are often linked to insights, self-reflections, change and growth for our clients. Yet every practitioner knows that sometimes we achieve this connection and sometimes we don't quite manage it. The process of engagement and attunement is elusive, but I believe the process of achieving emotional depth is no different in a triad to a dyad.

To work in a therapeutic triad and achieve relational depth is about communication that runs deeper than words. What's in your heart is more important than the words you use and that is a universal language. As practitioners we have an obligation to our clients, who exhibit courage and resilience daily. They struggle to express indescribable experiences but with the right interpreter can find the 'voice in a whisper' (Martin Luther King Jr, 2000, p. 2).

I would describe a therapeutic triad as like a group of musicians who are all playing different instruments. The music sounds infinitely better when they listen and respond to each other. With gifted communicators amazing things can happen.

Ten simple rules

Before you start:

1 Check what language the client would like to speak in during therapy. Ideally ask which gender they would prefer the interpreter to be.

2 Take the same care when employing an interpreter as you do when employing other members of staff. Only work with trained interpreters who understand professional boundaries. Trust your instincts; are they a gifted communicator that you feel in tune with?

3 Always meet a new interpreter before starting work. Communicate what you expect (we have a staff check list). Tell them what therapy/discipline/orientation you work from and what the aim of the sessions will be. Ask if they know

or have worked with your client in any other context. This may/may not prohibit work but will affect the early dynamics in the triad.

4 Use the same interpreter with the same client throughout the therapy, unless there is a problem. Continuity allows relationships to develop and trust and rapport to build.

At the interview:

5 Allow two or three minutes for the interpreter to introduce themselves at the first session. When contracting, emphasise that confidentiality refers to you both. The client needs to see you as a team and know that you will both be there for every session.

6 Remember you are in charge. Both the other participants in the triad are looking for you to take control and steer the session.

7 Always speak in the first person, direct your gaze and focus on the client. This will create intimacy and immediacy.

8 A successful triad is an ever-evolving and dynamic process. Work as a three-way team. This requires communication, planning and discussion when things go wrong. If it's not working, stop and say to both client and interpreter, 'Can we stop for a minute, something is not working properly'. Between you it can be sorted out.

9 Never speak to the interpreter in front of the client and not explain the conversation, even if it's nothing to do with the case.

Post interview:

10 Build in a five-minute debrief after every session. Ask the interpreter anything you are unsure of, especially about cultural or linguistic issues. You may have missed something nuanced and related to values or beliefs you are not aware of. To protect from vicarious trauma, check they feel okay too, especially if it has been an emotional session. This is probably the only time they will get to reflect on the session as interpreters do not receive clinical supervision, so you have a duty of care to them as well as your client.

References

Abbe, A., Gulick, L.M.V. and Herman, J.L. (2007) *Cross-Cultural Competence in Army Leaders: A Conceptual and Empirical Foundation*. Washington, DC: US Army Research Institute.

BACP (2018) *Ethical Framework for the Counselling Professions* [online]. Available at: www.bacp.co.uk/.../ethics.../ethical-framework-for-the-counselling-professions/ [Accessed 4 Jan. 2019].

Bot, H. and Wadensjö, C. (2004) 'The Presence of a Third Party: A Dialogical View on Interpreter Assisted Treatment'. In: J. Wilson and B. Drozdek (eds) *Broken Spirits: The Treatment of Traumatized Asylum Seekers, Refugees, War and Torture Victims* (pp. 355–378). Hove: Brunner Routledge.

British Psychological Society (2017) *Working with Interpreters*. [online] Available at: www.bps.org.uk/.../bps.../Working%20with%20interpreters%20-%20guidelines%. [Accessed 4 Jan. 2019].

Burck, C. (2004) 'Living in Several Languages: Implications for Therapy', *Journal of Family Therapy*, 26(4), pp. 314–339.

Century, G., Leavey, G. and Payne, H. (2007) 'The Experience of Working with Refugees: Counsellors in Primary Care', *British Journal of Guidance and Counselling*, 35(1), pp. 23–40.

Costa, B. and Dewaele, J.M. (2012) 'Psychotherapy across Languages: Beliefs, Attitudes and Practices of Monolingual and Multilingual Therapists with their Multilingual Patients', *Language and Psychoanalysis*, 1(1), pp. 18–40.

Cushing, A. (2003) 'Interpreters in Medical Consultations'. In: R. Tribe and H. Ravel (eds) *Working with Interpreters in Mental Health* (pp. 30–53). East Sussex: Brunner-Routledge.

Edwards, R. (1995) 'Working with Interpreters: Access to Services and User Views'. In: G. Wilson (ed.) *Community Care: Asking the Users* (pp. 54–68). London: Chapman and Hall.

Ekman, P. (2007) *Emotions Revealed: Recognizing Faces and Feelings to Improve Communication and Emotional Life*. New York: Henry Holt.

Elfenbein, H. and Ambady, N. (2003) 'Cultural Similarity's Consequences: A Distance Perspective on Cross-Cultural Differences in Emotion Recognition', *Journal of Cross-Cultural Psychology*, 34(1), pp. 92–110.

Farooq, S. and Fear, C. (2003) 'Working through Interpreters: Advances in Psychiatric Treatment', *Royal College of Psychiatrists Journal of Continuing Professional Development*, 9(2), pp. 104–109.

Gajwani, R., Parsons, H., Birchwood, M. and Singh, S. (2016) Ethnicity and detention: are Black and minority ethnic (BME) groups disproportionately detained under the Mental Health Act 2007? *Social Psychology and Psychiatric Epidemiology*, 51(5), pp 703–711.

Haggard, E.A. and Isaacs, K.S. (1966) 'Micro-Momentary Facial Expressions as Indicators of Ego Mechanisms in Psychotherapy'. In: L.A. Gottschalk and A.H. Auerbach (eds) *Methods of Research in Psychotherapy* (pp. 154–165). New York: Appleton-Century-Crofts.

Hall, E.T. (1959) *The Silent Language*. Garden City, NY: Doubleday.

Harris, C.L. (2006) 'When Is a First Language More Emotional?'. In: A. Pavlenko (ed.) *Bilingual Minds: Emotional Experience, Expression, and Representation* (pp. 257–283). Clevedon, UK: Multilingual Matters.

Hassan, J. (2009) *A House Next Door to Trauma: Learning from Holocaust Survivors How to Respond to Atrocity*. London: Jessica Kingsley Publications.

King, Martin Luther Jr. (2000) *Why We Can't Wait*. New York: New American Library.

Knapp, M.L. and Hall, J.A. (2006) *Nonverbal Communication in Human Interaction* (6th edn). Belmont, CA: Thomson Wadsworth.

Krause, I.B. (2002) *Culture and System in Family Therapy*. London: Karnac Publishing.

Learman, L. (2015) *A dialogue with three voices: The impact of interpreters on the therapeutic alliance when working with asylum seekers and refugees who have lived through traumatic experiences*. Unpublished professional doctorate, University of Manchester.

Mearns, D. and Cooper, M. (2005) *Working at Relational Depth in Counselling and Psychotherapy*. London: Sage Publications.

Mehrabian, A. (2009) *Nonverbal Communication* (3rd edn). New Brunswick, NJ: Aldine Transaction.

Miller, S.D., Hubble, M. and Duncan, B. (2008) 'Supershrinks: What Is the Secret of their Success?', *Psychotherapy in Australia*, 14(4), pp. 14–22.

Miller, K.E., Martell, Z., Pazdirek, L., Caruth, M. and Lopez, D. (2005) 'The Role of Interpreters in Psychotherapy with Refugees: An Exploratory Study', *American Journal of Orthopsychiatry*, 75(1), pp. 27–39.

Pavlenko, A. (2012) 'Affective Processing in Bilingual Speakers: Disembodied Cognition?', *International Journal of Psychology*, 47(6), pp. 405–428.

Quality Care Commission. (2010) *Count me in* [online]. Available at: www.cqc.org.uk/sites/default/files/.../count_me_in_2010_final_tagged.pdf [Accessed 4 Jan. 2019].

Raval, H. (2003) 'An Overview of the Issues in the Work with Interpreters'. In: R. Tribe and H. Ravel (eds) *Working with Interpreters in Mental Health* (pp. 8–29). East Sussex: Brunner-Routledge.

Ross, F. (2001) 'Speech and Silence: Women's Testimony in the First Five Weeks of Public Hearings of the South African Truth and Reconciliation Commission'. In: V. Das, A. Kleinman, M. Lock, M. Ramphelle and P. Reynolds (eds) *Remaking a World: Violence, Social Suffering and Recovery* (pp. 250–280). California: University of California Press Ltd.

Samovar, L. and Porter, R. (2004) *Communication between Cultures* (5th edn). Boston, MA: Wadsworth Publishing.

Stiff, J.B., Hale, J.L., Garlick, R. and Rogan, R.G. (1990) 'Effect of Cue Incongruence and Social Normation Influences on Individual Judgments of Honesty and Deceit', *Southern Communication Journal*, 55(2), pp. 206–229.

Summerfield, D. (2001) 'Asylum Seekers, Refugees and Mental Health Services in the UK', *Psychiatric Bulletin*, 25(5), pp. 161–163.

Tannen, D. (1980) 'Implications of the Oral/Literate Continuum for Cross Cultural Communication'. In: J.E. Alatis (ed.) *Georgetown University Round Table on Languages & Linguistics 1980: Current Issues in Bilingual Education* (pp. 326–347). Washington, DC: Georgetown University Press.

Trimble, M. (2012) *Why Humans Like to Cry: Tragedy, Evolution, and the Brain*. Oxford: Oxford University Press.

14

BEYOND RELATIONSHIPS

Into new realms in supervision

Allison Brown

Where are the edges, the endings and the beginnings within relationships? Where are the boundaries with multiple relationships and what of the blurred lines of professional awareness that so often replace clarity?

Part one

Once upon a time, there was a therapist who needed a new supervisor. Marie imagined someone who could really understand her way of working and be able to be genuine and real in the same way she was with the clients she worked with.

After months of research and searching she met a new supervisor and was initially impressed with how they appeared to be able to understand, empathise and relate to how she worked therapeutically. For the first time, Marie was tempted to take risks in what she shared about herself and her way of working with clients. In some supervision meetings she was able to sense a lot of unspoken feelings but often came away wondering if her own sense of unconscious processing could be trusted.

Marie felt that her new supervisor, Graham, knew this also, but didn't appear willing to share and she was unsure about whether this felt secure or not. Sometimes it was unnerving, and yet, she had a sense of intrigue that was exciting and had replaced the staleness of supervision relationships long outgrown.

This differing degree of depth took a while to adjust to. Marie likened it to client work, with a natural trust that would either develop or dissipate – the outcome as yet undecided.

Over time, this supervision relationship did indeed develop, and seemingly had quietly and subtly created a space that at every meeting took Marie on a journey through client work that virtually insisted she question every therapeutic rationale at a deep level. It became a space where the unravelling of her own emotional experiences alongside the disentangling of client work produced some completely new experiences of unconscious processing. It was a shared space of curiosity, of wondering about client work alongside the personal impact of the work, and of life and its flexing of boundaries and perpetual questioning of rationales and reason.

Discussions about clinical case work produced cyclical and parallel conversations about cases in which unconscious thinking and emotions were expressed. One particular case revolving around anxiety had created a strong reaction within supervision … Marie had struggled to get a clear grasp on the therapeutic work, which had made no sense within any conscious awareness. She had thought about this client on the drive to supervision and, during that journey, had been moved by the depth and beauty of the sunset which deepened in shades of red and golden amber with every mile travelled – she arrived at supervision feeling she had been following the setting sun so closely that she felt 'at one' with the world.

The session itself felt random, disjointed and yet strangely calm and safe – they talked of the therapeutic work and ideas of fear and foreboding. As they talked more of the struggle with anxiety, a sense of fear developed and she felt sick physically. She had felt vulnerable and in a particularly dark place that was unfamiliar to her. There was a door near her in the supervision room and, unexpectedly, Graham asked her about the fear behind the door. Marie felt as though if it opened she would be swallowed and lost within darkness forever and she felt detached, far from her own reality and sense of self, dissociated, out of control, delusional and frightened. This state of mind very slowly dissipated while they sat in silence on the edge of their chairs, waiting. Marie's physical position had changed – curled over at the front of her seat, her arms wrapped around each other tightly. As it dissipated, a sense of grounded, calm reality followed in which a more clear understanding of her own world, and the potential world of her client was gained.

Marie was shocked, and yet awestruck that such an experience could actually occur and be worked through, she felt drained, exhausted and exhilarated at the same time.

A few days later, the more conscious awareness of isolation that Marie had experienced allowed for more clear links to the actual therapeutic work to be made. Her awareness of a similarly felt sense within the client sessions gave rise to conversations about anxiety and the impact on the client's day to day life. In considering the darker edges to this anxiety, there began an exploration into early and enduring parental relationships which provided safety and security, and where the quality of those early attachments provided a clear sense of love and belonging for the client. Subsequent anxieties around the potential for loss of these key relationships and people gave a link to possible existential pain that was almost too much for the client to contemplate. The feeling of this experience during the session carried an intensity that could not easily be articulated, yet required an emotional strength to sit within. The client had not considered that their anxiety was linked to the fear of loss, and yet they were able to find ways to rationalise and consider these experiences in a more grounded way that enabled them to manage their day to day life with more ease.

Marie wondered whether she had been able to experience an aspect of the client's world that allowed insight to be explored within supervision and subsequently passed back into the client sessions – this potential for parallel process always intrigued. The relational connections within the client work seemed transient at times, with the intensity of connections and subsequent distance a regular part of experience and attachment.

One explanation offered regarding parallel processing in supervision is that it is a way of communicating unconscious aspects of the client work. Projections and projective identifications are worked up from the client–therapist relationship and unfold within the supervisory relationship. Carroll (2006) outlines 'the conduits for parallel processing are supervisees: they are the members of both systems and carry one system into the other'. Supervision, therefore, becomes the relationship where interactions, conscious and unconscious, between client and therapist can unfold but only if that supervision relationship can be alive to the possibility and remain aware of the implications of working with such processes.

Years later Graham offered some comments about his experience within the supervision session where this experience occurred. He had offered one or two observations on the apparent 'blanks' in the client's story so far, of possible pre-verbal experience for which there was no available 'language'. An image had appeared in his mind of what seemed an immense black void on the other side of the door that was alongside and behind where Marie was sat. This void seemed to lead all the way down to the centre of the earth and, trusting in the relational work, Graham felt compelled to share this image with Marie. On hearing his disclosure of this image, Marie acknowledged a sense of an intense fear and anxiety, feeling momentarily physically sick. They had mused on the possibilities around client unspoken dread, and whether Marie could tolerate it – Marie paused, reflected, and gradually re-grounded herself in the present moment, recognising the clinical potential in this shared parallel process phenomenon.

Graham also acknowledged independently that these processes would not have been possible without the level of trust and relational intimacy that had existed at this stage within the supervision relationship.

Within weeks however, these sessions were quickly replaced by the relentless journey of existence and she was astonished how her life could take such rapid twists and turns. Marie had to travel and visit her father. She had cancelled all appointments in order not to be disturbed, she wanted to see him without interruptions before he died.

Her supervision meeting had also been cancelled. Unfortunately, however, Graham appeared to have omitted to note the cancellation and contacted her to ask why she hadn't arrived. Marie was annoyed at the interruption which she had tried so hard to avoid. Her current circumstances took precedence, however, and her mind snapped back to remind her that she had more important things to worry about, she forgave the interruption and returned to the hospital bedside. The stark hospital images pierced her mind like daggers made of cold, clinical steel.

Much, much later, Marie returned to her supervision discussions and talked about a particular conversation with one of her own supervisees, who had been talking about a bereavement case and Marie was particularly moved about the impact of a parent's death for a young person. She wondered what it was like to know, as a parent, that you are dying. Marie mentioned this to the supervisee, phrased in a wondering and curious way – the supervisee was tearful and said that she also had been wondering about this. It was as though they could almost imagine being the dying parent and the supervisory work was about positioning the sadness of loss in the most accurate way possible.

The connection in the moment with her supervisee felt important to note, and this reverberating theme echoed back and forth within her own supervision. A seemingly key moment, where Graham disclosed the impact of the discussion for himself, of wondering what a dying parent may think and feel as opposed to a child's experience of that parent's death. The disclosure was unexpected, and added a new level to the reflections and awareness that seemingly discrete pieces of information have the capacity to produce a jolt in the awareness of others.

This disclosure left her thinking and pondering her own experiences of bereavement over the years and instead of becoming further embroiled in her past deep sadness she was curious about how her own experiences were woven through her therapeutic work on so many levels.

With the further passage of time, and with each supervision meeting, Marie realised that she was beginning to have a sense of change, of something shifting within the relationship. She reflected on her experiences of loss and the intricate, interwoven, complex fabric that supervision had become. She simultaneously craved a new supervision relationship and desperately wanted the current one to continue, but Marie realised there was a cyclical process that prevented any possibility of escaping her own personal grief. There were difficult decisions ahead and endings to be faced.

Eventually Marie followed through with the professional discussions about ending her current supervision because it had begun to be affected by the cumulative losses she had experienced. At times the supervisory relationship had reflected her relationships with her father and grandfather, sometimes keeping her trapped in a place of comforting memories. The strong transferences kept alive relationships with the dead in a way that Marie realised had got in the way of grieving. At the same time, she had a strong sense of being in a better position to make clear decisions and it was with relief that her need for change was acknowledged by Graham. So much in this relationship was unspoken and yet a shared awareness of the depth of work and connection allowed for a 'realness' that was unprecedented in her professional career.

Discussions with Graham about the depth of supervision relationships and the importance of being real and totally genuine within supervision and therapy followed, and she realised that for many years the unspoken words had been recognised and worked through on many levels. This depth of experiencing was able to affect personal relationships, work with supervisees, clients and colleagues alike; a genuine way of relating to others is key to the depth and quality of experiencing relationships.

Marie was ready to try new things again, to start a new supervision relationship with someone else, and it felt the right time to do so. In moments where eyes welled up and words were not spoken, she was fearful as well as adamant that her decision was the right option.

Marie and Graham talked about living and experiencing relationships, of therapy and supervision and how it was difficult and painful for her to contemplate letting go of the supervisory relationship. Relentlessly, personal experiences impacted her thinking and decisions like the heaviness of freight trains in the silent black night. Rationally, returning each time to her choices, she knew a change to another, new supervisor was the right choice, but the pulls were so very significant and fought hard not to be ignored.

Graham mentioned how deep, connected work could be about love and attachment; she became tearful and it reminded her of her father and grandfather. This final session ended, Marie questioned the decision but resisted the urge to turn round and retract it.

The weeks that followed involved a great deal of soul searching – her understanding had been clear, that this change would require that she revisit the loss of her father. What she hadn't bargained for was the fact that this loss was not going to be about his death but about his leaving her and her mother at the age of twelve. This was to become a process about intense anger – at a level of intensity she recognised immediately. This time though, she could not use the anger any longer as a cover for the pain of overall loss.

Part two ...

Once upon a time, there was a therapist who was unsure if they could go to work on this particular Monday. Her father had died on the evening of the Friday before and the level of rawness felt like a new cut, a deep knife wound through her entire body.

She had not actually been with him when he died – having sat at a hospital bedside most of the week she had returned home. During the afternoon, however, she was studying photographs and was surprised at how vivid the images became through her tears – knowing the inevitable loss would soon come. She talked to her father, and during this monologue felt a strange presence when she talked of her children and all the love they had had for him.

He, along with her grandparents, had been a key figure in her life – a relationship not without major challenges but one that had taught her the meaning of caring for others, of loving and forgiving. His death at the end had been unexpected on that particular evening, with nurses explaining how only that afternoon he had sat bolt upright in his bed with a large smile on his face – it was at the very same time as she had been sitting on the stairs a hundred miles away chatting away to him.

So, her children had gone to school, her husband to work, and so she also went to work with nothing but thoughts about her father running amok throughout her shredded mind. She did not undertake any therapeutic work for two weeks, but during this time she also experienced the death of her grandad, her father's father, and made plans for two funerals.

At the first one, her father's, she was accompanied by her husband and two children and spent the day preoccupied with their needs and support – she was proud of them. She had written some words about her father but was unable to even hear when they were being read on her behalf – cold, distanced, unemotional was how she got through that day. This, of course, was very far from the distraught truth of the emotions that were being held so very tightly inside.

Thoughts of her father were banished, and a card given to her by one of his work colleagues from when she was a child was accepted gratefully and ignored. Later, when she read the words, she dismissed the idea that her father loved her more than anything as a vicious lie in order to remain composed. She was angry that people could make such assumptions about love and the relationships of others. She had been angry since she was twelve years old when her parents separated and had carried this anger for the best part of thirty years. It was an anger so strong that it eclipsed all other emotions at times, numerous therapists had not been able to help her make any breakthroughs so she remained aware of it, and managed it on a relentless, sometimes daily basis.

Exactly one week later, she sat in the same funeral car, next to the same perfectly groomed dark green privet hedge waiting to bury her grandfather – without her own children this time. Tears flowed and she was able to remember how important this man was to her. A man who taught her to care for others no matter what, a man who had survived World War Two and yet never spoke of the emotional scars he carried, and a man who had to suffer hearing his own son had died while he was dying himself.

The emotional cost of this was too much – she returned to her home and returned to work. She used her colleagues for support, she tried her best to support her children but for many months this was done at the cost of her own grieving.

She very consciously did not take on any therapeutic work, but within the next four months two of her supervisees also lost their fathers and she turned to her own supervision to be able to continue to work effectively.

This process began to develop her own relationship with her supervisor to a significant depth while she balanced clinical work against a backdrop of grief and the busyness of life, which plodded on regardless of the weight of the losses she carried. The loss was so great that the old anger had no place within in it, and she often reflected on the impotence of being angry with the dead. These teenage feelings of anger slowly dissipated, leaving space required for grief and loss and pain that on some days felt impossible to bear.

With time, the balance returned and she began to work with new clients again, a decision that was taken with an internal agreement that there would not be any bereavement work initially. Over the next twelve months her clinical work increased and talking in supervision became an intricate web of case work, personal experience, deep connections and a growing feeling that the depth of discussions reminded her clearly of a lifetime of philosophical conversations with her father. Conversations held very close to her heart, that used to encompass anything from the best beer at the pub to the meaning of love and the universe! Her father, however, had developed a more rare form of dementia following a stroke earlier in his life and for the last few years he had been a shadow, who could not always be reached on that deep emotional level any more.

She missed her father greatly but as time passed, the memories of his death and the clear, stark hospital imagery lessened. The emotions, however, did not, and conversations in supervision reminded her of him and the lifetime of conversations about people and the world and the universe which she had shared with him. She liked this, and yet, it occurred to her that her own supervision was a relationship that also needed to change to release her from a cycle that linked her each time to death and loss and pain and then back to the excitement about pure possibility within human relationships.

Late into the supervisory relationship, Marie had discussed a supervision session of her own and the impact on herself and the therapist of Marie sharing an intuitive curiosity about being a dying parent. She had wanted to understand more about the processing of thoughts and feelings at the very edge of awareness but was unprepared for this to have a significant impact for both her and Graham. Graham had also acknowledged that this process had provided a curiosity for himself personally that had not been provoked in any of his own, past therapy. It felt significant.

She subsequently left this session questioning what it might be like to know that you were dying while unable to communicate with those around you. She acknowledged to herself for the first time that her father had known she was with him in his last days and hours. She wondered considerably about her father and remembered his last words spoken to her – she had buried this last memory behind intense anger. He had mouthed almost silently, out of view of other family that he loved her – she had forgotten. Remembering was liberating.

These tales revolve around a professional relationship that had been able to develop to such a point that being sufficiently secure and yet vulnerable was a prerequisite for change. Factors that were also a considerable necessity for exploring case work and working through significant unconscious material factors which made for the very best of therapeutic relationships.

Essentially any supervision relationship should have the capacity to work at such a depth of relating where meaning, genuine trust and realness operate throughout. Such relationships should be secure to allow significant known and unknown vulnerabilities to be explored.

The impact is clear to see, not only for those in the direct supervision relationship, but to clients, supervisees as well as personal relationships.

Ask anyone in the therapeutic world to describe the value and depth and meaning of their work and you will most likely get a very wide range of answers.

The range of answers will be linked to the individual therapist's viewpoint, and to some extent the model in which they trained. All descriptions, however, will also include the importance, and value, of the 'relationship' in some form or another. They will all talk about being genuine and real with the clients and therapists they work with.

Part three: searching for explanation

The research by Paul Nicholson in 2015 considered in part the therapists use of self in client relationships and how the idea of 'being real' supports good therapy and, it could be further argued, good supervision. The use of instinctive and intuitive practice is seen as key by the therapists within this research – they talk of care and love for the therapeutic work they do, and how a genuine and intuitive sense of working creates genuine relationships where significant change can occur.

Nicholson was particularly interested in considering how this intuitive dimension was personally accounted for within therapeutic practice and how development was influenced. What was identified through this research was a trend with experienced therapists to see the divide between personal and professional as indistinct, if existing at all. The idea of a division was considered difficult to define, but attempts to create a definitive separation were derided, particularly if it came in the form of withholding authenticity from counselling practice, with one therapist discussing 'this idea of a separation between private stuff and professional stuff? I'd love someone to show me a clear boundary, because it just doesn't exist' (Nicholson, 2015).

According to the interpreted findings from the research, using the self is primarily the action of offering observations – of your experience being with the client at that moment in time. It involves offering the client your opinion of what you see and hear, and think or feel in response to them. A large section of the available literature describes active decision making regarding the disclosure of our *in the moment* experience of being with the client (Rogers, 1975).

All participants declared that the sharing of observation was essential for effective therapy to take place but contingent on the specific primary condition that the therapist keep their disclosures centred entirely on the client's narrative and the client's perspective within it.

Use of self appeared to take two forms: the intuitive and the intentional. The consensus from the sample was that the spontaneous responding tended to be the most powerful and hold the most significance for the client.

When Marie spoke to her supervisee about an empathic sadness around being a dying parent, even though the supervisee's client was that mother's child who survived, she was both intuitively interested as well as having a parallel process awareness of potential transferential material. It was both a conscious decision to explore the process of therapy and supervision as well as being able to be sufficiently vulnerable to allow any subsequent conversation or feelings to be explored in depth.

Later, within Marie's supervision with Graham, the same mix of professional and personal insight and exploration gave rise to further professional development and personal awareness that neither could have predicted. These moments in time, which if missed or not acknowledged may be lost forever, are often key to the strength of therapeutic relationships.

Whether points in relational experiences are defined as 'moments in time', meetings at 'relational depth', 'moments of meeting' (Stern, 2005), 'meaning moments' (Nolan, 2015) or even approaching spiritual experiences, their existence has been shown time and again to have meaning, value and significance for individuals – experiences that Rogers (1986, p. 197) characterised as 'moments where it seems that my inner spirit has reached out and touched the inner spirit of the other. Our relationship transcends itself and has become something larger'.

Rogers also wrote:

> [W]hen I can relax and be close to the transcendental core of me, then I may behave in strange and impulsive ways which I cannot justify rationally, which have nothing to do with my thought processes. But these strange behaviours turn out to be right, in some odd way. At those moments it seems that my inner spirit has reached out and touched the inner spirit of the other.
>
> *Rogers, 1986, p. 197*

On a theoretical level the experiences of supervision described here travel much deeper than the transferences and parallel processing within 'parent–child' relating and into a more intense 'felt-sense' of the unconscious therapeutic material and phenomena very much 'out of initial awareness'.

Lyall Watson quotes Jung's ideas that the only part of us that is in close contact with our roots is the unconscious and that the real insights often exist in the loose ends, on the fringes of understanding. The truth, or our best approximation of it, is carried in the undercurrents of life (Watson, 1979, p. 12).

Ogden (2005) appears to describe similar experiences and insight, this time related directly to supervision in a comparable manner to the client experiences outlined by Rogers:

> [I]t was a form of bringing the entirety of oneself, the full depth and breadth of emotional responsiveness to bear not only on an analytic relationship but also on an interaction between supervisor and supervisee … it did not matter whether it was his or my own conscious, preconscious or unconscious responsiveness that took the lead at any given moment as we talked about our analytic work or what was happening between us … claims of ownership or credit due for originality or insightfulness held no purchase. All that seemed to matter was making a human connection and gaining a sense of what was true to the present moment, both of the analytic work and the supervisory work.
>
> *Ogden, 2005, p. 1275*

Such depth of experiencing brings with it risk, and vulnerability and a need to feel sufficiently safe to explore conscious and unconscious processes. If supervision is unable to provide such safety then the question remains – how can the therapy world support clients to explore their most painful experiences?

Ogden (2005, p. 1269) says of supervision:

> The supervisory frame is a felt presence that affords the supervisee a sense of security that his efforts at being honest in the presence of the supervisor will be treated humanly, respectfully and confidentially. The supervisee entrusts to the supervisor something highly personal – his conscious, preconscious and unconscious experience of the intimacy and the loneliness, the sexual aliveness and the deadness, the tenderness and the fearfulness of the analytic relationship.

The therapist's experiences described in this chapter embody these processes and indicate the depth and breadth of therapeutic possibility. Such depth of experience and exploration is only possible within a secure supervisory frame and relationship.

Security and safety within supervision are also key to the supervisory dreaming and fantasising about therapeutic work and the many levels of processing, summarised by Ellis (2017) when she discusses the nature of wasted time within client sessions and supervision, and the multi-faceted nature of understanding this process. Supervision sessions, and indeed client sessions where there is a sense of dialogue that is less structured, often give rise to new experiences and a developing of relationships and insights. Ellis talks about a sense of guilt and how such sessions can feel as though the time is wasted, or in some way give rise to a lower standard of therapeutic work. However, these are often the sessions and interactions where real awareness is gained and significant shifts in emotion can occur. The emotions felt by supervisors can give insight into the client worlds being explored in supervision – these emotional clues can be key to the depth of therapeutic work and yet can be so easily missed if the relational connections and resilience are not present. Emotions hidden within the client work can be identified and located, explored and passed back in a parallel way that provides intrigue and insight. Supervision that only focuses on the top level understanding of case work often does not give rise to such experiences unless the supervisory relationship is sufficiently safe to allow exploration into the unknown.

It could be argued that the real experiences described in part one above give an example of how open and honest sharing of perception and impact of the initial client work about death, had a subsequent and very clearly identified journey. The impact can be seen through the initial supervision session, the supervisor's supervision session and a subsequent personal impact on both supervisors before passing back into the client work via the ongoing regular supervision and client meetings. None of this insight would have been gained however without trust, when meaning and understanding of processes seemed very far away. Human existence and experience is developed around relationships both positive and negative. We learn from experience, from being able to share that sense of relating with another, and from being able to unpick and understand the detail in many different types of relationships. This in turn adds to a depth and richness of experience that shapes the persona and psyche. Frankl (2008) talked about the complexities of understanding alongside trust and a sense of humanity which he observed throughout his years in Auschwitz. He was an observer, a people watcher in the most horrific of circumstances and a key relationship builder. It could be argued that in many ways his observations could have been overshadowed greatly by his own life experiences. Instead, he writes, 'What is demanded of man is not as some existential philosophers teach, to endure the meaningless of life, but rather to bear his incapacity to grasp its unconditional meaningfulness in rational terms' (Frankl, 2008, p. 217).

Play and reverie, curiosity and searches for meaning become an inherent part of all therapeutic relationships, with clients and within supervision. These aspects are not possible unless 'held' and 'contained' by quality attachments. When we consider working therapeutically with children, for example, it is this very safety that allows for growth and development – play (and testing of experiences) is at the heart of relationships on many levels. For example, Winnicott (1997) said of 'The Piggle', 'it is not possible for a child to get meaning out of a game unless that game is played and enjoyed'. The very same essence can be applied to good therapy and good supervision relationships – we need a safe opportunity within which to 'play', allowing searching curiosity within all therapeutic work.

The supervision relationship in part one is demonstrative of a need for supervision to be safe, secure and yet challenging and open. Good therapy demands an ability and willingness to be vulnerable with clients – to be 'real'. When this happens clients often move to a place of vulnerability and healing themselves. Supervision, in turn, needs to provide space where therapists can take their deepest thoughts about their work and have these thoughts valued and considered. Good supervision is safe, and yet paradoxically fearless at the same time and, like Winnicott's work with 'The Piggle', good supervision can play, explore, remain curious, test awareness, produce change. Good supervision and good therapy change lives. Quality therapeutic relationships that give safety and space to be vulnerable have the potential to provide insight and awareness right the way through the therapeutic chain.

There is a richness to such experience that demands a sense of humility, of being at one with oneself and another person within a relationship that is both intimate, secure but at the very edge of awareness and human existential experiencing. Such experiencing should be embraced within the therapeutic profession and not dismissed within a world that spends less and less time focusing attention on the depth of therapeutic work in its entirety.

The dying man in part two above told his young daughter, over many, many years about the need to 'love and care for one's fellow man' along life's journeys. This was a message Marie never, ever forgot.

References

Carroll, M. (2006) *Counselling Supervision*. London: Sage.

Ellis, S. (2017) Apprehending the translucent in the art of supervision. *British Journal of Psychotherapy*, 33(3), pp. 297–311.

Frankl, V. (2008) *Man's Search for Meaning*. London: Rider Publishing.

Nicholson, P. (2015) An interpretive phenomenological analysis of how colloquial experience is understood to influence the 'use of self' in counselling practice. Unpublished Master's Dissertation, Leeds Metropolitan University.

Nolan, G. (2015) Perspectives at the edge of experiencing in clinical supervision. In: G. Nolan and W. West (Eds) *Therapy, Culture and Spirituality: Developing Therapeutic Practice*. London: Palgrave Macmillan (pp. 138–158).

Ogden, T.H. (2005) On psychoanalytic supervision. *International Journal of Psychoanalysis*, 86, pp. 1265–1280.

Rogers, C.R. (1975) Empathic: An unappreciated way of being. *The Counselling Psychologist*, 5(2), pp. 2–10.

Rogers, C.R. (1986) A client centred/person centred approach to therapy. In: I. Kutash and A. Wolf (eds) *Psychotherapist's Casebook*. San Francisco, CA: Jossey Bass (pp. 197–208).

Stern, D. (2005) *The Present Moment in Psychotherapy and Everyday Life*. New York: Norton and Company.

Watson, L. (1979) *Lifetide*. London: Hodder and Stoughton Ltd.

Winnicott, D.W. (1997) *The Piggle*. Harmondsworth: Penguin Books.

15

CLIENT WISDOM AND HOLISM IN ANTHROPOSOPHIC PSYCHOTHERAPY

John Lees

Introduction

In this chapter I will outline some basic principles of anthroposophic psychotherapy which is a spiritual and holistic approach to therapy inspired by the work of Rudolf Steiner. It aims to extend mainstream therapies by adding 'further knowledge' to them using 'different methods' (Steiner & Wegman, 1925/1983, p. 1): a statement made to medical doctors but applying equally to therapists. There is more-or-less one approach to Western medicine with its worldwide protocols but there are over 400 variations of therapy. Consequently, it is taught as a post-qualifying method for therapists already trained in other modalities[1] and each therapist develops a unique approach to anthroposophic psychotherapy which is informed by their prior training and experience.

My own approach contributes to contemporary innovations in psycho-social humanistically inclined relational psychoanalysis and recent psychosomatic research and practice (Dekkers, Dekkers, & Lees, 2018; Lees, 2016a, 2017). This focus reflects my training, professional development and interests; primarily relational psychoanalysis, intersubjectivity, attachment theory, neuroscience and body-orientated therapy. Other anthroposophic psychotherapists would add to other current therapeutic modalities. I will demonstrate four of the basic principles that underpin my anthroposophic psychotherapeutic practice.

First, my therapeutic technique focuses on the therapeutic relationship, as in contemporary relational psychoanalysis and humanistic thinking, and the existential phenomenological situation of the client. In other words I move between the life experience of the client and the here and now of the therapeutic session (Lees, 2016b).

Second, I regard the spiritual eternal self of the human being as the most powerful element in healing (Lees, 2013a, 2016b, 2018). This adds to such humanistic notions as the organismic self or Jungian thinking which sees the self as 'a priori existent' to our birth and as containing 'the seeds of the individual's destiny' (Samuels, 1985, pp. 90–91) and as the 'total, timeless man … who stands for the mutual integration of conscious and unconscious' (Jung, 1983). Yet, whereas Jungian therapy sees the self as an expression of a collective consciousness, I see it as individual.

Third, I focus on the client's sense of time (and space) and their relationship with the world around them. I view this in a broad way; namely, the whole environment, including the broader social, political and economic context. I also consider the client's sense of past, present and future including good, as well as painful, memories (Barnes & Lees, 2017; Dekkers-Appel, 2015; Dekkers-Appel & Lees, 2017; Lees, 2013b).

Fourth, I work wherever possible in an interdisciplinary way, particularly with holistic complementary and alternative medicine anthroposophic doctors, since I take the view that 'the spirit's power of expression is disturbed by the bodily organism' (Steiner, 1920/1975, p. 176). In anthroposophic psychotherapy, this principle goes much further than recent developments in neuroscience (Lees, 2011; Lees & Tovey, 2012), since it also looks at the effect of adverse child development on our internal organs (Rissmann, 2008). This principle is recognized to a limited degree in medical scientific research – the notion of allostatic load (McEwen, 2000) and the effects of 'the complex wandering of the vagus nerve affecting and being affected by most of the internal organs' (Levine, 2010, p. 96). However, in situations where an anthroposophic doctor is not available I improvise with psychotherapeutic technique – for instance, emulating the actions of the medicines.

I will demonstrate all of these principles further with a single case study.[2] In using case study methodology I will be adopting a form of practice-based research (Lees & Freshwater, 2008). This addresses the anthroposophical view that a descriptive approach in research is essential 'to penetrate into real life, into what actually happens in life' (Steiner, 1916/1999, p. 314) and that only after we have examined 'the individual case with all its idiosyncrasies is it acceptable to employ statistics' (Steiner, 1924/1998, p. 252). After looking at the case (the findings) I will describe the procedure I adopted in the research (the method). This reverses the usual order of sections in the write up of a research project where methodology and method precede findings. The reason for this is that the findings are of primary importance and I do not want the method to get in the way – merely to give an overview of the process I undertook in the research for those readers who wish to judge its veracity and rigour. Having said this, I should also state the obvious; namely that case study methodology has formed the basis of research in the psychotherapy profession ever since its inception. *Studies in Hysteria* (Breuer & Freud, 1895/1974) is, arguably, the first example of the genre. But, in view of its reliance on the perspective of the practitioner researcher, the method has been relentlessly critiqued over the years as being unscientific (Spence, 1997).

If you are not interested in the method I adopted, like those American therapists who gave low ratings in surveys examining the relevance of research to practice in comparison with other 'sources of information and learning such as colleagues, supervisors, personal therapy and clients' in spite of the fact that therapists in the USA 'undergo a highly research-orientated training' (McLeod, 1999, p. 6), then you might skip the methods section. For me the university methodology and methods industry is like looking at the mechanics of the flowers in the garden as opposed to appreciating their beauty and healing potential – and, in political terms, putting methodology and methods at the beginning of the research seems to constrain the researcher by creating a straightjacket for them before they do the research. But you must decide for yourselves.

Findings

Narrative analysis (see methods section)

Angela was in her 30s when I met her. She was diagnosed as having major depressive disorder with psychotic features and had been hospitalized on two occasions in her 20s. She did not think that she had had a particularly difficult childhood. Her upbringing was fine and 'her mother liked being a mother'. She 'loved being a mum', was a 'stay-at-home' mother, was 'dedicated' and 'worked hard'. Yet this did not quite add up for me. It was not compatible with the high levels of disturbance which she experienced in her life. In the study I will look at an earlier session about one month after I had begun to see her when I had a pre-arranged holiday. I will also look at two later sessions as the work was coming to a close.

The earlier session was the first version after my holiday break. During the break she texted me two times. The first text sent the day after the session before the break, stated that 'I'm not managing well this morning. Tired tearful and I want to give up'. The second text, sent four days before the sessions resumed, stated that: 'I feel afraid. I feel alone. And my head is getting strong with less meds. And my head is not good. I am exhausted'. I responded to both texts and, at the beginning of the next session, she said she had experienced an 'intensification' of issues that had built up over a period of time, that she had dealt with it by wrapping herself in blankets, that it was 'something to do with her mother' and that it reminded her of the age of 14 when her mother left home.

About 10 minutes into the session she said she needed to protect herself in relationships. It was not clear to me why she was saying this and so I asked her to give an example to locate the experience in space and time. She then said that someone had been speaking about her. This statement seemed to have a personality disordered element based on a paranoid distrust of others and so I asked her how she knew. In response, she referred to a remark by a colleague at work who said that she had heard that she had 'been inspired' by a workshop that she had attended. On realising that someone had actually spoken about her, and that it was not a fantasy, I continued to inquire about the incident. Angela then said that the colleague's remark made her feel 'cared for' but that the attention made her feel 'a bit like a child' and she rebelled against this feeling. She also said she didn't want to speak about the workshop 'because it felt too private', she 'didn't want anyone to change it' and 'it felt like taking away the experience'. I pursued this because I was puzzled and did not understand why she was feeling like this. She went on to say that she felt 'scared to talk about it' and then said 'I don't want to mess it up'. At this point, in response to my further inquiries, she said she did not want to say any more. So I simply said 'trust me'. She then cast her eyes downward and, almost immediately, without hesitation, jerked into speaking.

She spoke about the workshop and why it was important to her – how it was 'amazing' and had 'stopped that desperate feeling that … it will get better'. I did not understand what this meant but, rather than asking her for clarification, asked her to return to the specific incident and, in particular, her feelings about it. She then said that she felt as though 'people may be stealing something'. Her use of the word 'stealing' was striking. Although this was a variation on a previous statement about taking away her experiences, it had a strong impact on me. I felt as though something of deep significance had taken place. This resonated within me for some time. The discussion then opened up some information about her mother. She said she experienced her as wanting something, that this made her feel 'resentful' and that she thought she was 'trying to help' her mother 'too much'. In the course of this discussion, Angela calmed down and she made no further reference to her difficult experience. But such episodes reappeared periodically. It became clear, in a later moment of crisis when she was in an extremely vulnerable state, that the notion of things being stolen from her was a strong signature in her life, that it was the narrative that she lived with on a day-to-day basis and that it ebbed and flowed in intensity. I also developed the view that, in her 20s, it was so powerful that she preferred to cease to live her life rather than having things taken away and stolen and that she did this by becoming 'frozen', 'slowly shutting down', and not eating or sleeping. In fact she was quite explicit about this. She said 'I took myself out in my 20s' and that it was 'easier to go with the feeling that it doesn't matter' when facing problems in life although this scared her.

In the later stage of the work, when she was recovering, she experienced what I refer to as withdrawal symptoms (which is a common experience in any recovery). For Angela this began after about four years of therapy with me, an anthroposophic doctor and a eurythmy therapist. I will refer, in particular, to two sessions from the latter part of the fifth year of therapy. By that time she was saying things like, 'Each time I meet you it seems like the first time' and, after a three-week holiday break, that she managed to remember the sessions for two weeks after the previous session but by the third week 'I couldn't believe I could come any more' and that she 'was angry that I missed what was happening' in her life when I was away. We agreed that having the experience of always meeting me for the 'first time' was not easy but understandable in terms of her recovery and that losing the continuity of the sessions created a sense of anxiety. The fact that we were able to discuss the experiences in this way combined both the work on her existential phenomenological situation and working on the dynamics of our therapeutic relationship. In this session Donald Winnicott's paper on object use and object relating came to my mind (Winnicott, 1969).

During the following session after a one-week break because of Angela's holiday, I linked with the previous session, as I often do. Angela added to my formulations of the previous week by helping me to deepen my understanding of the two states she had previously referred to – seeing each session as the first one and difficulty in maintaining the continuity between the sessions. She also spoke about loneliness. This then led to a discussion about the old Angela (the poorly Angela, which we had referred to in earlier sessions) and the new Angela (Angela in recovery) and how the new Angela now had a sense of the future: a 'sense of being alone … where there are no people to look after you'. As she said this, I had another reverie of Donald Winnicott's paper (Winnicott, 1957) about the capacity to be alone in the presence of others which, as far as I could remember, described the process of maturation, as did the other Winnicott paper (1969). I didn't mention anything but she then said, 'On the way here I was thinking of things to say and now I can't think of anything'. In the course of the ensuing discussion she spoke about how on her holiday (in her mother's caravan with her mother and her sister) she had removed herself from the difficult interaction with her still very needy mother who 'talks, talks and talks' and 'tells me everything' by doing a large jigsaw to avoid 'getting pulled around'. She said she did the same thing when she was last in hospital where she felt 'threatened' and the jigsaw represented for her connecting what she was hearing by 'finding places for the pieces'. This then enabled me to suggest that she was perhaps feeling alone in their presence, in other people's presence and in mine.

Analysis of narratives (see methods section)

I will now examine how the work demonstrated the four principles I introduced earlier.

First, my principal reason for choosing Angela was to demonstrate how anthroposophic psychotherapy moves between the therapeutic relationship and the existential phenomenological situation of the client. As regards the therapeutic relationship, the narrative analysis demonstrated the establishment of a secure attachment base (Bowlby, 1988). She needed proximity to me assisted, in the early sessions, by texts. Toward the end of the work she responded well if she knew I was available but not so well if I was not (anger) because of an ambivalent attachment style (Main & Solomon, 1990), alignment and non-alignment, experiencing each session as though it was the first time, being angry, my reveries about Winnicott's two articles and the issue of loneliness. It also described the existential phenomenological state in her life – how she needed to protect herself in relationships, the sense that people may be stealing something, having difficulty in remembering the sessions, not believing she could come back to see me and removing herself from difficult interactions by doing a jigsaw.

Second, the work was founded on trust in Angela's potential for insight and wisdom. This was evident in the early stages (stealing something) and toward the end when she was able to show evidence of progression and maturation as expressed in the Winnicott reveries (Ogden, 1994). Her insight extended to the therapeutic work. She constantly inferred my 'intentions' and my 'motivational direction' (BCPSG, 2005), tuned in 'consciously and unconsciously' to my 'attitudes and feelings', was able to touch 'on sensitive aspects' of my character (Aron, 1991/1999) and had a capacity for 'implicit relational knowing' (Lyons-Ruth et al., 1998). She was thus an active player in the co-creational intersubjective dance which enabled us to be in a state of mutuality that resembled Benjamin's rhythmic third (Benjamin, 2004/2012) and provided moments of meeting, such as when she used the words 'stealing something' (Stern, 2004).

Angela's insight and wisdom was a double-edged sword. It was very helpful therapeutically. Her diagnostic comment that people may be stealing something was much more useful to me than major depressive disorder with psychotic features, and her description of doing a jigsaw in her mother's caravan – a self-care measure which she devised – was more useful to me for demonstrating progress than psychometric measures. And she also unwittingly supervised me with the Winnicott reveries. The case shows that clients are often wiser than the armies of professors, academics and senior practitioners who devise diagnostic manuals and conduct evaluation studies at great expense. But the self-same insight also led to hypersensitivity and caused her great pain and suffering.

Third, the sense of time and space is important since it locates us in the physical world and enables us to live our lives on the earth. Initially, Angela's experience was dominated by removing herself from the situations of her life in a timeless way. She wrapped herself in blankets, did not want to speak about the workshop 'because it felt too private' and ceased to live her life rather than having things taken away. This, in anthroposophical terms, stemmed from the fact that she was not bound to the physical world, preferred to return to her timeless and spaceless spiritual world. This meant she had little sense of the social and political context in which she was living. Yet she gradually connected more directly with time-space reality. As regards time she could distinguish, at different times, the poorly Angela and the new Angela in recovery, she could see that there would be a time, in the future, when she would not be able to see me anymore and would have to deal with the 'sense of being alone … where there are no people to look after you', although there was still some confusion when she experienced each session as the first session, although this was improving. As regards space, there was the mother who 'talks, talks and talks' and 'tells me everything', her mother's caravan with her mother and her sister but, significantly, her own capacity to deal with it by doing a jigsaw and putting the pieces together.

These changes were built on interventions that constantly aimed to connect her with space-time reality (Dekkers, 2015). These interventions addressed the part of her constitution that mediates between the spiritual and earthly worlds. One aspect of this is an 'intermediate' time body and this had been weakened because of attachment problems because of the needy mother[3] and this, in turn, hindered her capacity to call forth 'physical materials and forces into life' (Steiner, 1909/1963, p. 27) which locates us in space. This intermediate part of our constitution is the 'architect' of the physical body in that 'all the organs of the physical body are maintained in their form and structure by the currents and movements' of this intermediate body which is in constant 'living interflow and movement' (ibid., p. 43). Moreover, this weakened body affected the 'spirit's power of expression'. It was hindered in its activity because it did not have a 'bodily organism' in which to express itself. But now this intermediate body was becoming stronger.

Fourth, anthroposophic psychotherapy is, where possible, interdisciplinary, and if this is not possible the therapist has to improvise. In this case there was a doctor and a eurythmy therapist but I also improvised. To describe all of the interventions would take too long. So I will just mention one; namely how I improvised one of the medicines prescribed by the anthroposophic doctor.

Contemporary neuroscience would recognize Angela's tendency to become 'frozen' and to begin 'slowly shutting down' as a response to trauma by the autonomic nervous system (Rothschild, 2000). But anthroposophic medicine views the effect of her early life trauma on the internal organs as being more fundamental and preceding this. A crucial organ for Angela was the spleen which is medically understood as filtering the blood and as being part of the immune system. But Steiner goes further and sees it as isolating 'the circulation of the blood from all outside influences', adapting 'itself to the outside world' and becoming 'harmonious with it' (Steiner, 1911/1997). In other words it serves as a barrier to protect us from influences from the world around, particularly the states of mind of other human beings so that, for Angela, the attachment difficulties did not constantly repeat. The complementary and alternative medicine which addressed this was called *cichorium plumbo cultum*, a vegetabilized metal that combines chicory with lead. It is used for addressing psychological boundary disorder and dependency personality disorder by helping the healthy spiritual self to 'transform threatening sense experiences' as a result of strengthening 'the organism's boundaries and defences against the environment' (Committee,[4] 2009, p. 265). The nature of chicory and lead confirm their capacity to strengthen the immune system. Chicory is high in vitamin C and lead is used as a shield against X-ray and gamma-ray radiation and so is used in X-ray machines and nuclear reactors.

Most therapists do not have the luxury of anthroposophic medicine but one aspect of my research is to show how the actions of medicines can be reproduced by psychotherapeutic interventions (Lees, 2013a, 2013b, 2018). In this case the intersubjective therapeutic interaction described in the narrative analysis was intended to replicate the mechanisms of action by shielding Angela from the harshness of life today and this was driven by her creative 'I' and, in the process, strengthened the part of her being that calls forth physical materials into life.

Method

Anthroposophic psychotherapy, like all anthroposophical practical activities including teaching, farming and science, is based on Goethean science (Steiner, 1886/1978). This means that the primary focus is on the observation of phenomena. Having observed the phenomena we then inwardly work on the phenomena anthroposophically by developing Imaginations which reproduce the phenomena inwardly, Inspirations which bring it alive in our feelings, and Intuitions which enable us to act in response to the phenomena we originally observed – a process that is, in effect, a holistic spiritual version of existential phenomenology.

I began by selecting Angela from a number of clients who had given written informed consent to use clinical material for the purposes of research and teaching in accordance with the British Association for Counselling and Psychotherapy Ethical Framework (British Association for Counselling and Psychotherapy, 2018). I chose this to demonstrate one of the general principles outlined in the Introduction; namely, working with the therapeutic relationship and the client's existential phenomenological state. I originally had four cases lined up – one for each of the four areas. Then I whittled them down to two. But I then decided that there would be too much material and not enough words, and chose just one. So I had to demonstrate the four principles with just one case. This meant the design was flexible – a design that 'evolves, develops and (to use a term popular with their advocates) "unfolds" as the research proceeds' (Robson, 2002, p. 5), thereby emerging out of the research process.

The design was also affected by the fact that, as the practitioner researcher, I was a participant in the research field and so adopted the attitude of an engaged researcher participant rather than a detached and neutral observer. This meant that the boundary between me and the other participant, Angela, was obscured: it 'destabilized boundaries between myself, my research and those with whom I engage in my research' (Maxey, 1999, p. 203). The same can be said about the stages of the research process. In quantitative research, and also in most approaches to qualitative inquiry, the researcher engages in a linear process by dividing the research project into a series of stages – question, literature review, data collection, data analysis, results. Clinical practice can also be viewed in a linear fashion – problem/diagnosis treatment plan, putting plan into action, interpreting/learning, evaluating results. However, in this study the distinctions are not so clear-cut due to the fact that I constantly returned to the same experience to view it in new ways. As I did this, I raised new questions, necessitating new reading and viewing the material differently. So, for example, the literature become part of the ongoing process and not a section in an early stage of the project.

The data was recorded in clinical notes and subjected to a process of selection in order to prepare it for analysis. I then selected a few extracts that demonstrated the principles outlined in the Introduction, starting with demonstrating how the work moved between the existential phenomenological situation of the client and the therapeutic relationship. Yet in view of fewer cases I used more material from the case of Angela as the research proceeded in order to address all four areas.

The analytical strategy followed Goethe's dictum that 'every analysis presupposes a synthesis' or, put differently, 'separating and co-ordinating are two inseparable acts of life'. This involved three types of data analysis: narrative analysis, analysis of narratives and report writing.

1 The narrative analysis of extracts organized 'the data elements into a coherent developmental account' and, as such, was 'a synthesis of the data rather than a separation of its constituent parts' (Polkinghorne, 1995, p. 15). This aspect of the account thus reads, to some degree, as a story of the client interaction and the client's existential phenomenological state. So there are no references in this section.

2 The analysis of narratives had the specific aim of locating 'common themes or conceptual manifestations among the stories collected as data' (Polkinghorne, 1995, p. 13) – or specifically how the case demonstrates the four general principles outlined in the Introduction and how anthroposophic psychotherapy adds to other therapeutic methods.

3 The report writing also contributed to analysis (Clarkson, 1995; Richardson, 1994). It was, in effect, an 'analysis over time' lasting almost two months. This process included immersion, incubation and all the other stages of heuristic research (Moustakas, 1990) and many iterations. It had the secondary purpose of giving the account coherence, consistency and comprehensibility, thereby giving order and structure to the narrative, and exposing the nature of the 'social actions' which I undertook (Potter & Wetherell, 1987). I have thereby attempted to make my situatedness (Freshwater & Rolfe, 2001, p. 532) and my 'subjectivities and positionings', (Clarkson, 1995, p. 267) transparent to enable the reader 'to follow the progression of events and logic in the study as a way of establishing trustworthiness' (Freshwater, 2000, p. 110) and thereby observe my process of 'narrative smoothing' (Spence, 1997, p. 78), thereby evaluating my social actions. In other words, I have tried to create a text that attempts to undermine its own absolutist tendencies and shows, instead, that it is based on tentative hypotheses which are subject to revision, as in all research.

Another way of describing the analysis is to see it as reflexive. This can be understood in a number of ways. The definition I adopted was based on the notion of 'turning' or 'bending' something back on itself. Steier (1991, p. 2) refers to 'a turning back of one's experience upon oneself', while Freshwater and Rolfe (2001) discuss 'turning thought or reflection back on itself'. So, in the account, the clinical notes turned the work with Angela back on itself, the narrative analysis turned the thoughts underpinning my clinical notes back on themselves, the analysis of narratives similarly turned the narrative analysis back on itself, while this methods section has turned the process of thinking about the case back on itself, and writing up has involved the iterative process of constantly turning the thinking permeating my text back on itself.

Notes

1 Anthroposophic psychotherapy has been taught as a post-qualifying course in fourteen countries throughout the world. The second post-qualifying course in the

UK began at Emerson College in Sussex in October 2018 (www.emerson.org.uk/anthroposophic-psychotherapy).

2 The client has given written permission to use the material and I have also altered the material to preserve anonymity.

3 Steiner refers to this as the etheric body of formative forces.

4 Medical Section of the School of Spiritual Science; International Federation of Anthroposophic Medical Associations (IVAA); Association of Anthroposophic Physicians in Germany (GAÄD).

References

Aron, L. (1991/1999). The patient's experience of the analyst's subjectivity. In S. A. Mitchell & L. Aron (Eds.), *Relational Psychoanalysis* (pp. 243–265). London: Routledge.

Barnes, C., & Lees, J. (2017). The man who did not wish to come to earth: a case study. *Self and Society, 14*(1), 19–28.

BCPSG. (2005). The 'something more' than interpretation revisited: sloppiness and co-creativity in the psychoanalytic encounter. *Journal of American Psychoanalytic Association, 53*(3), 693–729.

Benjamin, J. (2004/2012). Beyond doer and done to: an intersubjective view of thirdness. In L. Aron (Ed.), *Relational Psychoanalysis Vol. 4* (pp. 91–123). Hove, Sussex: Routledge.

Bowlby, J. (1988). *A Secure Base: Clinical Applications of Attachment Theory*. London: Routledge.

Breuer, J., & Freud, S. (1895/1974). *Studies in Hysteria*. Harmondsworth: Penguin.

British Association for Counselling and Psychotherapy. (2018). Ethical Framework for the Counselling Professions. Retrieved 28 August 2019 from www.bacp.co.uk/media/3103/bacp-ethical-framework-for-the-counselling-professions-2018.pdf

Clarkson, P. (1995). *The Therapeutic Relationship*. London: Whurr.

Committee. (2009). *Vademecum of Anthroposophic Medicines*. Filderstadt: Gesellschaft Anthroposophischer Artzte.

Dekkers, A. (2015). *A Psychology of Human Dignity*. Great Barrington, MA: Steiner Books.

Dekkers, A., Dekkers, H., & Lees, J. (2018). Anthroposophy as an enrichment of psychotherapy. *Self and Society, 46*(1), 27–29.

Dekkers-Appel, H. (2015). *Changing social structures in a society in transition*. Unpublished manuscript.

Dekkers-Appel, H., & Lees, J. (2017). Addressing materialism and illusionism in anthroposophic psychotherapy. *Self and Society, 45*(1), 9–18.

Freshwater, D. (2000). *Transformatory Learning in Nurse Education*. Southsea: Nursing Praxis International.

Freshwater, D., & Rolfe, G. (2001). Critical reflexivity: a politically and ethically engage research method for nursing. *NT Research, 6*(1), 526–537.

Jung, C. G. (1983). *The Psychology of the Transference*. London: Routledge.

Lees, J. (2011). Counselling and psychotherapy in dialogue with complementary and alternative medicine. *British Journal of Guidance and Counselling, 39*(2), 117–130.

Lees, J. (2013a). Facilitating self-healing in anthroposophic psychotherapy. *Forschende Komplementärmedizin, 20*, 286–289.

Lees, J. (2013b). Psychotherapy, complementary and alternative medicine and social dysfunction. *European Journal of Psychotherapy and Counselling, 15*(3), 201–203.

Lees, J. (2016a). The future of psychological therapy. *Therapy Today, 27*(8). Retrieved September 2018 from www.bacp.co.uk/admin/structure/files/pdf/15648_all%20editorial%20ttsep%2016%20low%20res.pdf

Lees, J. (2016b). Microphenomena research, intersubjectivity and client as self-healer. *Psychodynamic Practice, 22*(1), 22–37.

Lees, J. (2017). The emerging therapeutic landscape of psychotherapy in the twenty-first century and the contribution of anthroposophic psychotherapy. *European Journal of Psychotherapy and Counselling, 19*(2), 141–157. doi: 10.1080/13642537.2017.1312476

Lees, J. (2018). Client insight and client as healer in anthroposophic psychotherapy. *Self and Society, 46*(1), 13–20.

Lees, J., & Freshwater, D. (Eds.). (2008). *Practitioner-based Research: Power, Discourse and Transformation*. London: Karnac Books.

Lees, J., & Tovey, P. (2012). Counselling and psychotherapy, complementary and alternative medicine and the future of healthcare. *British Journal of Guidance and Counselling, 40*, 67–81.

Lees, J. (2018). Relational psychoanalysis, anthroposophic psychotherapy and political turmoil. *Article under review*.

Levine, P. A. (2010). *In an Unspoken Voice: How the Body Releases Trauma and Restores Goodness*. Berlerley, CA: North Atlantic Books.

Lyons-Ruth, K., Bruschweiler-Stern, N., Harrison, A. M., Morgan, A. C., Nahum, J. P., Sander, L., et al. (1998). Implicit relational knowing: its role in development and psychoanalytic treatment. *Infant Mental Health Journal, 19*(3), 282–289. doi: 10.1002/(sici)1097-0355(199823)19:3<282::aid-imhj3>3.0.co;2-o

Main, M., & Solomon, J. (1990). Procedures for identifying infants as disorganised/disorientated during the Ainsworth Strange Situation. In M. Greenberg, D. Cicchette & E. M. Cummings (Eds.), *Attachment During the Preschool Years: Theory, Research and Intervention* (pp. 121–160). Chicago, IL: University of Chicago Press.

Maxey, I. (1999). Beyond boundaries? Activism, academia, reflexivity and research. *Area, 31*(3), 199–208.

McEwen, B. S. (2000). Allostasis and allostatic load: implications for neuropsychopharmacology. *Neuropsychopharmacology, 22*(2), 108–124.

McLeod, J. (1999). *Practitioner Research in Counselling*. London: Sage.

Moustakas, C. (1990). *Heuristic Research: Methodology and Application*. London: Sage.

Ogden, T. (1994). The analytic third: working with intersubjective clinical facts. *International Journal of Psycho-analysis, 75*, 3–19.

Polkinghorne, D. (1995). Narrative configuration in qualitative analysis. In J. A. Hatch & R. Wisiewski (Eds.), *Life History and Narrative* (pp. 3–23). London: The Falmer Press.

Potter, J., & Wetherell, M. (1987). *Discourse in Social Psychology*. London: Sage.

Richardson, L. (1994). Writing as a method of inquiry. In N. K. Denzin & Y. S. Lincoln (Eds.), *Handbook of Qualitative Research* (pp. 923–948). London: Sage.

Rissmann, W. (2008). Depressive disorders-anthroposophical insight and treatment using anthroposophical medicines and external applications. *Der Merkurstab (Journal of Anthroposophic Medicine)* Retrieved 20 March 2011, from www.merkurstab.de/Dateien/English/depression/4_Depression_Rissmann_engl_2008.pdf

Robson, C. (2002). *Real World Research*. Oxford: Blackwell Publishers.

Rothschild, B. (2000). *The Body Remembers*. New York: W.W. Norton and Co.

Samuels, A. (1985). *Jung and the Post-Jungians*. London: Routledge.

Spence, D. P. (1997). Case reports and the reality they represent: the many faces of Nachtraglichkeit. In I. Ward (Ed.), *The Presentation of Case Material in Clinical Discourse* (pp. 77–93). London: Freud Museum Publications.

Steier, F. (1991). Introduction: research as self-reflexivity, self-reflexivity as process. In F. Steier (Ed.), *Research and Reflexivity* (pp. 1–11). London: Sage.

Steiner, R. (1886/1978). *A Theory of Knowledge Implicit in Goethe's World Conception*. London: Rudolf Steiner Press

Steiner, R. (1909/1963). *Occult Science*. London: Rudolf Steiner Press.

Steiner, R. (1911/1997). *Occult Physiology*. London: Rudolf Steiner Press.

Steiner, R. (1916/1999). *The Meaning of Life*. London: Rudolf Steiner Press.

Steiner, R. (1920/1975). *Spiritual Science and Medicine*. London: Rudolf Steiner Press.

Steiner, R. (1924/1998). *The Book of Revelation*. London: Rudolf Steiner Press.

Steiner, R., & Wegman, I. (1925/1983). *The Fundamentals of Therapy*. London: Rudolf Steiner Press.

Stern, D. N. (2004). *The Present Moment in Psychotherapy and Everyday Life*. New York: W.W. Norton and Co.

Winnicott, D. W. (1969). The use of an object. *International Journal of Psycho-analysis, 50*, 711–716.

Winnicott, D.W. (1957). The capacity to be alone. *International Journal of Psycho-analysis, 39*, 416–420.

16

DWELLING ON THE EDGE

William West

Typically counsellors and psychotherapists have grown up on the edge of their families, sometimes spending a lot of their childhood alone, perhaps being the confidant/carer to siblings and occasionally to a parent, and mostly growing up too soon. Becoming a therapist as an adult, one can draw on these childhood experiences but there is a potential cost. Therapists are not the only ones who might find or see themselves as edge dwellers; for example, religious leaders, doctors and nurses – especially GPs and community nurses. But beyond these professional roles, dwelling on the edge is experienced by many others, again at a potential cost. These include people who are marginalised by the wider society, for instance refugees, immigrants, LGBT+ people, people who just look different, disabled people and people with mental health issues. Such groups can find themselves 'othered' by some of the wider populations.

Dwelling on the edge is not necessarily and always a wholly negative experience. It can be seen as liminality, as a choosing to not belong or be in one situation, place or group. It gives the person involved an interesting and potentially creative perspective on what might be under examined situations. Also, being on the edge in one scenario does not necessarily mean that it happens at all times in all situations.

In this chapter, I will explore the experience of edge dwelling, including the challenges, the costs and the potential benefits involved, largely drawing on my own experiences of my early years, working as a therapist, not wishing to be defined, being defined by others, attending a gay pride march, working therapeutically with clergy, and on the impact of suffering and death among friends and family.

Early years

> We have suggested that a primary theme in the descriptions of becoming a psychotherapist is that of being called upon to understand the nature of

> suffering, and one's own suffering in particular, and to seek to repair what has gone wrong in one's own life through the attempt to heal others.
>
> *Spurling and Dryden, 2014: 190*

Spurling and Dryden (2014) go on to suggest that the wound suffered by therapists in their early years is one of isolation or division from others. It is possible that this wound is never healed. Indeed, the phrase 'wounded healer' is used. Looking at the experiences of traditional healers or shamen, the active work by the healer on their woundedness is part of their preparation for becoming a practitioner. Indeed, Ellenberger (1970), in his seminal work on the discovery of the unconscious, suggested that both Freud and Jung processed their wounds and that training analysis involved future therapists undergoing Freudian or Jungian shamanic journeys.

I remember as a child feeling that I did not really belong in my birth family the way my sister did. For a while I entertained notions that I was adopted but my mother told too many stories about me as a baby for that to remain at all convincing. This sense of feeling different, of not truly belonging in the family home, led to my knowing as an adolescent that I needed to leave home. I planned the various ways I might do this from the age of fourteen! I needed to escape my family to find my true self. This pushed me to aim for university and to study there for a good career rather than something that was more dear to me.

Edge dwelling in therapy

A few years ago, I wrote in some detail about some of my therapeutic work with a Sufi client who chose to be called Matthew and who wrote about his experience also (West, 2004). One of the key moments in Matthew's therapy from my point of view was when we both went into a deep silence together. This silence was familiar to me from my experiences of meditation and of the silence of Quaker Meetings. However, I knew that I could not just give myself over to a deep altered state of consciousness in which I would lose almost all connection with ordinary consciousness. My primary task was to remain available to Matthew. So I remained on the edge of this deeper state of consciousness staying in touch with Matthew. I was surprised to discover that I could even speak to him without losing the depth I had reached (I say depth because it felt like I was going deeper inside myself).

So it seems to me that I was in quite a liminal state in this moment in Matthew's therapy with me. It felt like an exceptional version of a more common experience of feeling quite interconnected with a client; something that could be seen as 'relational depth' (Mearns and Cooper, 2005) or an example of Rogers' (1980) notion of 'presence' and Thorne's (1991) 'tenderness'. It is also useful to reflect on this experience in terms of Buber's (1923/1970) notion of the 'I-Thou' relationship. Buber suggests we can treat each other as an object and have an I-It relationship or we treat each other as subject or kin and have an I-Thou relationship. In healthy relating there will be movement between I-It and I-Thou forms of relating.

Reflecting on my inner experience of working with Matthew, described above, it might also prove helpful to consider Gendlin's (1996) notion of focusing. He uses focusing as a way of accessing what he calls the 'felt sense' during counselling sessions. This is a familiar, if somewhat controversial, practice within the therapy world, especially in the person-centred tradition. Gendlin locates this 'felt sense' as:

> The felt sense that I also call the edge of awareness is the centre of the personality. It comes between the conscious person and the deep universal reaches of human nature where we are no longer ourselves. It is open to what comes from those universals, but it feels like 'really me'.
>
> *Gendlin, 1984, p. 81*

This description of where the 'felt sense' is experienced echoes both my description of the deep level I reached inside while working with my client Matthew and also my spiritual moment in York Minster which I discuss in the next section. Gendlin's words suggest to me transpersonal and spiritual notions of our Higher Selves or Souls (Assagioli, 1986; Rowan, 2005) and of our often unexplored and undeveloped capacities to connect with everything by going deep inside our selves, even if at such a point a distinction between inner and outer is pretty irrelevant.

Liminality

A few years ago, I wrote a poem called 'Liminal' which reflected my frustrations at being expected to define myself in binary either/or ways. I recognise that these frustrations are not just about what people might expect of me; they are also my self-censorship.

Liminal
I refuse to be defined
As researcher or a practitioner
As a writer or
As an academic or
As middle class or
As white or
As religious or secular
As a healer or a therapist
As gay or straight.
I don't want to be defined
or boxed in
or shut out
Talk to me
Listen to me
Let us be
together

apart
human.
I want to be liminal!

These express the notion that to be liminal is to be more complete, more myself; it has a flavour of the spiritual or mystic experiences that I have in which I feel more truly myself when I am interconnected with life and creation as a whole. I have previously written about an experience that I had in York Minster.

> As I entered the cathedral I immediately felt a sense of being in a spiritual place, if you like I was awestruck. I made for the small chapel that I knew was set aside for silent prayer. Inside the chapel I was overwhelmed by the feel of the spiritual energy present and was moved to weep. I felt such a sense of gratitude at being able to feel this energy and also had a sense of being enabled to return to my true nature or spiritual self. This was immediately followed by a feeling of regret at not living enough from that true centre of mine. I spent some time in prayer for those close to me especially those in difficulties, and also spent some time in contemplative silence. I left the Minster feeling uplifted and cleansed and somewhat washed out.
>
> *West, 2004, pp. 2–3*

This was a relatively familiar experience to me that can occur in places of religion or religious significance including synagogues, mosques, temples, churches, stone circles but also simply outdoors in nature, especially at sunrises and sunsets.

Being defined by others

The trouble with the label 'counsellor' or 'psychotherapist' is that it causes other people to react to us in terms of what these words mean to them, both consciously and unconsciously. This is not always helpful or useful to us or them. In my early days as a therapist in the 1980s, I used to facilitate a number of one-off weekend therapy groups. There was an informal counter cultural network of mostly young people such groups appealed to. (This was before social media.)

I would find myself in social gatherings such as parties where I would be introduced to someone as 'Bill West'. I remember someone replying, "Oh, you're Bill West!" whatever that meant. Others might say, "Oh yeah, I have been meaning to come and see you/come to one of your groups". In these cases I would then need to carefully handle their approach to me, in this semi-public situation with drink taken. I reached a point where I did not want to be so visible – on duty, if you like – and so when asked what I did I replied, "I am a writer." This was true except I made no money from writing. I soon noticed that this produced a much more positive response from people!

Manchester Pride

This year (2018), for the first time ever, I finally got to take part in the Manchester Pride March. It was stunning; I enjoyed it so much and felt a real energy and excitement. I marched under the Unitarian banner. It felt so good to be seen among a religious group that welcomes and indeed marries LBGTQ+ people. The march was delayed for half an hour due to an evangelical Christian protest against it. This may well have added to the warmth of the reception we received from the large crowd, particularly from young people.

When we see some people as different or 'other' to our selves it can be the start of something not good, even toxic. Yes we all have differences around class, age, sex, race, gender, faith, disability and health. And these differences can be the basis of prejudice – conscious or unconscious. 'Othering' is one way of thinking about and catching hold of such a moment. Think about the wonderful T shirt that says 'Never kissed a Tory'. That is 'othering'. There are some decent good Tory voters out there and even the odd decent Tory member of parliament. OK the T shirt is a joke but it does point to very real danger.

So welcoming different people rather than 'othering' them changes our faith groups, social groups and classes, workplaces, etc. for the better. But it feels even more than that to me; when I stop 'othering' you I also stop 'othering' myself. When I get forms that ask me: am I single, married, divorced, etc. or straight/heterosexual, gay, lesbian, trans, etc., I feel this is missing the real or fuller me. It is no longer whether I have sex with someone that defines who I am, it is whether I love them or not. This may reflect my age but I am glad to know this and it feels like it is part of my ongoing experience since the Manchester Pride March.

Working with clergy

In the last couple of years, I facilitated a Reflective Practice group for some clergy. This group met every month for a couple of hours and group members were able to reflect on their work. It had a huge impact on me, including challenging my assumptions about ministers, some of which were buried quite deeply in me. I am not myself ordained, although my evolving religious faith is very important to me. It was, therefore, curious to be facilitating a group whose members shared a role that I had never experienced. It also contrasted with my experience of group and individual supervision of therapists and trainee therapists. In such groups we also share the same ethical stance. I found that I was working with a group whose members were 'edge dwellers' and, in my own case, I was an edge dweller to this group.

Various other insights emerged for me over the course of this group. I found myself developing deep admiration and respect for the ministers involved, especially their 'on call' status which was even more intensive if they lived near to their church. I also noticed the disappearance of the traditional role of the clergy wife. These days many clergy partners have their own careers and the more recent role of the clergy husband does not carry the same expectations as the (traditional) clergy wife does. However, ministers remain central figures for their congregations. The women clergy in my group were clearly under differing stresses and expectations from their congregations as were the men and they were often also wives and mothers.

I was touched by the faith of clergy in my group and this had a deep impact on my own religious journey at that time. Some of the life challenges they faced echoed those of mine to a greater or lesser extent. It was clear that their faith had not made them perfect nor insulated them from suffering.

I remain fascinated by our religious and spiritual journeys and by the relationship between our faiths and the counselling encounter.

Approaching the final edge?

Having begun the process of 'retirement' some four years ago, I am aware that I could see myself as 'living on borrowed time' and I remember my late father commenting on how in his day most men died within eighteen months of retirement. I have also been to too many funerals of late; some of them for people even younger than me. And I have a dear friend who recently spent six months in hospital – mostly in intensive care – and who nearly died three times. Thankfully he is now recovering slowly. And dementia is taking its toll on people close to me.

This is changing how I see life and existence and, of course, suffering. Suffering is fundamental to the theory and practice of therapy and of religion. Both therapy and religion tell us about the steps we can take, if we so choose, to minimise suffering. But to love is to suffer. If I love you I will suffer and, perhaps even worse, if I love myself I will suffer despite how self-compassionate I try to be.

So I find that I am currently experiencing existence as weirder than I used to understand it. This challenges my person-centred optimism – I remember reading a chapter by Carl Rogers entitled 'Growing old: older and growing', but on re-visiting it recently I did not share its largely optimistic tone. However, at one point in this chapter he states: "Writing is my way of communicating with a world to which, in a very real sense, I feel I do not quite belong" (Kirschenbaum, and Henderson, 1990, p. 44). This echoes my own experience and is an expression of Rogers as an edge dweller.

The suffering I face also challenges my religious faith – although that is probably another story or book chapter! It is clear that our design as humans, if we view ourselves as designed, does usually involve us experiencing intense suffering at a number of points in our lives. So there must be some purpose, some value to achieve from experiencing suffering. Certainly it undermines our egos which may be no bad thing. It seems to invite humility and (self) compassion.

Curiously, this current stage of my life's journey has been helped by attending meetings of a Death Café held locally in Manchester. In the Death Café meetings I have been to, you sit around a table in a small leaderless group of five or six people – drinking tea and maybe nibbling on a cake – and share your thoughts about death and dying. It works surprisingly well; I usually come away feeling surprisingly uplifted. It is great that I am having these conversations with strangers and that I am free to voice any concerns and to share any related events that have happened or might happen in my life.

Recently, while singing a hymn during a Unitarian Sunday service, some words came to me out of the blue and I had to stop singing while I pondered their meaning. These words said, "We are meant to be broken because we are not angels". Dwelling on these words I thought about the idea that we need to be broken to allow the light in. I also thought of us as crooked trees that cannot be straightened out as psychoanalysis might lead us to hope; and to see the beauty in the crookedness. I also muse a lot these days around the differing ways that flowers die – some have a late flowering; some go quickly; some slowly. In the end they all die but their seeds do have a chance to germinate.

I recently revisited Erikson's stages of human psychosocial development.[1] There are now nine stages and the collaborative part played by his wife Joan is acknowledged. I seem to fit the eighth stage – late adulthood, being 60+ years old, the existential question being, 'Is it OK to have been me?', a lot of reflection on life which leads to either integrity or despair or perhaps a mixture. The significant relationship is with mankind or my kind. For me this includes God, whatever is meant by that word! This does fit my developing sense of having a different relationship both with existence and with the people in my life.

My life as a person and as a therapist has been all about making sense of things, initially mentally but gradually more and more holistically – emotionally, embodied and spiritually. All this still becomes clearer in those moments of mystical bliss that I am still blessed to experience from time to time. This feeds my optimism, at least for a while. And suffering, like everything else that is human and incarnate, does end. Who knows what is next? Meanwhile, in the moment, I experience gratitude to be alive and well.

Conclusion

In this chapter I have reflected on dwelling on the edge, on liminality, and on what this means both within the world of counselling practice but also in life. This includes some of the potential downsides involved. I am strongly convinced that we all need to find a way of living with difference without being (too) threatened by it, whether within us, outside us or both. Indeed we need to see difference as a nudge toward personal growth and development which is what counselling and also the spiritual journey are all about. In so doing we leave behind limited notions of who we are and what human existence is all about.

Note

1 https://en.wikipedia.org/wiki/Erikson%27s_stages_of_psychosocial_development

References

Assagioli, R. (1986) Self-realisation and psychological disturbance, *Revision* 8(2), pp. 21–31.

Buber, M. (1923/1970) *I and Thou*. Edinburgh: T & T Clark.

Dryden, W., & Spurling, L. (2014) (Eds) *On Becoming a Psychotherapist*. London: Tavistock/ Routledge.

Ellenberger, H. (1970) *The Discovery of the Unconscious*. New York: Basic Books.

Erikson, E. (2019) Erikson's stages of psychosocial development. https://en.wikipedia.org/wiki/Erikson%27s_stages_of_psychosocial_development (accessed 13/02/2019)

Gendlin, E.T. (1984) The client's client: The edge of awareness. In: R.F. Levant & J.M. Shlien (Eds), *Client-centred Therapy and the Person-centred Approach: New directions in theory, research and practice* (pp. 76–107). New York: Praeger.

Gendlin, E.T. (1996) *Focusing-oriented Psychotherapy: A manual of the experiential method*. New York/London: Guilford.

Kirschenbaum, H., & Henderson, V.L. (Eds) (1990) The Carl Rogers Reader. London: Constable.

Mearns, D., & Cooper, M. (2005) *Working at Relational Depth*. London: Sage.

Rogers, C.R. (1980) *A Way of Being*. Boston, MA: Houghton Mifflin.

Rowan, J. (2005) *The Transpersonal: Spirituality in psychotherapy and counselling*. London: Routledge.

Spurling, L., & Dryden, W. (2104) The self and the therapeutic domain. In: W. Dryden & L. Spurling (Eds), *On Becoming a Psychotherapist* (pp. 186–210). London: Tavistock/ Routledge.

Thorne, B.(1991) *Person Centred Counselling: Therapeutic and spiritual dimensions*. London: Whurr.

West, W. (2004) *Spiritual Issues in Therapy: Relating experience to practice*. Basingstoke: Palgrave Macmillan.

IN CONCLUSION

William West and Greg Nolan

Where does this leave us?

Humankind suffers – it seems to be part of our DNA. It also seems that from our earliest days some of us have offered pastoral care and 'counselling', whether within a religious context and/or a healing framework or informally within (extended) family and community life. How we think about, discuss and frame this has altered over time as we have evolved from hunter-gatherers to farmers to the Industrial Revolution and city life, and now we are experiencing the electronic revolution.

In these current times of great change, for many of us our understandings of what counselling is, what it can do for us, and how best to offer/frame it, has to evolve. As must its relationship with other approaches to helping – think medicine, and psychology – and also its part in the wider society.

Competing political and economic pressures that demand Darwinian notions of survival, have seemingly fed a sense of heightened existential anxiety, particularly evident in the UK with the consequences of the banking and financial crises of the last decade. Those under threat from socio-economically insecure environments, or those who find themselves trapped within local internecine wars, some fed by globally competing political interests, are increasingly driven to leave their homes or escape the aftermath in order to find a better life and sustain their survival. Perhaps not since the World Wars of the 20th century have there been so many displaced human beings on the move for these reasons; the impact down the line on international, national, regional and local interests only serves to feed further anxieties into those communities that are already challenged by socio-economic disadvantage, undermining the potential for welcome toward those similarly, or even more in need.

Training and practice in the psychological therapies, the organisations and systems that seek to facilitate support for clients in the face of such pressures, have a responsibility to take note of, and react accordingly to, these wider factors. There is an imperative need to understand and acknowledge the contexts that clients can bring with them when attempting to make sense of the sometimes 'nonsensical'. All too often practitioners can, in the eyes of those seeking help, be seen as being blinkered toward clients' contextual realities, and the enormity of finding ways of making sufficient meaning. Some practices in the helping and caring professions have perhaps become ossified, overly determined by dependency on lead bodies, training institutions and universities that together rely on their competing labels of professional identities. These promoted practices can be too often driven by service funding that requires statistical evidence of tick-box 'success' in the numbers receiving 'treatment' through bureaucratically prescriptive protocols, clients endlessly recycled through under-resourced systems 'delivered' by overstretched practitioners, and graduate and postgraduate research projects supported through funding that predetermines the parameters of hypothesis, rather than encouraging 'blue sky' thinking, the intuitive thought and creative discovery. Political dogma and power-driven doctrinal ideology continue to challenge practitioners' capacity to respond and remain sensitive to individual and collective cultural change; there is a consequent need to recognise and adapt support for service users and clients that would better reflect the realities of rapid change in contemporary social communities.

In counselling and psychotherapy, the clinical and supervisory frames, as containers, can offer unique and privileged experiences of relational intimacy, as professional practitioner and fellow temporal human, being alongside and with others' need. Cumulative hours of attentive focusing, person-with-person while being open to reflection in the moment, frissons the fibres of relational awareness, sensitises neuronal and visceral openness toward the intuited thought, permits the unbidden image and thought that feeds reflective insight. Within such privileged situations we are perhaps doing no more than re-opening and honing access to those heightened perceptions that were phylogenetically evolved in palaeological self-preservation, being alert to each and every micro-moment, one or more of which may have signalled a threat to continuing existence.

Bearing witness with emotional distress in helping and caring is a vocational imperative that drives practitioners within the mental health field; the personal cost of being-with the other in our temporal human frailty is not to be underestimated. In their practice our authors have risked extending the boundaries of academic theory and therapeutic practice. While being mindful of ethical and professional exigencies in the care of their clients, they have developed innovative ideas and shared insights informed through findings from research projects and reflections on experience. Their writing has presented examples of candid openness toward self and professional awareness, evolving notions of personal identity, exploring individual and collective cultural contexts in applying findings from research, and helping ways toward new knowledge in the development of good practice and supervision.

This gives us confidence that the therapy world can respond creatively to the evolving needs of our clients and society as whole; in this context we trust that these chapters offer the reader opportunities for reflection in enhancing practice. It has never been enough for therapists merely to deliver good care to individual clients. The role of the wider society in health and wellbeing for all remains paramount, and therapists need to work toward their eventual redundancy by dialoguing with the wider society. This book is hopefully part of such a process.

INDEX